BUCKLAND'S BOOK OF SPIRIT COMMUNICATIONS

About the Author

Raymond Buckland came to the United States from England in 1962. He had written television comedy scripts for ITV's *The Army Game* series and a pilot, *Sly Digs,* for BBC-TV. He was also personal scriptwriter for the popular British comedian Ted Lune. In the past thirty years he has had over thirty books published—fiction and nonfiction—by such publishers as Ace Books, Warner Books, Prentice Hall, Samuel Weiser, Inner Traditions International, Galde Press, Citadel, Visible Ink Press, and Llewellyn Worldwide, Ltd., with more than a million copies in print and translations in sixteen foreign languages. He has also written newspaper and magazine articles and five screenplays. Two of his books are each in their thirtieth printing. His *Gypsy Witchcraft and Magic* received the 1999 Visionary Award for nonfiction and the *Buckland Romany Tarot* received the 2001 Visionary Award.

Considered an authority on the occult and the supernatural, Raymond Buckland served as technical advisor for the Orson Welles movie *Necromancy* (later retitled *The Witching)* and has also worked as an advisor for a stage production of *Macbeth* with William Friedkin, director of *The Exorcist.* He is of Romany (Gypsy) descent and, as such, is an authority on the Gypsies, four of his books dealing with that subject. He has lectured at colleges and universities across the country, including Pennsylvania State University, University of Western Illinois, University of North Dakota, New York State University, Kent State (Ohio), and San Diego City College. He has been the subject of articles in such newspapers and magazines as *The New York Times, Los Angeles Times, New York Daily* (and *Sunday) News, National Observer, Cleveland Plain Dealer, Look Magazine, Cosmopolitan, True,* and many others.

Raymond Buckland has appeared on numerous radio and television talk programs, including *The Dick Cavett Show, Tom Snyder's Tomorrow Show, Not For Women Only* (with Barbara Walters), *The Virginia Graham Show, The Dennis Wholley Show,* and the *Sally Jessy Raphael Show.* He has been seen on BBC-TV England, RAI-TV Italy, and CBC-TV Canada. He has appeared extensively on stage in England and played small character parts in movies in America.

He has taught courses at New York State University, Hofstra University, New Hampshire Technical College, and for the Hampton (Virginia) City Council, and been a featured speaker at the Tidewater Writers Conference and other writers' workshops. He is listed in a number of reference works including *Contemporary Authors, Who's Who In America, Men of Achievement,* and *International Authors and Writers Who's Who.* Today he lives on a small farm in north-central Ohio.

Many of Llewellyn's authors have websites with additional information and resources. For more information, please visit our website at http://www.llewellyn.com.

BUCKLAND'S BOOK OF SPIRIT COMMUNICATIONS

RAYMOND BUCKLAND

Llewellyn Publications
Woodbury, Minnesota

SECOND EDITION, REVISED & EXPANDED
Fifteenth Printing, 2019

First edition, eight printings
(Previously titled *Doors to Other Worlds*)

Book design by Becky Zins and Kimberly Nightingale
Cover design by Kevin R. Brown
Interior illustrations © 2004 by Lauren Foster-MacLeod pages 5, 14, 50, 52, 76, 81, 124, 110, 124, 178, 221
Interior photos courtesy of Fortean Picture Library pages 19, 23, 71, 85, 92, 98, 148, 194
Interior photos courtesy of Prints and Photographs Division, Library of Congress pages 25, 26, 36, and 171
Interior photos courtesy of NSAC, Lily Dale, NY pages 94, 95
Interior photos courtesy of Lily Dale Assembly, Lily Dale, NY pages 24, 33, 94, 95, 195
Interior photos courtesy of Psychic Press, Ltd. pages 150 and 166
Interior photos courtesy of John G. Wolck pages 93 and 97
Interior photos courtesy of M. G. de Fontenay page 164
Interior photos courtesy of Raymond Buckland pages xvi, 2, 3, 36, 74, 88, 89, 90, 117, 122, 135, 138, 145, 165, 176, 193

Library of Congress Cataloging-in-Publication Data
Buckland, Raymond.
Buckland's book of spirit communications / Raymond Buckland.—2nd ed., rev. and expanded.
p. cm.
Rev. ed. of: Doors to other worlds. 1st ed. 1993.
Includes bibliographical references and index.
ISBN 13: 978-0-7387-0399-2
ISBN 10: 0-7387-0399-0
1. Spiritualism. I. Buckland, Raymond. Doors to other worlds. II. Title.

BF1261.2.B78 2004
133.9–dc22 2003066115

Llewellyn Publications
A Division of Llewellyn Worldwide Ltd.
2143 Wooddale Drive
Woodbury, MN 55125-2989
www.llewellyn.com

Printed in the United States of America

Other Books by Raymond Buckland

Advanced Candle Magic (Llewellyn, 1996)

Amazing Secrets of the Psychic World (Parker, 1975) *with Hereward Carrington*

Anatomy of the Occult (Weiser, 1977)

The Book of African Divination (Inner Traditions, 1992) *with Kathleen Binger*

Buckland's Complete Book of Witchcraft (Llewellyn, 1986, 2002)

Buckland Gypsies' Domino Divination Deck (Llewellyn, 1995)

Cardinal's Sin (Llewellyn, 1996)

Cards of Alchemy (Llewellyn, 2003)

Coin Divination (Llewellyn, 1999)

Color Magick (Llewellyn, 1983, 2002)

The Committee (Llewellyn, 1993)

The Fortune-Telling Book (Visible Ink Press, 2003)

Gypsy Dream Dictionary (Llewellyn, 1990, 1998)

Gypsy Witchcraft & Magic (Llewellyn, 1998)

Here is the Occult (HC, 1974)

The Magic of Chant-O-Matics (Parker, 1978)

Mu Revealed (Warner Paperback Library, 1970) *under the pseudonym "Tony Earll"*

A Pocket Guide to the Supernatural (Ace, 1969)

Practical Candleburning Rituals (Llewellyn, 1970, 1976, 1982)

Ray Buckland's Magic Cauldron (Galde Press, 1995)

Scottish Witchcraft (Llewellyn, 1991)

Secrets of Gypsy Fortunetelling (Llewellyn, 1988)

Secrets of Gypsy Love Magic (Llewellyn, 1990)

Signs, Symbols & Omens (Llewellyn, 2003)

The Tree: Complete Book of Saxon Witchcraft (Weiser, 1974)

Truth About Spirit Communication (Llewellyn, 1995)

Wicca for Life (Citadel, 2001)

The Witch Book (Visible Ink Press, 2002)

Witchcraft Ancient and Modern (HC, 1970)

Witchcraft From the Inside (Llewellyn, 1971, 1975, 1995)

Witchcraft . . . the Religion (Buckland Museum, 1966)

Solitary Séance (Llewellyn, 2011)

Tarot Kits and Videos

The Buckland Romani Tarot (2000)

Gypsy Fortunetelling Tarot Kit (1989, 1998)

Witchcraft . . . Yesterday and Today (1990)

For Tara

and in memory of my father and Uncle George

We are all agreed that the present state of things is a scandal to the enlightened age in which we live, that the dispute as to the reality of these marvelous phenomena of which it is quite impossible to exaggerate the scientific importance, if only a tenth part of what has been alleged by generally credible witnesses could be shown to be true—I say it is a scandal that the dispute as to the reality of these phenomena should still be going on, that so many competent witnesses should have declared their belief in them, that so many others should be so profoundly interested in having the question determined, and yet the educated world, as a body, should still be simply in an attitude of incredulity.

Professor Henry Sidgwick

Table of Contents

Acknowledgments

Many thanks to all the people at Llewellyn who made this book possible.
Thanks also to the National Spiritualist Association of Churches, the Lily Dale Assembly,
Ron Nagy and Joyce LaJudice of the Lily Dale Museum for their support and encouragement.

Preface

ALTHOUGH LARGELY BASED on my previous book *Doors to Other Worlds*, this is in many ways a new book. It is a workbook. It includes exercises and each lesson ends with a set of examination questions. There is also a list of essay projects, though they can also be used by a group as discussion subjects. The book can be a reference work, an educational tool, a tool for mediumship development, or for Spiritualism as a way of life. It can be used by the individual or by a group, such as a Home Development Circle. As a group, read it through together—exploring and questioning, and doing the exercises either together or individually. From there, go on to other books in the bibliography.

As you'll read in the introduction, Spiritualism is where I started my trek along the road to spiritual enlightenment. From time to time, over the (many) years, I've come back to Spiritualism. I feel I'm now back to stay. Recently I have taken workshops with such great mediums as Anne Gehman and John Edward. I'm back to reading and rereading the many books on the history and practice of Spiritualism. I'm also presenting and refining my own workshops on the subject.

This book has been a joy to write and is one of which I am very proud. I hope it will bring as much joy and pride to many others. Spiritualism is a practice—it can even be "just a hobby"—or a religion (not a division of Christianity, by the way, but a religion in its own right) and a way of life. The main tenet of Spiritualism is "that communication with the so-called dead is a fact, scientifically proven by the phenomena of Spiritualism."* It is also, then, a means of bringing tremendous solace and relief to those who have "lost" loved ones. It shows that, in fact, those loved ones have not been entirely lost—they are still within reach, and still in contact.

**NSAC Spiritualist Manual:* Declaration of Principles.

Many of the phenomena of Spiritualism surprise (even shock) the senses of modern man and woman. This is the price we pay for the "advancement" of civilization. We've been taught to distrust what our unconscious knows to be true. Young children still accept, as normal, much that is found in Spiritualism—such things as seeing their "dead" relatives, hearing voices, simply knowing certain things they haven't been told. Many older people have managed to return to that innocence. And I use the word innocence advisedly. It is not naiveté. It is not a gullibility, or any form of weakness—far from it; I view it as a strength.

In neopaganism, Wicca, and the many back-to-reality movements, millions of people are rediscovering these lost links with aspects of themselves that had become buried under the artificial shell of modern-day living. I hope this book can help you break out of that shell and find a whole new world of enlightenment, and excitement, awaiting you.

In love and light,
Raymond Buckland
Ohio, 2004

Introduction

UNCLE GEORGE WAS my father's brother and someone of whom I was very fond. He was no more than five feet in height and had the most infectious laugh I have ever come across (almost a giggle!). He and my aunt Doris, together with my mother's brother and his wife, had left England in the early 1930s and emigrated to the United States. Unfortunately, Uncle George developed health problems—the climate of New York's Long Island did not agree with him—and, just before the start of World War II, he and my aunt returned to England.

Uncle George had the most wonderful stories to tell of America, especially about Prohibition, and I would listen to him for hours. He was also an excellent artist and encouraged me in my drawing: pen and ink, pencil, and charcoal.

Uncle George and Aunt Doris were Spiritualists. I don't know if they were of that affiliation before they left for America or whether that was something they became members of during their sojourn abroad. But again and again Uncle George would regale me with wondrous stories of mediums he had witnessed and séances he had attended, both in America and in England. He told of miraculous healings he had seen performed by the late Harry Edwards and others.

When I was about twelve years old, Uncle George loaned me a book on Spiritualism. I don't remember which one it was but I read it and devoured it. I asked him for more, which he was only too happy to provide. I was always a voracious reader and I quickly worked my way through all the spiritualist books he had. I then headed for the public library.

This was the beginning of my interest in matters metaphysical. I slowly but surely worked my way along the library shelves, from Spiritualism into ghosts, ESP, magic, witchcraft, divination, and so on. I was never to look back. Doors had been opened to me, which, in turn, led to other doors . . . I had been introduced to a wide subject that would keep me captivated for the rest of this lifetime. I often look now at my personal library of some five thousand such books and murmur my thanks to Uncle George.

In my late teens and into my early twenties I found that a number of my close friends had a similar interest in the possibility of spirit contact. In my London flat we would get together once a week and work with a Ouija board, or with automatic writing, or with another method of spirit contact. None of us were gullible nor were we total skeptics. We kept careful notes, tried to keep open minds, and carefully examined everything that happened. And some striking things did happen.

One evening we were using a board when the spirit we contacted claimed to have been a brother of mine. It (or "he") went on to say, "I died newborn." I had only one brother to my knowledge and at that time he was still alive, so I later questioned Uncle George and showed him what I'd received. He told me something I hadn't known—and certainly no one else present could have known. He told me that my mother had had a stillborn child two years before the birth of my older brother! Later my mother confirmed this.

Another time we contacted the spirit of a man who had been hanged for a murder he didn't commit (or so he claimed). He gave us the name of the woman he was supposed to have killed, also the name of the church where she was buried, and the year she was buried (1847, as I recall). None of us had heard of the church but a study of a map of the Greater London area confirmed that there was such a place. The following weekend we all traveled to the church and spent a good couple of hours or more moving through the cemetery, studying the gravestones. We couldn't find one for the woman in question. However, the church had been badly bombed during the war and many grave markers were missing. On the pretext of doing genealogical research, I wrote to the vicar and asked if he had any record of

Uncle George

such a woman having died on such a date. I received a prompt reply. Apparently the church records had been placed in safekeeping for the duration of the war. In checking through them, the vicar confirmed that there had indeed been a woman of the name given, who had been buried on that particular date in the churchyard.

To a young man such as myself, starting out along the path of psychic research, these and many other examples were enough to not only hold my interest but to start me forward on a spiritual quest. I learned that, although not Spiritualists themselves, my father and mother had traveled a similar route, holding séances with Uncle George and Aunt Doris and several other friends in the early years of their marriage, before George and Doris emigrated.

Over the many years since then I have never lost my interest in Spiritualism. When I, in my turn, immigrated to the United States and took up residence on Long Island, New York, I went to occasional séances and, over several years, investigated many haunted houses there. When I bought and lived in a nineteenth-century home in New Hampshire, I found I was in the company of at least two ghosts, both of whom made themselves visible to me and to others. In the mid 1970s, in Virginia Beach, Virginia, I held the position of Education

Director for the Poseidia Institute, which was one of the early organizations working with channelers and psychics. And during my eight years in southern California, I attended a number of séances at churches and at Harmony Grove Spiritualist Community. It was in San Diego that I finally came to realize that I had some small gift of mediumship myself, suddenly finding myself describing long-dead friends and relatives to a group of people, some of whom I knew and some of whom were strangers to me. More recently, I have spent time at the famous Lily Dale Assembly, a Spiritualist community in upper state New York, and have taken courses with mediums Anne Gehman and John Edward.

I find that more and more people are turning to Spiritualism. There seems to be a veritable renaissance of interest in it—from talking boards, to séances, to all forms of mediumship. Such mediums as John Edward have popularized Spiritualism through the televising of open séances. There is so much about the subject that makes the most remarkable sense. Extra sensory perception, or ESP, has been well proven for many years. If we are able to communicate with one another mind-to-mind in the flesh, then why not in and out of the flesh? From earliest times, teachings and writings have held that the spirit lives on after death. Then why should we not be able to make contact with that spirit? I believe that we can. By the time you have worked through this book, I think you will agree with me.

Uncle George still looks down on me, as do my parents and my grandparents. They have all been dead many years (recently my brother and my son have joined them), yet they are all still very much a part of me. And this is one of the greatest pleasures of Spiritualism—knowing that you never really lose anyone . . . not even to death.

Raymond Buckland

LESSON ONE

What is Mediumship?

Beginnings

In some of my books I have spoken of the earliest beginnings of religio-magic and described the probable actions of Paleolithic peoples in their attempts to communicate with deity. Certainly we know that the earliest humans needed success in hunting in order to survive and, from extant cave paintings, carvings, and clay models, we know that "magic" was performed immediately before their all-important hunts. We also know from these sources that humankind called upon deity to bring success to this magic, thereby making these hunts fruitful.

From the painting known as "The Sorcerer" in the Caverne des Trois Frères, in Ariége, France (see page 2), it can be seen that a member of the tribe would dress in the skins of a stag and wear the mask and horns, or antlers, of the animal—playing the role of the God of Hunting—in order to lead a ritual designed to bring success to the hunt that would follow. As part of his role, the person playing the part of the Hunting God would almost certainly have spoken as that deity, directing the hunters in their pantomimed actions. So what he might well have been doing, whether or not he realized it, was "channeling" the deity; actually allowing the Hunting God to speak through him.

Channeling

Channeling is a phenomenon that has become popular in recent years, with any number of people publicly going into trance and allowing "entities" to speak through them to their audiences. In public halls, on television, on video tapes, these channelers can be seen and heard. Though not claiming to be a plenipotentiary for "God," many of them do claim that they are bringing the voice, and the teachings, of an entity who has never previously

Follow after charity and desire spiritual gifts . . . that ye may prophesy.

1 Corinthians 14:1

A medium is a connecting link between this physical world and the world of spirit. Anyone can learn to act as that link. Anyone can become a medium.

Lady Ann M. Burdock

---

lived on this earth but who dwells, or has dwelled, on some far distant planet or even in some other dimension. (I'll speak more on this in lesson 15.)

Channeling can be found throughout the ages; from those early cave-dwelling days continuously through to present-day examples. The ancient Egyptian priests would frequently play the part of one or another of their many gods and goddesses. Once again we have extant examples of the paraphernalia used (for example, the mask worn when representing Anubis, the jackal-headed god). The sibyls of ancient Greece were regularly consulted by a populace who desired to speak with their deities. The Romans, too, had their soothsayers and seers, who passed on the words of the dwellers on Mount Olympus. In the Mayan temples the priests played the part of their gods, giving or relaying instructions and advice to the people.

Paleolithic cave art

In the Bible, in 1 Corinthians 12 and 14, there are exhortations for all to use their gifts of prophesy and other spiritual gifts. Throughout the Middle Ages it was common to consult with those who had access to the land beyond death through the rituals of necromancy. In eighteenth- and nineteenth-century Haiti, the slaves developed their own form of religion to produce Voodoo, a combination of their native African beliefs and practices, mixed in with those of the indigenous Indians, and with what they saw as the power of the Catholic Church. In Voodoo, the sole purpose of many of the gatherings is to speak to the deities, who "appear" by possessing one or another of the worshippers and speaking through them. In modern-day Panchmuda, India (northwest of Calcutta), similar rites are held each year at the Temple of Manasa for the Snake Festival, when the Serpent Mother takes possession of her worshippers. Writers, musicians, and artists have long composed through a process of channeling. Wolfgang Mozart heard music in his head and simply wrote down what he heard, never changing or modifying it. In the mid-nineteenth century came the birth of the present-day Spiritualist movement, with the Fox sisters of New York, in 1848, discovering a simple method to communicate with the spirits of the dead (see lesson 3).

It can be seen, then, that there is nothing new in channeling, be it bringing messages from those who have died and passed on, producing advice from extraterrestrial entities, or speaking the words of divinities. The channel is a medium through which the information is produced. (What that information is, how accurate it may be, and from whence it comes, are questions we will address later in this book.) Anyone can act as such a channel, or medium. Some people seem more readily attuned to the position than others, but we all have the capability. Most mediums and channels work consciously and have, indeed, spent time in training to achieve their results, yet some act completely spontaneously and unconsciously.

Possession

Mediumship is not the same thing as possession. In possession an undesirable spirit or entity takes over the body of a living human, forcing out and overriding that human's spirit. It possesses and refuses to give up possession unless driven out . . . though there are actually far fewer cases of true possession than late-night movies and the sensational media would have you believe. In mediumship the living human may voluntarily allow another spirit to make use of his or her vocal cords, hand and/or arm muscles, or other parts of the body; but never giving up total control of the entire body . . . it is a mutual agreement that can be terminated at any time. Under the proper circumstances there is absolutely no harm that can come to the medium, though it may be wise to use some precautionary measures "just in case." These I'll deal with, in detail, elsewhere.

In many types of mediumship, however, there is no giving up of any of the medium's organism whatsoever. For example, with clairvoyance and clairaudience the medium is simply seeing and hearing and then relaying what he or she sees or hears. It is only in such forms as direct voice, automatic writing, and the like that there is ever any degree of use of the medium's body.

In this book I will be dealing mainly with mediumship in the sense of obtaining information from the spirits of those who have died and passed on but, toward the end of the book, I'll also look into channeling of other entities. Throughout the book I'll address developing your own abilities in the various

Voodoo possession

aspects of mediumship. Here practice will be the keyword. But with practice, one thing needs to be borne in mind: don't overdo things. Don't try to do something—be it crystal-gazing, clairvoyance, or psychometry—and keep trying till you are blue in the face! Apart from getting discouraged, you'll rapidly terminate your interest in that specific art, and perhaps the whole field of mediumship, and you'll drag down your psychic defenses to the point where you could suffer both physically and emotionally. It is much better to take small bites on a regular basis; then you'll progress, gain in strength, and much sooner reach the goals you have set for yourself.

Exercises

At the root of all psychic development is good breathing. In my book *Amazing Secrets of the Psychic World* (coauthored with Hereward Carrington), I spoke of the life-giving property of fresh air and the fact that simply by breathing fully you contribute to living fully. Some of the exercises I gave were:

1. Stand before an open window, or out of doors, free from all restrictive clothing. Exhale forcibly, bending the body forward and relaxing the muscles. Then stand up straight and place both hands over your abdomen. Now breathe as deeply as possible against those hands, expanding the abdomen as much as possible without allowing the chest or ribs to expand at all. Again exhale forcibly.

2. After five or six such breaths, place your hands on either side against your ribs. Now breathe in deeply, pressing out the ribs but without allowing either the abdomen or the upper chest to expand more than a little.

3. After five or six breaths, place your hands on your upper chest, just below the neck, and breathe with this portion of the lungs, without allowing either the ribs or the abdomen to expand.

4. You will find that it's not so easy to control your breathing. After you have mastered it, however, you can go on to the next step, the complete breath:

5. Take a number of good, deep breaths, starting with expanding your abdomen, then the ribs, then the upper chest, one after the other in the one breath. Try to control this intake in the three stages, one after the other. Then, as you become more accomplished, merge them one into the next so that you have something akin to a rolling motion as the breath moves up the body. Breathe in through your nose and out through either your nose or mouth.

From there continue with establishing a mental image of the breath as you breathe it, in the form of light. See it coming into your body and filling it. As you breathe out, see the light forcing out all the negativity in the form of dark colors: black, dark browns, greens, and reds. You can imagine the light entering from wherever seems most comfortable to you—through the third eye; into the heart; up from the ground through your feet . . . whichever you prefer. Just be consistent and always see it entering at the same place.

For the exit of the negativity, see it being driven out of all your bodily orifices, one after the other, and end with it leaving through all the pores of the skin. End with the whole body—every little extremity—completely filled with fresh, vibrant, positive light.

Trance Development and Chakra Enhancement

Analyze your "falling asleep" pattern. Try to catch yourself at just the point of falling asleep and to "hold on to yourself," as it were, as long as possible in that state until you can hold no more and you actually do fall asleep. This is excellent practice so that you will always be in control of yourself, no matter how deep the trance you enter.

> Spirits do not belong perpetually to the same order. All are destined to attain perfection by passing through the different degrees of the spirit-hierarchy. This amelioration is effected by incarnation . . .
>
> **Allan Kardec**

The physical body is connected to the etheric or spiritual body at centers known as chakras (pronounced "shock-ruz"). Part of the development of any psychic and spiritual ability is to stimulate those chakras by raising what is known as the kundalini power—power that travels through the body and generates energy. The chakras are linked with actual physical glands, and there are seven of them. The first, lumbar (or base) chakra, is at the gonads; the second, spine chakra, is at the adrenals; the solar plexus chakra is at the lyden; the heart chakra is at the thymus; the throat chakra is at the thyroid; the third eye chakra is at the pineal, and the crown chakra is at the pituitary. Here is what I say about chakras and kundalini in my book *Buckland's Complete Book of Witchcraft* (Llewellyn, 2002):

> *In meditation the mysterious psychic energy can be sent up through these centers. This very potent force is called the kundalini, or "Serpent Power." As this mighty force begins to flow within you, these vital psychic centers—the chakras—begin to open in successive order.*
>
> *As the vital forces begin to flow through the nervous system, the individual achieves a sense of well-being and peace. The subconscious begins to clear itself of the negative and undesired patterns of feelings and images that have been programmed into it through your lifetime. The cosmic force of the kundalini very naturally operates in a calm, relaxed, contemplative atmosphere. As the succession of opening chakras continues, your awareness and perception of life flows continually from within. A new vibrancy permeates your being.*

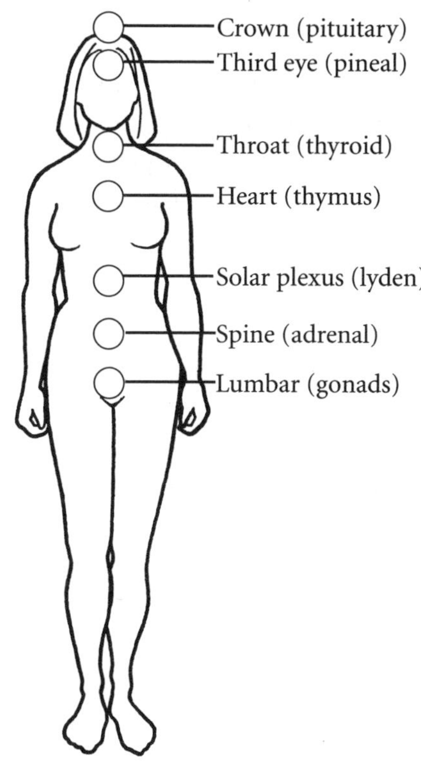

Chakra centers

Exercise

Getting the kundalini power to flow through the chakras very definitely sets up a new vibrancy. But how to get that power to flow? The first step is to do your deep breathing, as in the exercises above, then to awaken the chakras as follows.

Each of the seven centers is associated with a color, going through the spectrum. The base chakra is red, the spine chakra is orange, the solar plexus chakra is yellow, the heart chakra is green, the throat chakra is blue, the pineal chakra is indigo, and the crown chakra is violet. Imagine each of these centers, one at a time, and see it enveloped in its specific color. Concentrate your energies first on the base

> Mental attitude is also important. Practice should be initiated with the positive thought that it will produce the desired results. It helps tremendously to "get into the mood," as it does in the case of most undertakings which require concentration and skill.
>
> **Omar Garrison**

---

chakra, and see it enveloped in a swirling ball of red light. Imagine this light ball spinning around, clockwise, getting faster and faster. After a few moments of this, see the ball of light moving up to the position of the second chakra, at the adrenals. As it moves up, see it gradually changing color to orange, so that by the time it gets to that second chakra position it is pure orange. Again, have it swirl around and around. Then move the ball of light on up to the third chakra, at the solar plexus, changing the light to pure yellow as it moves. Go on up through all the chakras until all have been vitalized in this fashion. Finish off by changing the color to white and seeing the ball of light grow larger and larger until it envelops your whole body.

It is important that the chakras be awakened in the right order, from base to crown. You will find you feel a sensation of warmth with, perhaps, a faint pricking at each center, as you "awaken the fiery serpent."

The English medium Ivy Northage suggests that you might also imagine each chakra center as a flower and see it opening up. Eastern philosophy links the centers with the "thousand-petaled lotus," but you can see the chakras as any flower you wish. A different flower at each center, if you would like, though please be consistent and always have that same one at the same center. As the light swirls about it, see the petals slowly open and fold back until the whole bloom is there. If you can tie-in a psychic smell of the flower at that point, that would be wonderful. Then move that colored light on up toward the next chakra.

Raising Your Vibrations

We are all vibrations. Everything is made up of vibrating matter; be it a tree, a rock, a blade of grass, or a human being. We are vibrating matter. The world of spirit is vibrating at a different rate from the physical world, so if we can raise our vibration rate sufficiently it will facilitate our communication with the second level.

A worthwhile suggestion is given by Jon Klimo in *Channeling* (Tarcher, 1987) for raising your vibrations. Imagine a dial, with an attached knob, fastened to yourself. See it calibrated from one to ten. The dial is to indicate the raising of your consciousness vibrations. In your meditative state, start to turn the knob and see the needle on the dial move up from zero to one. Feel, sense, and know that your vibrations are moving up toward the ideal of being on a completely spiritual level; where you are at one with your higher self. Slowly turn the knob on up to two, then three. Take your time with this. Adjust your senses with each turn of the knob. It may take a number of sittings before you feel able to get as high as ten and be at one with your higher self. Don't rush this; take it a little at a time. As you raise your vibrations, also feel your emotions being cleansed.

Examination Questions for Lesson One

1. Are mediumship and channeling relatively modern phenomena? If not, how far back do they go?

2. What does Wolfgang Mozart have to do with mediumship?

3. What is the Bible's attitude toward the practice of mediumship and channeling?

4. What is the difference between a medium and someone who is possessed?

5. Does a medium surrender his or her body completely to the spirit coming through?

Profile

John Edward

John Edward was born John Edward McGee, on Long Island, New York, in 1969. He was an only child. His father, Jack, was a New York City cop and his mother, Perinda, was a secretary. John's grandmother had read tea leaves and his father admitted to having had a number of personal psychic experiences in his younger days. John's parents separated when John was eleven.

John's mother was a regular attendee at local psychic fairs and frequently had psychics come to the house. It was at one such home gathering that John encountered Lydia Clar. Clar claimed that the main reason she was at the house was to give John a sense of direction and to encourage him in developing his own psychic abilities. From a very young age, John had experienced various phenomena, such as astral projection, and had displayed psychic talent, speaking knowledgeably of relatives he had never met and who had died long before he was born. Yet despite this, John himself was a great skeptic of all psychic matters. As a teenager, however, he did buy himself a deck of tarot cards and started reading them for others. Another friend, Shelley Peck, also became close as both a friend and advisor. Very quickly, John went on to do readings at psychic fairs and rapidly developed a following because of the accuracy of his readings. He had premonitions, such as of the *Challenger* disaster, the Oklahoma City bombing, and the crash on Pan Am's flight 103 in Scotland.

At college, John studied Health Care Administration and Public Administration. He went on to work at a hospital for several years as a phlebotomist. But as his psychic and medium gifts developed, he realized that he needed to devote full time to them and, at age twenty-six, left the security of his hospital employment. When his mother died, on October 5, 1989, he started looking for the signs that the two of them had agreed she would send, to confirm her continued existence in the afterlife. Although one of the signs came at the funeral, John had to wait several years before he got the other confirmations.

John became a regular guest on the *Larry King Live* television show, and others. In 1998 he published his first book, an autobiographical work titled *One Last Time.* He also appeared in an HBO television special, *Life After Life.* By the year 2000, John had his own show, *Crossing Over,* which was to become a major success and to make John a star. It was syndicated in the United States and eventually appeared in other parts of the world, including Australia. His second book, *Crossing Over With John Edward,* was an instant bestseller. In 2001 an unfair attack was made on John and the show by *Time* magazine, when a journalist named Leon Jaroff wrote a story of half-truths, innuendos, and pure speculation. He wrote it without ever interviewing John, without attending the show, and with talking to only one (for some reason disgruntled) audience member named Michael O'Neill. Despite strong letters to *Time* from network executives, and consideration of a lawsuit, the magazine declined to print a retraction, thus demonstrating yet another flaw in journalistic integrity in these present times. In contrast, scientific tests were carried out at the University of Arizona in Tucson, using five top mediums: John Edward, George Anderson, Anne Gehman, Suzane Northrop, and Laurie Campbell. The whole session was televised and included a hookup of nineteen electrodes to the head, to measure heart and brain whilst doing Spiritualist readings. The final results showed that while a group of control subjects (non-mediums) scored 36 percent accuracy, the true mediums scored an average of 83 percent accuracy.

Today John lives with his wife Sandra, and their two Bichon Frises, Jolie and Roxie, in Long Island, New York. His time is taken up with his television show, with private readings, and with lecturing and giving workshops. His great success is a testament to what has been repeatedly described as his down to earth approach, and obvious sincerity.

LESSON TWO

The World of Spirits

A 1980 Gallup Poll revealed that as many as 71 percent of Americans believe in an afterlife. Orthodox theology has brainwashed many of us to believe in a "Heaven" and a "Hell," as the two ultimate destinations for our soul, or spirit. (I prefer the word "spirit" and will stick with that throughout this book.) The Roman Catholic Church also throws in "Purgatory" as a third intermediate state. As Hereward Carrington pointed out, in *Your Psychic Powers and How To Develop Them* (Dodd Mead, 1920):

> *When in this state (Purgatory), souls may be helped either by those who have passed over or by the prayers of the living. It will thus be seen that, in this respect at least, the Catholic church approaches nearer than any other religion the doctrines of Spiritualism!*

In many religions, as in Spiritualism, there is no such division into two or three parts. The afterlife is in just one place; neither "good" nor "bad," having neither rewards nor punishments. Andrew Jackson Davis coined the term "Summerland" for this afterlife world (picked up by Gerald Gardner and used by today's Wiccans). It's a place very much like our present earthly plane, yet on the next, more advanced, level of existence. The information about this next plane has come to us from a wide variety of sources and, as might be expected, is very contradictory.

Looking into the Spirit World

Where do these reports come from? Who gives them? In recent times a large number of "near-death experiences" have been documented. Raymond Moody and Elisabeth Kübler-Ross, among others, have written extensively on the descriptions of what has been found by people who have briefly "died" and passed over, only to return. But for centuries there have

> The distinctive contribution of Spiritualism to the enlightenment of mankind is to show that our continued existence after death is not pious hope but a demonstrable fact.
>
> **W. H. Mackintosh**

> Spirits differ very widely from one another as regards their knowledge and morality, it is evident that the same question may receive from them very different answers . . . exactly as would be the case if it were propounded alternately to a man of science, an ignoramus, and a mischievous wag. The important point . . . is to know who is the spirit to whom we are addressing our question.
>
> **Allan Kardec**

> On the whole, Christianity has tended to be better at depicting hell than heaven or any of the other places. The demons and the tortures of hell have an immediacy and richness of texture generally lacking in the corresponding descriptions of heaven, which is most often some vague and ethereal place where angels sit around on clouds playing harps and singing hosannas.
>
> **Carol Neimen and Emily Goldman**

---

also been excursions into the spirit world undertaken by shamans, seers, and clairvoyants. Moses, Swedenborg, Andrew Jackson Davis, and others have recorded what they have found. More importantly, perhaps, we also have a wealth of material given to us through mediums, directly from spirits of the dead, describing their new world in minute detail. From this we have a fairly complete representative picture of the spirit world.

Death will not make you omniscient. Far from it; you enter the new life still carrying with you all the beliefs, prejudices, and opinions that you had here on earth. If you believed in reincarnation before death you will almost certainly find it confirmed after death. Yet, if you did not believe in reincarnation prior to death you are just as likely to find that "confirmed" after death!

It seems that the most devoutly religious find what they expect—an afterlife that is much as their teachings have led them to believe it to be—whereas the not-so-devout find it to be more like the physical plane they just left. How can there be this difference? It seems likely that those who have been indoctrinated with certain expectations will find those expectations satisfied, at least for a period. Then gradually, it seems, they are brought to see that not everything is exactly as they were taught. In this way there is no great shock to them on passing over. So, reincarnation—and other major beliefs—may or may not be a fact, but it will take a while in the afterlife to find out. Just because a spirit, returning through the agencies of a medium, states that he or she has found a particular thing to be so, does not necessarily mean that it is so.

How, then, can we judge anything that is relayed to us through a medium? Much the same way as here on earth. We must listen to the reports, consider the majority voice, and then go with what makes most sense to us, as individuals. It won't be confirmed or denied until we make that passage ourselves, and then probably not for some time after.

It does seem certain that there are a number of levels, variously described as "zones" or "spheres,"

At first one wanders . . . through the dark . . . then one is struck with a marvelous light; one is received into pure regions and meadows.

Plutarch

My involvement with paranormal phenomena has convinced me that the whole experience is simply an extension of our natural awareness and mental abilities. The phrase "life after death" presupposes a following event, when it seems to me to be a parallel existence which is continual. The before, after and during is purely relative to the observer.

Michael Bentine

The detailed and graphic descriptions of the afterlife that are supplied by Spiritualist communicators contain some uncanny similarities with many ancient religious concepts.

Sue Leonard

That transitional state we call death leads us into a period of rest, followed by our recent earth life review from which we can assess lessons learnt to add to those already learnt in the process of the evolvement of the soul . . . Having left our physical body behind on the earth plane, we are then our astral body or true self which is remarkably like our physical body at its best.

David Bassant

---

through which we must progress. Our rate of progression is entirely up to us. For the duration of this book I will describe this earthly plane as the first level and that immediately following death as the second level. Apparently, communication between two adjacent levels is easier than communication between separated levels. In other words, it is easier for us to make contact with those who have died relatively recently than with those who have been dead a considerable time and have passed on to higher levels.

Also, it is possible to "visit" a lower level (e.g. as with a spirit from level two materializing briefly in level one), yet not possible to move up before your time to a higher level.

Meeting "God"

All reports received through mediums seem to indicate that spirits do not have any immediate confrontation with any infinite intelligence; they do not pass directly into the presence of God or Goddess. As they progress in spiritual perception and understanding, however, they do seem to gradually perceive that the universe, far from being chaotic due to pure chance, is, in fact, orderly and systematic. There seems the possibility of it being governed by some Supreme Intelligence. Whether or not that Intelligence, if it does exist, is eventually encountered is unknown to us here on level one . . . and probably on the next few levels also.

The Spiritual Body

From spirit contact we learn that on the second level we retain the same appearance that we had here on level one, with one exception. The exception is that we may assume the state/development of that body we most prefer. In other words, if I end life with a bald head and a paunch, I can regain the slim, trim shape of my youth merely by wishing it so! Similarly, someone who went through life crippled can be fit and healthy in the afterlife.

But how is it, then, that a medium contacting your grandparents (for example) describes them as they were when they died—old and withered, with white hair and stooped shoulders? It is simply that, for the time of the séance, the communicating grandparent assumes the body by which you are most likely to remember him or her, to make recognition easier. After the séance, they will almost certainly revert to their preferred appearance.

Spirit Speech and Travel

Conversation between spirits is probably on a telepathic basis. Whether or not their lips move may depend upon how long they have been on the second level. It's like it is in our dreams, where we can be aware of what someone is saying without their actually "mouthing" it. In our dreams this seems quite natural, and so it would be in the spirit world. When communicating through a medium, however, I'm sure that most spirits seem to speak as we do on this level, if only to facilitate the medium's reception and understanding.

The body as we know it has an invisible double, known as the ethereal or astral body. It is an exact duplicate of its physical counterpart. In fact this astral body may well be our actual "spirit." In dreams, or what we think of as dreams, the astral body travels about at will, meeting the astral bodies of others, both living and dead. Remembrance of these travels and meetings are what we later recall as "dreams."

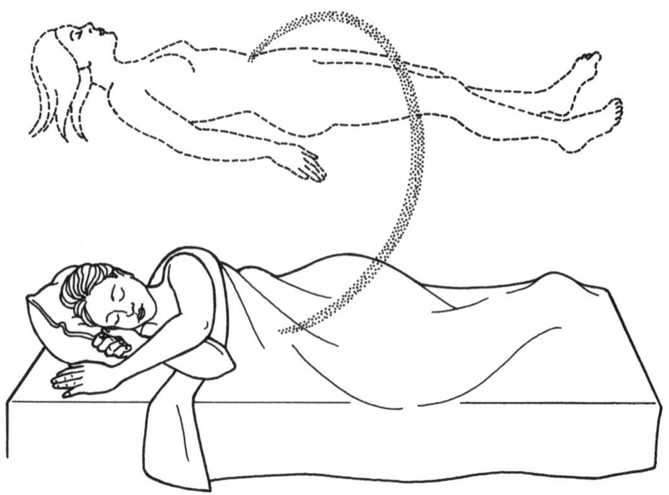

Physical and astral bodies

On the astral plane, our astral bodies can move with the speed of thought. Think you are in a particular location and so you are . . . even if it's halfway around the world. This may seem incredible until you consider the speed of such things as radio waves. These travel around the world at the speed of light—one hundred and eighty-six thousand miles a second; the equivalent of traveling four hundred and fifty times around the world in one minute! Such being the case, it's not unreasonable to accept that thought can move just as fast. And, as with thought, so with the spirits of the dead. They can relocate as fast as thinking.

Other Life Forms

In shamanism it is accepted that all things have spirits be they animal, vegetable, or mineral. Certainly, if you break down all things to their atomic and then subatomic levels, they are mostly space with little obvious difference between animal, vegetable, or mineral. This space could well be the "spirit" in shamanism that is found in all things, and by which all things are interconnected in the web of life.

What we perceive as a tree in this world is only the outward manifestation of the real spiritual tree lying within it, and this is true of all physical manifestations that we see in nature. Every physical body has a corresponding spiritual body behind it. Indeed, this fact gave rise to the famous "Doctrine of Correspondences" put forth by Swedenborg. As Hereward Carrington says:

> *This correspondence throws a little light on the bewildering fact that spirits often speak of spirit-gold, spirit-marble, spirit-houses, spirit-books, etc., as if they were tangible realities—not, of course, that these are sublimations of corresponding objects of earth, existent throughout but different as to material, yet sufficiently alike to be called by the same name. In other words, these spirit-objects are expressed in a different vehicle of the nature that is to us, externalized as gold, marble, etc. . . . We must endeavor to realize the reality of the spiritual world, which we have been unaccustomed to think of as in any way substantial owing to the teachings of theology.*

"Evil" Entities

Later I will speak more on the possibility of encountering anything "evil" in the spirit world, but for now let's simply consider that negative forces traditionally seem drawn to the darkness while positive forces are drawn to the light. As we progress, spiritually, we speak of "the light dawning," and of "coming into the light." This doesn't necessarily mean that we emerge from a material darkness and enter a material light, but rather that we go through a process of psychic evolution corresponding to this. Yet in near-death experiences, those who have "died" and returned always seem to speak of entering a tunnel of bright light, often so bright that they cannot see what's at the end of it. Very literally, they are "coming into the light."

Spiritually and parapsychologically, we speak of moving "lost souls," "earthbound spirits," "ghosts," forward into the light, so that they may progress.

Transition

What happens at the moment of death? Many people are afraid of dying, yet it seems there's really no need for this fear. One of the joys of Spiritualism, to my mind, is that it proves the continuance of existence after death, and thereby removes the primary fear of ending everything. As will be seen in progressing through this book, even communication with loved ones is not necessarily ended at death.

In astral projection, our ethereal double slips out of our physical body and goes on its way, preserving its connection to the physical body with an infinitely elastic silver-colored cord. When we dream, our invisible double also slides out of its shell and goes off, stretching its cord behind it. At death it is the same process; the spirit separates from the physical shell and leaves. The only difference is that at death there is no preserved connection by the cord. It separates, and, therefore, there is no going back.

It would be interesting to know if, in cases of the "near-death experience"—where someone has, to all intents and purposes, "died" yet later comes back—the silver cord is there or not. My suspicion would be that yes, it's still there.

Here is a typical death experience, related by a departed spirit speaking through a medium:

> *When I awoke in the spirit-life and saw that I still had hands and feet and all the rest of the human body, I can't say what feelings took hold of me. I realized that I had this body . . . a spiritual body, but a body. Imagine being reborn, free from the decaying flesh. I gazed on weeping friends with a saddened heart, mingled with joy, knowing that I could still be with them daily, though unseen and unheard. Then I felt a light touch on my shoulder and turned to find many loved ones who had long since departed life on earth; all there to greet me and help me move on.*

Many records of near-death experiences speak of leaving the body, going toward a bright light—oftentimes down a sort of tunnel—and seeing deceased loved ones there. In these experiences these loved ones often tell the spirit to return; that the time had not yet come to pass completely over.

So there's no pain in death. On the contrary, there's frequently escape from pain. The moment of death, when the spirit slips from the physical shell, is the moment that any pain that was present disappears. The only real pain of death is, in reality, the pain of those left behind, believing that they have forever lost the deceased. But for the deceased there is now joy and happiness.

Examination Questions

1. Do Spiritualists believe in a heaven and a hell?

2. Where do Spiritualists get their ideas of what constitutes the world of life after death?

3. Do you meet God when you die?

4. If your deceased uncle had been badly crippled with arthritis for many years before he died, and a clairvoyant medium described him that way, does that mean we have to live with our infirmities in the afterlife?

5. What is the connection between dreams and the afterlife?

6. Is dying a painful experience?

7. Once your spirit enters the afterlife, will it have knowledge of all things, perhaps being able to see into the future?

8. Two spirits—a brother and a sister—come through at a séance. The brother claims that there is such a thing as reincarnation; the sister says there is not. Who is right?

9. Are there trees and plants, birds and rocks, in the afterlife?

10. What happens, at death, to the silver cord that joins our physical and spiritual bodies? How far does it have to stretch?

Profile

Jeane Dixon

Jeane Dixon was born Jean Pinkert, in Medford, Wisconsin, on January 3, 1918. She grew up to become one of the best-known, if controversial, psychics of recent times—her possible prediction of the death of President John F. Kennedy catapulting her into the limelight.

Jeane was born to a wealthy lumber family that moved to California when she was still young. Jeane attended high school in Los Angeles and took some training toward becoming an actress and singer. At the age of eight she had her fortune told by a Gypsy, who said that she would become a famous seer. In 1939, at the age of twenty-one, she married James L. Dixon, an automobile dealer. They moved to Detroit and started a real-estate business.

During World War II, Dixon entertained servicemen by making predictions. This she did through the Home Hospitality Committee, organized by Washington socialites. When the couple moved to Washington, D.C., they continued in real estate and Dixon continued with her predictions.

A devout Roman Catholic, Dixon saw no problem with giving predictions, saying "a revelation is something special. Sometimes two, three, or even four years go by without God granting me a revelation, and then some mornings I wake up and feel inspired and know that something great is going to happen." She went on to say: "Another but a less certain way through which I receive knowledge of future events is what I call the 'psychic way.' Often when I meet people and shake their hands, I feel vibrations. But sensing and interpreting these vibrations, I can tell many things about that person. I 'see' even more if I have a chance to touch their hands with the tip of my right hand. My fingers are supersensitive, and many times a gentle touch enables me to pick up an individual channel of communication with eternity." She claimed she could see the past, present, and future.

Jeane Dixon

It was Ruth Montgomery's trumpeting of Jeane Dixon's claimed prediction of the assassination of President Kennedy that brought her most firmly to public attention. Ruth Montgomery was a newspaper political columnist who wrote the book *A Gift of Prophesy: the Phenomenal Jeane Dixon*, published in 1965. The book sold more than three million copies and launched Dixon on the lecture circuit. But the basis of the book left many in doubt. In an article in Parade magazine, in 1956, it was stated: "As for the 1960 election, Mrs. Dixon thinks it will be dominated by labor and won by a Democrat. But he will be assassinated or die in office." Dixon also said, however, that the occurrence would "not necessarily (be) in his first term." At another time she made the statement that "During the 1960 election, I saw Richard Nixon as the winner." At that time, she went on to add that "John F. Kennedy would fail to win the presidency." She also predicted that World War

III would start in 1958, that there would be a cure for cancer found in 1967, and that the Russians would put the first man on the moon. In 1956 she said that Indian Prime Minister Nehru would be ousted from office (yet he served until his death in 1964). She also said that Fidel Castro would be overthrown.

Dixon did make some very dramatic, and accurate, predictions, however. She warned movie actress Carole Lombard not to travel by air just a few days before the actress died in a plane crash. She similarly predicted the death of Dag Hammarskjöld, also in a plane crash. But most of her predictions were couched in such a way that she could claim to have been right no matter what happened.

LESSON THREE

The History of Spiritualism, Part One—The Early Years

The Episode at Hydesville

As stated in lesson one, Spiritualist phenomena have been manifesting for thousands of years. The ancient Greek oracles channeled by going into trance and speaking with a changed voice and personality. The sixteenth-century Tremblers of Cevennes, Germany, went into trance, spoke in tongues, communicated with spirits, and cured sickness. In the Bible the "Woman of Endor" (it was only King James who labeled her a "witch"; nowhere in the text is she so described) is an out-and-out Spiritualist medium, producing exactly the same phenomena that mediums have been regularly producing in séance rooms for the past one hundred fifty years.

But the modern Spiritualist movement was more firmly established—founded, if you like—in 1848, in the state of New York, as the result of publicity afforded the happenings at the Fox homestead in Hydesville, Wayne County.

Ever since moving into the house on December 11, 1847, the Fox family had been plagued with strange sounds echoing through the wooden cottage. There were knockings and rappings the origins of which neither John Fox nor his wife Margaret was able to trace. They tried all the obvious possibilities, such as loose shutters and window sashes, frequently getting up in the middle of the night to go searching through the house, candle in hand.

On the night of Friday, March 31, they and their two daughters had just retired to bed when the noises once again started up—in particular what sounded like someone or something rapping sharply on wood. Here is a statement made by Mrs. Margaret Fox:

God allows the spirit, as its free will develops, to become the master of its choices.

Allan Kardec

Let it then be clearly stated that there is no more connexion between physical Mediumship and morality than there is between a refined ear for music and morality. Both are purely physical gifts . . . There is simply no connexion at all between the two things, save that they both have their centre in the same human body.

Sir Arthur Conan Doyle

Be not simply good; be good for something.

Henry David Thoreau

It was very early when we went to bed on this night—hardly dark. I had been so broken of rest I was almost sick . . . I had just lain down. It commenced as usual. I knew it from all the other noises I had ever heard before. The children, who slept in the other bed in the room, heard the rapping, and tried to make similar sounds by snapping their fingers.

My youngest child, Cathie, said, "Mr. Splitfoot, do as I do," clapping her hands. The sound instantly followed her with the same number of raps. When she stopped the sound ceased for a short time. Then Margaretta said, in sport: "No, do just as I do. Count one, two, three, four," striking one hand against the other at the same time; and the raps came as before. She was afraid to repeat them . . .

I then thought I could put a test that no one in the place could answer. I asked the "noise" to rap my different children's ages successively. Instantly, each one of my children's ages was given correctly, pausing between them sufficiently long to individualise them until the seventh, at which a longer pause was made, and then three more emphatic raps were given, corresponding to the age of the little one that died, which was my youngest child.

I then asked: "Is this a human being that answers my questions so correctly?" There was no rap. I asked: "Is it a spirit? If it is, make two raps." Two sounds were given as soon as the request was made.

The Foxes went on with their questions and slowly learned that the spirit was a thirty-one-year-old man, a peddler, who had been murdered in the house. Mrs. Fox called: "Will you continue to rap if I call in my neighbors, that they may hear it too?" The raps were affirmative. She called in her neighbor, Mrs. Redfield. The testimony continues:

Mrs. Redfield is a very candid woman. The girls were sitting up in bed clinging to each other and trembling in terror . . . Mrs. Redfield came immediately (this was about half past seven), thinking she would have a laugh at the children. But when she saw them pale with fright and nearly speechless, she was amazed and believed there was something more serious than she had supposed. I asked a few questions for her and she was answered as before. He told her age exactly. She then called her husband, and the same questions were asked and answered.

Fox family home

The Foxes went on to call in the Dueslers, the Hydes, the Jewells, and several others.

On first looking at the phenomenon it would seem to be typical of poltergeist activity. There were young children in the house: Margaretta was seven and Cathie, or Kate, was ten years of age. With children of that age it's not uncommon for there to be spontaneous physical activity brought about by raw energy, for want of a better word, thrown off by the children. But the Fox episode differs from "normal" poltergeist activity in that the noises responded intelligently to questions. Indeed, they acknowledged being a "spirit." Poltergeist activity is completely unpredictable and uncontrollable, so here was a very real difference.

It is a little-known fact that the house had a prior history of strange noises. The tenants previous to the Foxes were a Michael and Hannah Weekman, who vacated the premises because of the noises. Before the Weekmans was a couple named Bell.

With the crowd of neighbors in the house that Friday night, the spirit was thoroughly tested with questions of all sorts. All were answered to the satisfaction of the questioners. The spirit also gave all the details of his murder, which was done with a butcher knife and in order to steal his money. Margaret Fox and the two girls left for the night, leaving the house overflowing with people, and still the rapping continued.

The next evening, Saturday, it was said that as many as three hundred people gathered to witness the rapping. The spirit claimed that its body had been buried ten feet below the surface of the ground. Immediate excavations turned up hair and bones, pronounced by medical experts to be human. But it wasn't until fifty-six years later that the whole skeleton was discovered. According to a report in the Boston Journal of November 23, 1904, parts of a basement wall collapsed and revealed an entire human skeleton . . . together with a peddler's tin box! The peddler's name was Charles B. Rosna.

Earlier a maid named Lucretia Pulver, who had worked for the Bells when they lived in the house, testified that she remembered a peddler once stopping there. Lucretia was sent off for the night and when she returned the next morning she was told the peddler had left. In her statement Lucretia said that both she and a friend, Aurelia Losey, had subsequently heard strange noises in the house during the night. The Bells were never charged with the murder.

Box of murdered peddler Charles B. Rosna

Andrew Jackson Davis

The birth of Spiritualism, in the Fox home, had been predicted. On that same March 31, 1848, a man who became known as the "Poughkeepsie Seer" wrote in his journal:

> *About daylight this morning a warm breathing passed over my face and I heard a voice, tender and strong, saying: "Brother, the good work has begun—behold a living demonstration is born." I was left wondering what could be meant by such a message.*

Obviously it referred to the Hydesville rappings. Andrew Jackson Davis was born in 1826 and grew up with little schooling. In his first sixteen years he only read one book, yet by the time he was twenty he was to write what Sir Arthur Conan Doyle has called "one of the most profound and original books of philosophy ever produced."

At the age of twelve Davis started to hear voices, giving him advice. On this advice he convinced his father to leave their native Blooming Grove, on the Hudson River, New York, and move to Poughkeepsie. His father was a weaver, then later became a shoemaker. A year or so later Davis began seeing things: at his mother's death he saw a beautiful house in a wonderful land of brightness, and knew it was where his mother had gone.

A traveling showman introduced Davis to hypnotism. It was found that while in trance the boy had tremendous clairvoyant powers, so much so that a local tailor named Levingston quit his profession to work full-time with Davis, diagnosing disease. Davis said that the human body became transparent to his spirit eyes—which actually seemed to work from the position of the third eye. Each organ then stood out clearly and with a radiance that was only dimmed by disease. Davis was also able to diagnose at a distance, his astral body soaring away over the land to the person whose body he needed to view.

One day in 1844, Davis suddenly left Poughkeepsie and, in a state of semitrance, wandered forty miles away into the Catskill Mountains. He later claimed that while there he met and talked with the spirits of Claudius Galen, a second-century Greek physician,

Andrew Jackson Davis

and Emanuel Swedenborg. Swedenborg was a brilliant eighteenth-century Swedish seer who was the first to explain that death means no change; that the spirit world is a counterpart of this physical world.

In 1845, in his nineteenth year, Davis felt the need to write a book. He broke his partnership with Levingston and teamed up with a Dr. Lyon, from Bridgeport, as hypnotist for this work. Lyon gave up his practice and took the young man to New York, where a Reverend William Fishbough also gave up his work to act as secretary and take the dictation Davis gave while in trance. In November, 1845, Davis began to dictate his great work: *The Principles of Nature, Her Divine Revelations, and a Voice to Mankind.* The dictation lasted for fifteen months.

Dr. George Bush, a professor of Hebrew at the University of New York, was present at many of the trance utterings. He later said:

> *I can solemnly affirm that I have heard Davis correctly quote the Hebrew language in his lectures (dictation), and display a knowledge of geology that would have been astonishing in a person of his age, even if he had devoted years to the study. He has discussed, with the most signal ability, the profoundest questions of historical and Biblical archæology, of mythology, of the origin and affinity of language, and the progress of civilization among the different nations of the globe, which would do honor to any scholar of the age, even if in reaching them he had the advantage of access to all the libraries of Christendom. Indeed, if he had acquired all the information he gives forth in these lectures, not in the two years since he left the shoemaker's bench, but in his whole life, with the most assiduous study, no prodigy of intellect of which the world has ever heard would be for a moment compared with him, yet not a single volume or page has he ever read.*

By the time he was twenty-one, Davis no longer needed a hypnotist, being able to put himself into light trance. Later still, his writing was purely inspirational. He attracted the attention of numerous famous personalities, Edgar Allan Poe among them, and he became a prolific author. His psychic development continued. One time he sat beside a dying woman and observed every detail of her spirit's departure from the body, detailing it in his book *The Great Harmonia* (1852).

Much of Davis's work reflected Swedenborg's earlier thoughts but, as Sir Arthur Conan Doyle said (*The History of Spiritualism,* 1924):

> *They went one step farther, having added just that knowledge of spirit power that Swedenborg may have attained after his death . . . Is it not a feasible hypothesis that the power that controlled Davis was actually Swedenborg? . . . But whether Davis stood alone, or whether he*

Spiritualism presents one very curious aspect. This consists of investigators discovering facts in psychic science which nobody but the learned newcomer into psychical research ever discovered before, with the result that dozens of words are coined which, on inquiry, turn out to mean exactly the same thing. Worse still, some of them deliberately put on blinkers and refuse to recognize their own conclusions when they awake to the startling discovery that they are merely supporting already well-founded Spiritualistic conclusions.

Harry Boddington

The Spiritualist who really wishes to lead a spiritual life must strive at all times to see and think only of the higher and more beautiful things that he sees around and about him.

H. Gordon Burroughs

---

was the reflection of one greater than himself, the fact remains that he was a miracle man . . . (who) left his mark deep upon Spiritualism.

The Fox Sisters

The Fox family had been greatly disturbed by the events at the house. Margaret Fox's hair turned white within a week of the affair. The two children were sent away; Kate to stay with her brother, David, in Auburn, and Margaretta to stay with her sister, Leah (married name Fish), in Rochester. But "the raps continued in the house even after they had left." (*Encyclopedia of Psychic Science* Nandor Fodor, London, 1934).

A strange factor was now to appear . . . not only did the raps continue at the house, but they also followed the girls to their new abodes. In Rochester, Leah, a staid music teacher, was suddenly exposed to violent disturbances. The phenomenon reverted to poltergeist-like outbursts, with Margaretta and Leah the targets of pinpricks and of flying blocks of wood. Leah said that:

Pins would be stuck into various parts of our persons. Mother's cap would be removed from her head, her comb jerked out of her hair and every conceivable thing done to annoy us.

Fox sisters

It took a while for them to remember that they had been able to converse with the spirit in the Hydesville house, through asking for raps in answer to questions. They started again to ask questions, and once again they got answers. Then they got the most important message of all:

> *Dear friends, you must proclaim this truth to the world. This is the dawning of a new era. You must not try to conceal it any longer. When you do your duty, God will protect you and the good spirits will watch over you.*

From that moment, the messages started to pour forth.

On November 14, 1849, a group of people met at Corinthian Hall in Rochester and a panel was formed to investigate the girls. This panel determined that there was no fraud involved in what was produced. Many present were not satisfied with this report, however, and demanded that a second committee be formed. This was done and the second group reached a similar conclusion. They stated that when the girls were "standing on pillows, with a handkerchief tied round the bottom of their dresses tight to the ankles, we all heard rapping on the wall and floor distinctly."

As interest in the phenomenon spread, so it was found that other people were able to act as channels, or "mediums," for the spirits. Leah's ability developed and she found herself so much in demand that she had to give up her music teaching and became the first professional medium.

The sisters started a tour, going to Albany in May of 1850 and then on to Troy. In June they were in New York. There, Horace Greeley, editor of the *New York Tribune,* investigated them. He was joined by Fenimore Cooper, George Bancroft, the poets Willis and Bryant, and others. Greeley reported in his newspaper:

> *We devoted what time we could spare from our duties out of three days to this subject, and it would be the basest cowardice not to say that we are convinced beyond a doubt of their perfect integrity and good faith in the premises. Whatever may be the origin or cause of the "rappings," the ladies in whose presence they occur do not make them. We tested this thoroughly and to our entire satisfaction.*

The early rappings gave way to other phenomena; table tipping, automatic writing, materialization, and even levitation. In 1853 it was reported that Governor Talmadge was levitated whilst sitting on a table! The governor also claimed that he had received direct writing from the spirit of John C. Calhoun.

Mediums started springing up all over the place. Not surprisingly, many of them were exposed as frauds. The phenomena were of the sort that could be produced fraudulently and therefore many charlatans tried to "jump on the bandwagon." Exposures became almost commonplace and finally even reached out toward the Fox sisters themselves. They were accused of producing the raps by "cracking" their knee joints and toe joints! In fact an alleged "confession" was presented by a relative, a Mrs. Norman Culver, who claimed that Catherine had told her that this was how they worked. In trying to explain how the raps could continue at an investigation where the committee held the ankles of the sisters, Mrs. Culver said that they had their servant rap on the floorboards from down in the cellar.

There were several problems with this accusation. The investigations in question had been held in the homes of various members of the committee plus in a public hall, and at the time the Fox sisters didn't have a servant! Not only that, but a Mr. Capron was able to show that at the time of the so-called "confession," Kate Fox was actually residing at his home, seventy miles distant!

Unfortunately the accusations did damage the reputation of the Fox sisters and for a time they found themselves with few defenders, other than Horace Greeley. There was tremendous pressure put upon

> Be not forgetful to entertain strangers: for thereby some have entertained angels unaware.
>
> **Hebrews 13:2**

> To many . . . the central interest of psychical research will still lie in the kinds of psychological dynamics within the individual human being which appear to give rise to telepathic and other paranormal events.
>
> **Gardner Murphy**

---

the sisters at this time; pressure to "perform." Precautions for mediumship were then unknown. In her autobiography, Mrs. Hardinge Britten speaks of talking to Kate Fox at a Spiritualist gathering and describes her thus:

> *Poor patient Kate, in the midst of a captious, grumbling crowd of investigators, repeating hour after hour the letters of the alphabet, while the no less poor, patient spirits rapped out names, ages, and dates to suit all comers.*

Interestingly, although the method of producing the sounds was frequently questioned, and many and marvelous explanations were forthcoming, seldom did anyone question the incredible amount of information that was produced; information that was unobtainable elsewhere and that, invariably, was absolutely correct. For example, from 1861 to 1866, Kate worked exclusively for the New York banker Charles F. Livermore, bringing him endless messages and information from his late wife, Estelle. During all that time, Estelle actually materialized and also wrote notes in her own handwriting; all information that would have been unknown to Kate but which Livermore was able to accept.

In 1852, Margaretta married the famous Arctic explorer, Dr. Elisha Kane. In November, 1858, Leah married her third husband, David Underhill, a wealthy insurance man.

In 1871, Kate visited England, where the first Spiritualist church had been established in Keighley, Yorkshire, in 1853. Her trip was financed by Livermore, in gratitude for the years of consolation that she had brought him. He wrote:

> *Miss Fox, taken all in all, is no doubt the most wonderful living medium. Her character is irreproachable and pure. I have received so much through her powers of mediumship during the past ten years which is solacing, instructive and astounding, that I feel greatly indebted to her.*

In England Kate sat for the well-known psychic investigator and physicist Professor William Crookes, among others (Sir William Crookes invented the tube that made possible the invention of x-rays). At one of the séances, a London Times correspondent was present. In light of earlier accusations made against the Fox sisters, claiming that they made the rapping noises with their joints, it is interesting to read the Times' correspondent's report. He said that he was taken to the door of the séance room and invited to stand by the medium and hold her hands. This he did "when loud thumps seemed to come from the panels, as if done with the fist. These were repeated at our request any number of times." He went on to give every test he could think of, while Kate gave every opportunity for examination and had both her feet and hands held securely.

Of one séance Crookes wrote:

> *I was holding the medium's two hands in one of mine, while her feet rested on my feet. Paper was on the table before us, and my disengaged*

hand was holding a pencil. A luminous hand came down from the upper part of the room, and after hovering near me for a few seconds, took the pencil from my hand, rapidly wrote on a sheet of paper, threw the pencil down, and then rose above our heads, gradually fading into darkness.

In December 1872 Kate married H. D. Jancken, a London barrister and one of England's early Spiritualists. They were to have two sons, both of whom were extremely psychic before Jancken died in 1881. In 1876 Margaretta traveled across the Atlantic to visit her sister.

Denunciation and Retraction

A quarrel developed between the three sisters, with Kate and Margaretta eventually siding together against the older Leah. Hearing of a growing problem of alcoholism in her sisters—especially Margaretta—Leah tried to have Kate separated from her two children. It has been suggested by such people as Sir Arthur Conan Doyle that this may have prompted an attack by Margaretta, who had been through some severe financial problems. (Additionally, she had come under strong Roman Catholic influence, pressuring her to acknowledge that her gift was actually a gift from the devil) Margaretta swore to avenge herself and her sister against Leah.

Thinking to hurt Leah by harming the entire Spiritualist movement, Margaretta wrote a letter to the New York Herald in which she denounced the movement and promised a full exposure of it. This she tried to do before a panel, in August 1888. The following month, Kate came over from England to join her. Although Kate didn't promise any exposé, she did seem to back her sister in the fight against Leah. In the Hall of Music, on October 21, 1888, Margaretta made her repudiation, claiming that all had been faked. She even managed to produce some minor raps to back up what she was saying. Kate kept silent, though by doing so she seemed to endorse her sister's statements.

Suddenly, on November 17, less than a month later, Kate wrote to a Mrs. Cottell:

I would have written to you before this but my surprise was so great on my arrival to hear of Maggie's exposure of Spiritualism that I had no heart to write to anyone.

The manager of the affair engaged the Academy of Music, the very largest place of entertainment in New York City; it was filled to overflowing. They made fifteen hundred dollars clear.

I think now I could make money in proving that the knockings are not made with the toes. So many people come to me to ask me about this exposure of Maggie's that I have to deny myself to them. They are hard at work to expose the whole thing if they can; but they certainly cannot.

On November 20, 1889, about a year after the "exposé," Margaretta gave an interview to the New York press:

Would to God that I could undo the injustice I did the cause of Spiritualism when, under the strong psychological influence of persons inimical to it, I gave expression to utterances that had no foundation in fact. This retraction and denial has not come about so much from my own sense of what is right as from the silent impulse of the spirits using my organism at the expense of the hostility of the treacherous horde who held out promises of wealth and happiness in return for an attack on Spiritualism, and whose hopeful assurances were deceitful.

She was asked "Was there any truth in the charges you made against Spiritualism?" to which she replied, "Those charges were false in every particular. I have no hesitation in saying that . . . When I made those dreadful statements I was not responsible for my words. Its genuineness is an incontrovertible fact."

Asked what her sister Catherine thought of her present course, she said: "She is in complete sympathy with me. She did not approve my course in the past."

The three Fox sisters died within a year or two of each other; Leah in 1890, Catherine in 1892, and Margaretta in 1893. The final word on them comes from a woman doctor—not a Spiritualist—who attended on Margaretta at her death. At a meeting of the Medico Legal Society of New York, in 1905, Dr. Mellen stated that Margaretta was lying in a bed in a tenement house on Ninth Street. According to the doctor she was unable, at that time, to move hand or foot. Yet knockings came from the wall, the floor, and from the ceiling, in answer to Margaretta's faint questions. "She was as incapable of cracking her toe-joints at this time, as I was," said the doctor.

French Forerunner

While so much was going on in America, there was independent work progressing in France. A simple, untrained mechanic named M. Cahagnet, who was not particularly well read or well educated, became interested in mesmerism (the precursor of hypnotism). Finding that he had skill as a mesmerist, Cahagnet worked with various subjects and was able to bring about cures for various disorders and diseases. He decided to devote his life to this work but became somewhat nonplused when some of his subjects, instead of simply following his directions while in trance, started to "wander off into space" to what they described as "the land of spirits." They described people whom they emphatically declared to be the souls of those who had previously lived on earth. M. Cahagnet tried hard to get these subjects to return to his direction, but they continued with what he termed "wild hallucinations." People came to witness what was taking place and, from among them, some recognized some of the spirits as dead relatives. So began a long series of experiments by Cahagnet, the results of which he finally presented in a book titled *The Celestial Telegraph,* or *Secrets of the Life to Come.* An English translation of this book was made in 1848—the year of the Fox sisters' phenomena.

It might also be worth mentioning that Joseph Glanville (1636–1680), who has been called the father of psychical research, conducted séances at Ragley Castle, in England, with Dr. Francis van Helmont, Dr. Henry More, and Robert Boyle. At these sittings, mediums demonstrated the art of communicating with the world of spirits. At that time it would have been classed as a branch of necromancy.

Examination Questions

1. Where was the "birthplace" of Spiritualism, and what family was responsible for it?

2. How did the spirit initially communicate with the questioners?

3. Was there any indication that this momentous occasion would take place and, if so, who received word of it?

4. Who was the well-known editor—and of what newspaper—who joined with other famous personalities to investigate the Fox sisters, on their first tour in 1850?

5. Which of the Fox sisters worked for many years with the New York banker Charles F. Livermore, and why?

6. Kate, Leah, and Margaretta Fox had a falling-out, with two of them aligning against the third. Which of the sisters made a supposed exposé against which other sister? Was there ever a retraction of this accusation?

7. How did Andrew Jackson Davis dictate his books? Did he always work in the same way?

8. Could Andrew Jackson Davis speak and/or write any languages other than English?

9. What unusual happening took place at the death bed of Margaretta Fox in 1893?

10. Who was the French mechanic who discovered contact with the world of spirits?

Profile

Abraham Lincoln

Abraham Lincoln (1809–1865) attended many séances, even having some at his own home. He was as much a Spiritualist as anything else. He was not of any particular Christian faith, although he certainly did seem to believe in an Infinite Intelligence. In the days before the Civil War only 25 to 35 percent of the population actually belonged to a Christian denomination. The vast majority did not belong to any church, though most seemed to have believed in an afterlife. Spiritualism competed with Christianity and, in the latter part of the nineteenth century, became the fastest growing religion in America.

The Lincolns had lost three of their four sons to childhood diseases so it was natural that Mary Todd Lincoln, the president's wife, would want to attend séances. Colonel Simon F. Kase told of one notable one, which both he and the president attended in the home of a Mrs. Laurie. The Laurie's daughter, a Mrs. Miller, was the medium and she played the piano while in trance. As she played, two legs of the instrument levitated several inches off the floor then repeatedly banged back to the floor to beat time to the music. As it kept rising up, Kase, a judge, and two soldiers who were present all climbed on the piano together but were unable to make it settle down again until the medium stopped playing. It was reported that the legs rose as high as four inches off the floor.

Abraham Lincoln had many prophetic dreams, including one of his own death. In early April 1865, he dreamed he was lying in bed when he heard the sound of sobbing. Getting up and leaving his bedroom, he went into the East Room of the White House where he saw a line of people filing past a catafalque. They were all paying their respects to the figure lying in state, guarded by four soldiers. The face of the figure was covered so, in the dream, Lincoln asked one of the soldiers who had died. The soldier replied, "The president. He was killed by an assassin." Lincoln later told his wife, Mary, and several friends about the dream. It was later that same month that he was shot and killed by John Wilkes Booth. Another of Lincoln's prophetic dreams was of a damaged ship sailing away with a Union ship in hot pursuit. Lincoln had this dream on a number of occasions, each time just before an important Union victory.

Spirit painting of Abraham Lincoln

At one séance the Lincolns attended a teenage girl approached the president. It was Nettie Colburn Maynard, a young medium. In trance, she began to lecture Lincoln on the necessity for emancipation. She spoke to him for almost an hour, stating that the Civil War could not come to an end until all men were free. When Nettie came out of her trance and saw to whom she had been speaking, she ran from the room in fright and embarrassment. But two days later, when Lincoln and his wife were at another séance, Nettie appeared again and did the same thing, lecturing the president about freeing the slaves. Kase reported that "President Lincoln was convinced as to the course he should pursue; the command coming from that all-seeing Spirit through the instrumentality of the angel world was not to be overlooked . . . thus the prediction of the medium was verified."

In 1854, ten years before the end of the Civil War, 15,000 Americans had petitioned Congress for a scientific study of Spiritualism, but the request was denied. The tremendous death toll of the war led to even more of an interest in—if not a need for—Spiritualism.

LESSON FOUR

The History of Spiritualism, Part Two—Later Development

At first glance it would seem surprising that so many fully developed mediums came forward so shortly after the "birth" of Spiritualism through the Fox sisters. But Sir Arthur Conan Doyle explains it this way:

> *It was no new gift (the Fox sisters) exhibited, it was only that their courageous action in making it widely known made others come forward and confess that they possessed the same power. This universal gift of mediumistic faculties now for the first time began to be freely developed.*

As Judge John W. Edmonds had said earlier (*Spiritualism,* New York 1853):

> *For the previous ten or twelve years there had been more or less of (mediumship) in different parts of the country, but it had been kept concealed, either from fear of ridicule or from ignorance of what it was.*

Ridicule was a major factor. As mentioned in the previous chapter, many of the phenomena of Spiritualism were easily duplicated by the unscrupulous. There were scandals and exposures galore, both real and fabricated. One major scandal was that involving Professor Robert Hare, one of the best-known scientists of the time. He had to give up his professorship at Pennsylvania University and was publicly denounced by the professors of Harvard. But the scientists made fools of themselves. As Conan Doyle describes it:

> *The crowning and most absurd instance of scientific intolerance—an intolerance that has always been as violent and unreasonable as that*

of the mediaeval Church—was shown by the American Scientific Association. This learned body howled down Professor Hare when he attempted to address them, and put it on record that the subject was unworthy of their attention . . . however . . . the same society at the same session held an animated debate as to why cocks crow between twelve and one at night, coming finally to the conclusion that at that particular hour a wave of electricity passes over the earth from north to south, and that the fowl, disturbed out of their slumbers, and "being naturally of a crowing disposition" registered the event in this fashion!

One important development was that of private mediumship, in the sense of those who discovered they had mediumistic ability but did not exhibit it in public, using it solely for their own private purposes. A large number of men and women, many of them well-known in other circles, discovered an ability to communicate with the spirits and proceeded to do so in their own homes, with only family and close friends in attendance.

Development in England

In 1852 an American medium named Mrs. Hayden visited England, followed shortly after by a Mrs. Roberts. Although they both did very well financially, they received mixed reviews. Some prominent men and women attested to the genuineness of their phenomena while others found their activity very difficult to accept.

By the following year, the continental craze of table tipping reached English shores and became very popular. So popular, in fact, that scientists such as Faraday, Braid, and Carpenter took notice and talked of it in terms of odylic force, electricity and magnetism.

There then followed a slight slump in interest until 1855, when Scottish-born Daniel Dunglas Home (pronounced "Hume") arrived there from America. He had been practicing for several years and was to develop into one of the finest mediums of all time. He stayed only a short while, but returned four years later, to stay. Home was responsible for the acceptance of Spiritualism by such figures as Thackeray, Anthony Trollope, Robert Bell, Lord Lytton, Lord Adare, the Earl of Dunraven, the Master of Lindsay, and Lord Brougham.

Daniel Dunglas Home

Perhaps the most famous of Home's feats was his levitation out of one window and in at another, seventy feet above the ground. It occurred at Ashley House, Victoria Street, London. Present were Lord Adare (the sporting young Irish peer), his cousin Captain Charles Wynne, and the Honorable Master of Lindsay (later Earl of Crawford and Balcarres). Both Adare and Lindsay wrote separate accounts of what happened that evening.

After a normal beginning to the séance—normal for Home's séances, that is, with telekinetic phenomena and the appearance of an apparition—Home began to pace the floor. He was in a trance state, as he had been all evening. He walked through to the next

> Spiritualism is a religion for those who find themselves outside all religions; while on the contrary it greatly strengthens the faith of those who already possess religious beliefs.
>
> **Sir Arthur Conan Doyle**

> The result of the experiments with Eusapia (Pallandino) at Naples convinced (Everard) Fielding (of the S.P.R.) that the long debated physical phenomena of Spiritualism actually occurred and in spite of the criticism leveled against the report he was never inclined to waver substantially from this position. From any point of view, the report was one of the most masterly inquiries ever undertaken.
>
> **E. J. Dingwall**

---

room and a window was heard to be raised. Lindsay states that he heard a voice whisper in his ear, telling him that Home would pass out of one window and in at another. The next moment they all saw Home floating in the air outside their window.

There was no ledge of any sort between the windows, which were nearly eight feet apart and seventy feet above the ground. Although there was no light on in the room, the moon provided sufficient illumination for all to distinguish each other and to see quite clearly the furniture in the room.

After remaining in position for a few seconds outside the window, with his feet about six inches above the sill, Home opened the window and "glided into the room feet foremost." Adare went to close the window in the adjacent room and found that it had only been opened twelve to fifteen inches. Home was asked how he had managed to pass through so small a space, and replied by showing them. Adare describes it: ". . . he then went through the open space, head first, quite rapidly, his body being nearly horizontal and apparently rigid. He came in again, feet foremost; and we returned to the other room."

Later, when Home came out of his trance, he was "much agitated; he said he felt as if he had gone through some fearful peril, and that he had a most horrible desire to throw himself out of the window."

Other mediums arrived from America, amongst them Mrs. Emma Hardinge Britten, the Davenport brothers, Lottie Fowler, and Henry Slade. By that time the focus was on spirits actually speaking through the medium, rather than conversing by way of raps. Slate writing was also introduced, as was billet reading, spirit photography, apports, and telekinetic demonstrations. (All of that will be examined later in this book.)

In December of 1861, Queen Victoria's beloved husband, Prince Albert, died. Within days a young boy named Robert James Lees, living in Leicester, went into trance and received a message from the departed prince. The message was for the queen and was published by a newspaper editor who happened to be at the séance with Lees. Queen Victoria already had an interest in Spiritualist matters and, seeing the report, sent two representatives to see Lees. The two used false names. The boy again channeled information from Prince Albert, recognized the two royal visitors, and called them by their correct names. He went on to write a letter to the queen, while in trance, in which he called Her Majesty by a private name used only between the husband and wife. The queen was so impressed she had the thirteen-year-old Lees brought to court and held several séances with him. Later her personal manservant, John Brown, took over as the medium through whom Albert chose to speak with her. Lees went on to become one of Britain's leading mediums of the time.

It took a while for the native English mediums to stand up and be recognized. Among the first were Mrs. Marshall, Mrs. Everitt, Edward Childs, William Howitt, William Wilkinson, and Mrs. Guppy. The British National Association of Spiritualists was founded in 1873 (reorganized in 1884 as the London Spiritualist Alliance), the Psychological Society of Great Britain in 1875, and the prestigious Society for Psychical Research in 1882.

Professor Henry Sidgwick was the first President of the S.P.R. (Society for Psychical Research). He was, at that time, the most influential professor at Cambridge University. In his first presidential address, Professor Sidgwick said:

> *We are all agreed that the present state of things is a scandal to the enlightened age in which we live, that the dispute as to the reality of these marvelous phenomena of which it is quite impossible to exaggerate the scientific importance, if only a tenth part of what has been alleged by generally credible witnesses could be shown to be true—I say it is a scandal that the dispute as to the reality of these phenomena should still be going on, that so many competent witnesses should have declared their belief in them, that so many others should be so profoundly interested in having the question determined, and yet the educated world, as a body, should still be simply in an attitude of incredulity.*

The S.P.R. did important work with many well-known researchers over the years, continuously investigating. It did later suffer severe criticism for its slowness, however, especially in investigating physical phenomena.

Many other organizations sprang up over the years, including the Marylebone Association of Spiritualists, the British College of Psychic Science, London Spiritualist Alliance, the British Spiritualist Lyceum Union, the Spiritualist National Union, and the Spiritualist Association of Great Britain.

Up until 1951, it was possible for any séance to be raided by the police and for the medium to be arrested and charged with fraud . . . under the old Witchcraft Act of 1735. In 1951 this Witchcraft Act was finally repealed and was replaced by the Fraudulent Mediums Act. This latter stated that mediumship was legal so long as it was not done "with intent to deceive," or used "any fraudulent device." Modern-day fake mediums have been charged under this new Act, a good example being the case of Helen Duncan, repeatedly caught in fraud, usually in materializations.

Development in America

There was a brief period where spirit communication was claimed as the basis for various free-love and community property groups, such as John Murray Spear's New Motor Movement and Reverend Scott and Thomas Lake Harris' Mountain Cove Settlement. Certainly the simple rappings of the Fox sisters paled beside the sudden panorama of psychic phenomena: phantom hands, levitation, psychometry, full-form materializations, slate writing, pellet reading, spirit photography, and the playing of musical instruments by ghostly hands.

In 1873 there was the first camp meeting, at Lake Pleasant, Massachusetts, and in 1885 there was the foundation of the American Society for Psychical Research (today having nearly three thousand members and a library of over nine thousand volumes).

Two of the most striking mediums to come forward were Mrs. Leonore E. Piper and Mina Stinson Crandon—known as "Margery." Mrs. Piper (1859–1950), described as "the foremost trance medium in the history of psychical research" (*Encyclopedia of Occultism and Parapsychology,* Leslie A. Shepard editor, Avon, New York, 1978) was the cause of the conversion to Spiritualism of such eminent people as Sir Oliver Lodge, Dr. Richard Hodgson, and Professor

James Hyslop. Her mediumship started at the age of eight, when she received word from the spirit world of the death of an aunt. At age twenty-two she married William Piper, of Boston. Professor James investigated her mediumship, as did Dr. Richard Hodgson. Hodgson has been described as "the keenest fraud-hunter, the most pronounced skeptic, (who) took every precaution to bar the possibility of deception." In 1898 Professor James wrote *(Psychological Review):*

> *Dr Hodgson considers that the hypothesis of fraud cannot be seriously maintained. I agree with him absolutely. The medium has been under observation, much of the time under close observation, as to most of the conditions of her life, by a large number of persons, eager, many of them, to pounce upon any suspicious circumstance for (nearly) fifteen years.*

Indeed, for decades Mrs. Piper was subjected to the most stringent of tests and was never once found wanting.

"Margery" was also from Boston and was the wife of Dr. L. R. G. Crandon, Professor of Surgery at the Harvard Medical School for sixteen years. Margery's first sitting took place in May, 1923. She showed great ability at table tipping but quickly developed to trance and direct voice. Automatic writing, psychic music, and other spectacular phenomena followed. A group from Harvard, including Prof. William McDougall, Dr. Gardner Murphy, and Dr. Roback, started investigating Margery. She was subsequently given rigorous examination by groups in France and England. With the strictest of controls she continued to produce outstanding phenomena. In London, famed investigator Harry Price had developed a fraud-proof table; in ordinary light Margery twice levitated it to a height of six inches or more.

A *Scientific American* committee used instruments such as sealed glass jars, scales, and electric bells to test Margery. Dr. E. J. Dingwall, as part of another committee, stated:

> *Phenomena occurred hitherto unrecorded in mediumistic history . . . the mediumship remains one of the most remarkable in the history of psychical research.*

It is recorded that Abraham Lincoln was very much into Spiritualism, attending séances in New York, with J. B. Conklin, and in Washington, D.C., with Mrs. Cranston Laurie and Nettie Colburn (later to become Mrs. Maynard). Nettie, who was in her late teens at the time, went into trance at one Washington séance attended by Lincoln, and approached the president. She told him, in eloquent words, of the importance of emancipating the slaves. When she came out of trance she was so overcome at finding herself standing talking to the president that she ran off. On a subsequent visit to the Laurie residence, however, Lincoln was again lectured by the entranced Nettie and again she emphasized the necessity to free the slaves. She also stated that from the time of such a proclamation from him there would be no defeat of the Union army. As it turned out, after Lincoln did issue his proclamation on September 22, 1862, there was nothing but Union army success.

The present-day legal position of mediums varies from state to state, there being no equivalent to the British Fraudulent Mediums Act in the United States. For this reason, if no other, most mediums go under the somewhat protective shell of ordination; adopting the religious title of "Reverend."

Development Circles

On both sides of the Atlantic ordinary people were drawn to this new phenomenon of communion with the spirits of the dead. Groups of people, many times just family members, got together to "sit in circle" and try to develop their own mediumistic talents. Frequently, the Circles were started by people who had heard the claims of the Spiritualists, or had attended a demonstration, and whose curiosity led to them trying to make contact themselves. With no

> Why do you want to open the outside door when there is an inside door? Everything is within.
>
> **Yogaswami**

> My experiences with mediums, good, bad and indifferent, are probably as wide as those of any living man. . . . I have sat in America . . . At home there are few mediums of the last twenty years whom I have not sampled . . . Hence, if I have formed conclusions they have been based upon wide experiences. I have always taken copious notes of my cases . . . With so much practical work behind me the reader can imagine my feelings when in a public debate upon the subject [of Spiritualism] with Dr. Haldane of Cambridge my distinguished opponent said, "I once knew a medium." In my reply I asked him what he would think of me if I contradicted him upon some point of chemistry, and said, "I have once been in a laboratory."
>
> **Sir Arthur Conan Doyle**

---

television to distract them, these Circles would often continue for years, and a number of fine mediums came into being as a result of them. In England there is still a great interest in such Home Circles; more so than in America, it seems.

A big boost—if that is the right word—was given to the Spiritualist movement with the start of World War I. This was a time when young men were being killed on the battlefields; when wives and mothers were losing those they loved. Spiritualism offered a means to renew contact, if only temporarily, and to find satisfaction in the knowledge that there was indeed a life after death. The time between the two wars was one of the most active for Spiritualism.

Spiritualism as a Religion

Before the end of the nineteenth century many Spiritualist organizations were calling themselves "churches," though the Roman Catholic Church early on decided that Spiritualist phenomena were the work of the devil (notwithstanding 1 Corinthians 12 and 14). The Anglicans were more tolerant, though far from actively promoting mediumship. Indeed, in 1953 there was the establishment of the Churches' Fellowship for Psychical and Spiritual Studies. The Fellowship organized conferences and study groups, lectures, and workshops, dealing with mediumship, healing, and psychic development.

On the whole, however, the organized churches were against Spiritualism. Yet to the Spiritualists themselves there was an undeniable link between proof of survival and many of the church teachings. And certainly a number of the returning spirits took the opportunity to preach the beliefs they had held while in their physical shells.

Not all Spiritualist organizations wanted religious affiliation. The Spiritualists' National Union has consistently refused to adopt specific Christian doctrine. So much so, in fact, that it led to the formation, in 1931, of the Greater World Christian Spiritualist League. The S.N.U. is the largest national organization in Britain and, although organized in "churches," represents the non-Christian element in Spiritualism. The G.W.C.S.L. represents the Christian element. In America groups include the National Spiritual Alliance of the United States of America, the National Spiritualist Association of Churches, the National Spiritualist Association of the United States, and the Universal Spiritualist Association. Internationally, there are the International Spiritualist Federation (headquartered in Paris, France) and the International General Assembly of Spiritualists.

In America today there is more of a tie-in with religion—specifically Christianity—than is found in Britain, with many Spiritualist churches having regular services of hymns, prayers, Bible-reading and sermons, along with their message giving. Yet Spiritualism remains a movement rather than an organization, with a large number of totally independent groups and autonomous "churches."

Spiritualism in Europe and South America

In France, Baron du Potet was fascinated by Spiritualist phenomena, as he had been for years with mesmerism. He published his *Journal du Magnétisme,* which covered twelve years of his investigations, from 1836 to 1848. In this journal he spoke of direct voice trance speaking, levitation, clairvoyance, materializations, apports, healing, and many other phenomena. Another baron—Baron Guldenstubbe—was the man who introduced table tipping to France, from the United States. This became a craze that then swept into England. It is still very much practiced today.

In Italy the most striking medium was Eusapia Palladino (1854–1918); in many ways as spectacular as D. D. Home. In later years she was, on several occasions, caught out as a fraud, but these few instances could never eclipse the vast majority of her séances undertaken in the most rigid of investigative circumstances, totally precluding falsity.

Palladino never managed levitation on the scale of Home's window-to-window maneuver, but levitation of objects she did do. One such event occurred at a sitting with Camille Flammarion and Guillaume de Fontenay. Before the séance, Flammarion made a detailed investigation of the room. He checked windows and doors, curtains and drapes, chairs, the sofa . . . everything. He looked for electrical wires, batteries, any form of concealed mechanism, but found nothing. Madame Zelma Blech, the hostess, stripped and searched the medium but found nothing suspicious. The sitting then took place in full light and is comprehensively described by Flammarion in *Mysterious Psychic Forces* (Unwin, London, 1907):

> *The medium sits before the curtain, turning her back to it. A table is placed before her—a kitchen table made of spruce, weighing about fifteen pounds. I examined this table and found nothing in it suspicious. It could be moved about in every direction.*
>
> *I sit at first on the left of Eusapia, then on her right side. I make sure as far as possible of her hands, and her feet, by personal control. Thus, for example, to begin with, in order to be sure that she should not lift the table either by her hands or her legs, or her feet, I take her left hand in my left hand, I place my right open hand upon her knees, and I place my right foot upon her left foot. Facing me, M. Guillaume de Fontenay, no more disposed than I to be duped, takes charge of her right hand and her right foot.*
>
> *There is full light . . . At the end of three minutes the table begins to move, balancing itself, and rising sometimes to the right, sometimes to the left. A minute afterwards it is lifted to a height of about nine inches, and remains there two seconds.*
>
> *In a second trial, I take the two hands of Eusapia in mine. A notable levitation is produced, nearly under the same conditions. We repeat the same experiments thrice, in such a way that five levitations of the table take place in a quarter of an hour and for several seconds the four feet are completely lifted from the floor, to the height of about nine inches.*

Another Frenchman, Hypolyte Leon Denizard Rivail (1804–1869), was told by a medium that in one of his previous incarnations his name had been Allan. A second medium said that in another lifetime it had been Kardec (or Kardek). Rivail therefore adopted the name "Allan Kardec" and as such became the father of "Spiritism." Spiritism is the term used for the popular form of Spiritualism found in both France and South America. Kardec worked with a number of early mediums, and through them accumulated a vast amount of information relating to the progress of the human spirit. Foremost in that information was the belief in reincarnation, something not necessarily accepted by all Spiritualists in either England or America.

The medium Kardec worked with was Celina Bequet (also known as Celina Japhet). Celina channeled information from both her grandfather and from Anton Mesmer, and gave out medical advice. Kardec organized the mass of material obtained through Celina and, without mentioning her name, published much of it under the title *Le Livre des Esprits* ("The Spirits' Book"). Eight years later, in 1864, he published *Le Livre des Mediums* ("The Mediums' Book"), which included most of the balance of Celina's material.

From his writings, Kardec's form of "Spiritism" was picked up in South America, most notably in Brazil, where it has also become known as "Kardecism." One of the tenets put forward by Kardec was that charity was essential for salvation and the greatest act of charity is to bestow health. From this, psychic healing developed and grew to where Brazil became one of the most active countries practicing it today. There are many Brazilian Spiritist hospitals where medical doctors work side by side with mediums. In 1925, Jeronimo Candido Gomide founded a Spiritist community—Palmelo; the only one of its kind in the world—where the mentally ill could be treated. Today Palmelo has over two thousand inhabitants, including a large number of mental patients.

Another form of South American Spiritism is Umbanda; a cross between Spiritualism and Voodoo. It is similar to the practice of Candomblé, found in Bahiá and Recife. In Umbanda the priestess, acting as a medium, is known as a *cavalo,* or "horse." She is only permitted to invoke disembodied spirits. The rites can take place almost anywhere out in the open, but it is preferred that they be close to water. In Candomblé the medium may only invoke "nature spirits," for it is believed that to bring the shades of the dead could cause "remnants of the suffering world" to return also.

In Voodoo itself is found a ritual that is almost totally Spiritualistic in nature, even to the extent that the priestess plays the part of a medium. I described it in my book *Anatomy of the Occult,* (Samuel Weiser, New York, 1977):

> *(This Haitian ritual) is called Retrait de l'esprit de l'eau (Return of the spirits from beneath the water). A small canvas, tent-like enclosure is erected in the hounfor. Inside are placed various small offerings, together with a tub of water and a stool for the "Mambo" (Priestess) to sit on. The Mambo enters and the entrance-flap is closed and secured after her. Several "hounsi" (initiates) then sit or lie on the ground before the structure, each holding a "govi" (the earthenware jars that house the spirits of the dead). As the people gather around, the Mambo can be heard chanting in "langage," a secret ritual language. There is a litany as she calls on the "loa" (gods), and the people respond. This litany may last for a half-hour or more. Eventually, however, there is silence.*
>
> *A sharp cry from the Mambo is the signal for the first hounsi to slip her govi under the canvas, into the tent. After a moment the sound of rushing water is heard, soon followed by a strained, rather hoarse, voice. The voice will call the name of one of those crowded around the tent. It is invariably recognized as being the voice of a dead relative. A conversation between the two (spirit and living relative) will ensue, sometimes with the Mambo putting in a word here and*

The middle of the twentieth century finds science in full retreat from the mechanistic outlook that characterized it in the nineteenth and early twentieth centuries. God, whom (Auguste) Comte ushered politely to the door of the universe, is now back in the living room and very much at home. Indeed, the prediction of Steinmetz that the greatest scientific discoveries of the twentieth century would be in the realm of the spirit is now in a fair way to being proved true.

Alson J. Smith

The superstition of the past is the science of the present, the proverb of the future.

Stewart Edward White

---

there. It is not unknown for the Mambo to be speaking at the same time that the dead ancestor is speaking.

The ancestor may be consulted on family matters; his advice may be asked on a variety of things. He, or she, may have some vital message to impart. At one such séance that I witnessed, the voice of a recently deceased man informed his daughter that a neighbor had borrowed a sum of money just prior to the father's death. No one else knew of the loan so, at the death, the neighbor had kept quiet thinking he would never have to repay it. He little thought of his lender returning from the grave to demand repayment to his daughter!

All the while the voices are speaking there is heard the rushing of waters in the background. Although the Mambo has a bowl of water in the enclosure with her, this background noise is not one that can be reproduced using that bowl . . . When the voice has been heard the govi is returned, under the flap, to the hounsi and the next jar taken in.

Interestingly this is, in its turn, very similar to the Yuwipi Vision Talk Ceremony of the Oglala Sioux Amerindians. The shamanic Yuwipi refers to himself as Tunkasila, meaning "interpreter" or "medium." In the sweat lodge he simply speaks with the spirits and tells the others what they say. But in the Vision Talk Ceremony, the Yuwipi is covered with a cloth and securely bound. All light is extinguished and then the singers start their songs. In the darkness various sacred rattles are heard. The clatter of them resounds around the blackened room, as they strike against the walls, ceiling, and floor. Then small sparks are seen as they sound, as though the rattles were metal striking against flint. These sparks signal the arrival of the spirits—spirits in the sense of an ancient race of pygmy-like warriors to whom the Yuwipi speaks. There is more singing and dancing by the participants, which leads to a healing for those in the hut who need it. Those being healed often will hear the spirits speaking directly to them; whispering into their ear as the healing progresses. They may even feel the spirits touch them. As the ceremony finishes, the lights are brought back and the Yuwipi is found kneeling in his inner sacred circle, the cloth that had covered him folded neatly beside him and the cord rolled up and lying on top of it.

Examination Questions

1. Why were there no other mediums known before the Fox sisters? How did people with the mediumistic gift protect themselves from ridicule?

2. What Spiritualist craze swept Europe in the early 1850s, and was it taken seriously when it arrived in England?

3. Who was the Scottish-born medium who floated out of a window in front of prominent witnesses? Was levitation his only gift?

4. Who was the boy Robert James Lees? What made him famous?

5. What prestigious society was founded in 1882? What were the aims (in general terms) of this society?

6. Why were mediums in England open to arrest and on what charge? When was the law changed in this respect; what Act was replaced with what Act?

7. Such prominent men as Sir Oliver Lodge, Dr. Richard Hodgson, and Professor James Hyslop were converted to Spiritualism after investigating a leading American medium. What was her name and for how long was she subjected to tests?

8. What nineteenth-century American president was fascinated by Spiritualism and attended a number of séances? Who was the young medium who lectured him on political matters while in trance? On what matter in particular did she lecture him?

9. Why did the Roman Catholic Church feel threatened by Spiritualism? What was the attitude of the Anglicans?

10. Frenchman Hypolyte Leon Denizard Rivail changed his name after being told, by two different mediums, what his name had been in previous lifetimes. What did he take as his "new" name? In what part(s) of the world did he become most influential with regard to Spiritualism? What was his term for Spiritualism?

Profile

Morris Pratt

Although little is known of the early life of Morris Pratt, it is on record that he visited the Lake Mills, Wisconsin, Spiritualist Center in 1851 (just three years after the Fox Sisters' ground-breaking experiences with Spiritualism). As a result of this visit, he became deeply interested in psychic phenomena and in what had become the religion of Spiritualism.

Pratt was well educated to the point where he frequently got into arguments with Christian ministers who criticized Spiritualism. On a number of occasions he was even evicted from churches because of his outspokenness. At one time, he was fined for his controversial actions. But, dedicated as he was to the promotion of this new religion, he recognized the need for a large number of educated proponents to spread the word and to address the opponents.

Pratt had recognized his own spiritual guide, in the person of a Native American. This guide told Pratt of various mineral deposits unknown to any other white man. Pratt then promised, "If I am made rich, I will give part of it to Spiritualism." On the information, he invested in a company that was later to become the very profitable Ashland Mine of Ironwood, Michigan. In just a few months, he made over two hundred thousand dollars. Morris Pratt didn't forget his promise. He used part of his profits to advance Spiritualism. In 1889 he had built and dedicated a building as a temple, at Whitewater, Wisconsin. When opened, it consisted of a number of lecture rooms, an office, chapel, and dormitories. It was deeded as the Morris Pratt Institute, though it quickly became known locally as "the Spooks' Temple." Over the years, however, the Pratt Institute earned the respect of the local citizens and even gained national fame. Today it has become the "Mecca of Modern Spiritualism."

LESSON FIVE

Spirit Guides

Meditation

Next to the belief that contacting the spirit world is possible, relaxation is key. You'll get nowhere if you are tense. Practice relaxation by way of meditation. Properly used, meditation can open the door to individual growth and personal advancement. And it's a practice that is simplicity itself.

There are many different ways to meditate. Transcendental Meditation has been very popular in the past and is still used by many. Edgar Cayce's is another common method as are various forms of Buddhist meditation. There are a number of variations on the theme. Once again there's no one right way; find what is right for you by experimentation . . . try different methods. Here is my own method—one you might try.

Exercise

First of all you must feel comfortable and secure. Wear loose, comfortable clothing—just slipping on a robe when you first get up in the morning, before you dress, and going straight to your meditation can be a good idea. Meditate somewhere where you know you will not be interrupted; where you can sit quietly for ten or fifteen minutes without being disturbed. Disconnect the telephone, turn off your pager and cell phone, make sure there is no television or radio noise, and lock the door.

Sit in a comfortable chair that has a straight back and armrests. I'd suggest removing your shoes. In workshops with medium Anne Gehman, she repeatedly said, "Avoid rubber soles!" Rubber, after all, is an insulator, so to avoid rubber-soled shoes makes a lot of sense. You want to have contact with the ground—directly or indirectly with the earth—so don't cut off that contact with a layer of rubber. Better to have leather-soled shoes but

> The whole area of spiritual service is governed by vibrations. The guides are responsible for harmonizing these vibrations with a medium, communicating spirit, and recipient. This trinity remains unchanged whatever expression of mediumship is used. The doorkeeper controls the motivation of these vibrations to the varying degree the spiritual service demands . . .
>
> No guide can use the sensitive without his assurance that harmonious vibrations can be maintained . . . While all spiritual service is coordinated with the guides, they cannot continue with any effort without his permission. His responsibility, however, like the guide's, ends with legitimate spiritual activity.
>
> **Ivy Northage**

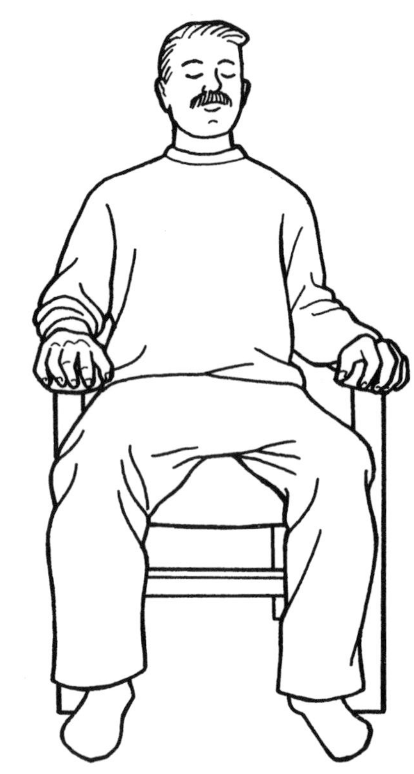

Meditation

better still to remove the shoes. Sit with your feet flat on the floor and your arms on the armrests. Be able to sit there for about fifteen minutes without discomfort. Early morning or late evening is a good time for meditating. Not only is exterior noise likely to be less but the general "vibes" of the atmosphere are more conducive to relaxation. Whenever you do it, try to always meditate at about the same time each day. Just once a day will do; twice a day (morning and evening) is better.

Start to relax your body by doing a few head rolls. Close your eyes and let your head come forward on your chest. Start to roll it around: up onto your right shoulder, to the back, around to the left shoulder and back to where you started, down in front. Roll it around three times and then reverse the process and go back around three times the other way.

Now bring your head back upright and hunch up your shoulders; up as close as you can get them to your ears. Hold them there for a moment, and then let them relax and drop. Do this three times.

Take three good, deep breaths. Really fill your lungs as you inhale, and then squeeze out every last little bit of air as you exhale. (Some people like to visualize themselves breathing in white, positive light and then breathing out all negativity.)

Now, breathing normally, concentrate on relaxing your body, taking it through from toes to head a little at a time. Focus your attention on your toes and feel them relaxing. Feel tension going out of them; any little aches and pains disappearing. Continue through to your feet as a whole—the balls of the feet, the soles, the heels, the ankles. You make it happen that they relax. Feel them relax. Then take that relaxation up to your calves. Feel those calf muscles relaxing! Move on to the knees.

Continue in this fashion throughout the entire body: thighs and upper legs, groin, buttocks, hips, spine, stomach, back, chest, shoulders, fingers, hands, wrists, lower and upper arms, neck, throat, chin, jaw, eyes, cranial area, ears, scalp . . . relaxing every muscle, vein, nerve and fiber. If you are familiar with hypnosis you may recognize this as an induction technique. It is very effective (and can be used, as will be seen later, for bringing on mediumistic trance).

When you have relaxed in this fashion you can simply sit there and enjoy it, or you can go on to do other psychic work. In Transcendental Meditation you would concentrate on a mantra—a short word or phrase (more just a sound than an actual word) to keep any thoughts from intruding as you sit and relax. But meditation is actually an excellent time to permit entry of certain things. Ignore mundane thoughts—"Oh boy! When I've finished here I've got to go out and mow the lawn," or "The rent is due tomorrow and I haven't got the money." Try, as much as possible, to think of nothing in particular. This is not easy but it can be done, and is the reason for the TM mantra. The trouble with something like a mantra is that it keeps out the worthwhile along with the mundane. Often it's in meditation that you get your first contact with spirit, or with your spirit guide. In Buddhist meditation it is said that you should simply accept these extraneous thoughts, acknowledge them, and let them go. Shortly, I will give a guided meditation that will bring you into contact with your spirit guide(s). For now, however, just use meditation as a tool for learning to relax totally and completely. If something should come, just accept it but don't dwell on it. Simply try to keep your mind as blank as possible.

Your conscious mind is like a spoiled child, it is constantly demanding attention. But it can be disciplined. It can be taught to sit quietly and wait. Once this happens you will start to get positive results. Sit in meditation and relax. Enjoy it. Ten minutes is probably enough time to start. You can gradually increase this to fifteen or even twenty minutes, if you wish.

At the end of your meditation period, reverse your relaxation technique: go through your body from the top of your head down to your toes. This time, however, feel your muscles awakening, feeling fresh and energized, ready for anything you want to tackle. Finish up by opening your eyes and, after a couple of minutes of reorientation, standing up. You should feel great!

Safeguards

"Like attracts like" is the adage, and it has proven to be true. For this reason you really need have no fear of attracting to you evil entities of any sort, while practicing your mediumship. Yet this is certainly a common fear among newcomers to Spiritualistic phenomena. Indiscriminate use of items like Ouija boards has brought problems to some people in the past, which has helped give rise to this apprehension. But, as I say, like attracts like. In other words, if you're the sort of person who is positive, seeking to help others through your mediumship, and looking to advance spiritually, then you'll attract nothing but good to you. You really have nothing to fear. On the other hand, if you are the sort who takes delight in playing pranks with a sadistic twist to them, are not averse to swindling people out of their savings, and wouldn't think twice about dealing in stolen goods, then you might well draw similar spirits to you! And along with such negative spirits you might well attract negative "entities," for want of a better term; elemental beings from other realms who might be looking for a means of entry into this one. Ivy Northage (previously quoted) says:

> *I am often asked if psychic activity invites evil spirits. Accepting a reasonable and sensible*

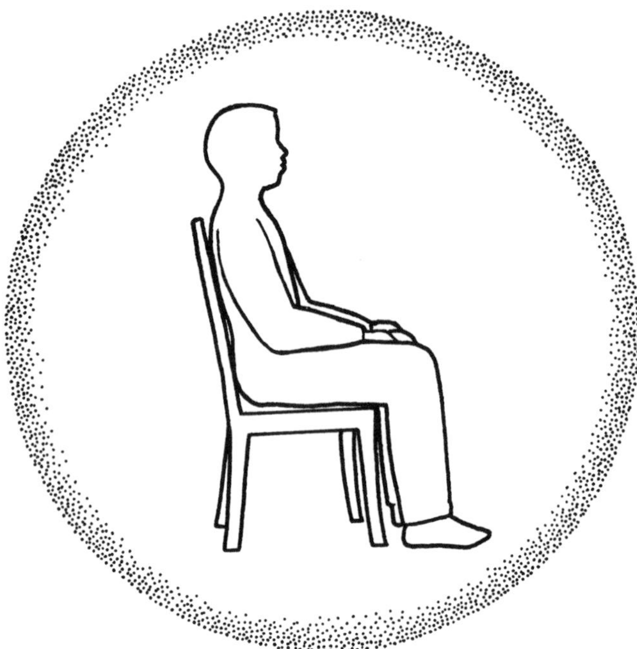

Protective pschic shell

approach to all such phenomena, the answer is a positive no. Like attracts like, and someone sincerely desirous of developing their gifts for the good of humanity can not be in touch with evil. It should be remembered, however, that psychic ability on the astral level is as a light in a foggy street. Therefore, uncontrolled or denied the spiritual stimulus of upliftment afforded by the guides, it can expose you to mischievous or lost spirits that, once attached, can be difficult to dislodge without firm refusal of psychic activity on the part of the medium.

With all of this in mind, it behooves the sensible medium always to take some precautions just in case. It takes but a moment to erect a psychic barrier around you, so why not do so every time you prepare to do any sort of psychic work? And I would even include your meditation. Here is a simple little cleansing and protection process you can go through right before you meditate, right before you try table tipping, psychometry, automatic writing, or a full-blown séance. In other words, every time.

Exercise

Sit quietly for a moment, eyes closed, feet flat on the floor, hands loosely in your lap or on the arms of your chair. Breathe deeply and evenly, and calm yourself. Then, as you breathe, imagine that with each intake of breath you are drawing into your body the soft, positive, blue light of protection; as you breathe out you are pushing out all negativity. Feel this blue light (some people prefer to "see" a white light or a golden one; use whichever color you feel most comfortable with) coming up into your body through your feet. Feel and sense that it is coming up from "Mother Earth"; from the great goodness of nature. Even if you are sitting in a room several floors up in a building, you can still sense this energy coming up out of the ground and then slowly climbing up through the building until it reaches your floor and your feet. Look upon this as an attunement with nature and with all the positive aspects of the myriad forms of life in and on the earth.

As you breathe in and out, feel/sense your body filling with this positivity and driving out all the negativity until you are completely filled with good energy. Then keep going for a while. "See" the light expanding until you are totally enclosed in a sphere of it; a ball of light with you in its center. This is your protective shell. This is the egg of which you are the yolk. Nothing negative can break through it. Know this, and accept it. It will serve and protect you.

If you are of an especially religious turn you might want to add the saying of a prayer to this practice. You can do this as you work on the power/light building. Another alternative is to see white, gold, blue, or whatever color light descending from "above" (from God/Goddess/All That Is) and entering your body at the crown of the head or the position of the third eye, rather than coming up from the ground.

Do not hesitate to do anything that will give you an added sense of security and protection. But at

> The idea of a guardian angel is one of the truisms that organized religion has not destroyed. For indeed, we do have guardian angels or guides who intervene for us and assist in our earthly missions . . . There are many types of guides, and to me, guardian angels and guides are one and the same. Before we were born, we mapped out a blueprint for our life's journey. When we veer off our life's path, usually a guide will help us get back on track.
>
> **James Van Praagh**

---

the same time don't, please, scare yourself into believing that you are about to embark on a perilous journey that is fraught with danger and from which you may not return! As I said earlier, there is probably no need for this protective measure at all; we are just doing it to err on the side of safety. So do it as a matter of course, then carry on without thinking anything more about it. You will be fine.

Spirit Guides and Guardian Angels

The belief that human beings have spirit guardians watching over them is found in many ages and many societies around the world. The ancient Greeks, Romans, Egyptians, the Chinese, African tribes, Amerindians, in the Old Testament and New, in Mohammedan belief—everywhere is found one or another aspect of this belief.

Spiritualism certainly agrees that we each have a spirit guide. It is not someone we choose; they choose us. Also, you may have more than one. Some mediums find they have one guide who works with them in clairvoyance, for example, and another who works with them to do automatic writing, or physical mediumship. There are some mediums who specialize in psychic healing (see lesson fourteen) and have a whole group of guides, some or all of whom were doctors in their earthly lives. It's also possible for a guide to work with more than one medium. And not all guides were, necessarily, once on this plane. There are some who have never manifested here.

One point to keep in mind is that your importance does not increase in proportion to the number of guides you have! If you hear a medium constantly speaking about his or her large number of guides, it may just be the ego that is being stroked. You can be just as good a medium—probably better—with only one guide.

If your guide gives you details of his or her previous life/lives on the physical plane, accept it as something interesting but don't dwell on it. It's only natural that you should look for some personal details of your guide's previous existence, but to get too caught up in what they did, where they lived, etc., is to detract from your main purpose, which is to do the work you have chosen to do.

The Doorkeeper

The term "doorkeeper," or "gatekeeper," is often given to the one guide who works most closely with you in mediumship. He or she is the one who organizes the spirits on the second level, ready to come through you to the sitters on this level. He will ensure that the spirits are there and will help them, if necessary. He will also keep away any unwanted spirits, should any unsavory types be attracted for whatever reason. The late medium Ena Twigg's personal guide and doorkeeper was "Philip," Estelle Roberts' was "Red Cloud," Arthur Ford had "Fletcher," Ivy Northage has "Chan," and William Rainen has "Dr. Peebles." (Not every medium is necessarily aware of his or her doorkeeper, however. For example, the New York medium George Anderson doesn't mention one and neither does San Diego's Chris Meredith.)

> Many teachers urge that our motives for spiritual development should be of the highest, and that we must avoid getting carried away by our own sense of importance.
>
> A guardian angel is the same as or similar to a spirit guide . . . Our personal guardian angel is with us from birth until we make our transition. So is the gatekeeper, but they are not the same. One has not lived in human form while the other has.
>
> **Elizabeth Owens**

Free Will

Another name sometimes used for a guide is a "spirit control," though this is more of a misnomer since, as I say, they do guide rather than control you. Another term occasionally used is "spirit associate."

We all have free will, so our guides do not interfere with the way we live our lives. That doesn't mean to say that they wouldn't try to influence you if they saw you seemingly bent on self-destruction. I'm sure they would. But any such interference would always be by suggestion, usually subtle, so that the last word is definitely yours.

Your guide would never lead you astray or cause you to do anything negative or destructive. If ever you feel you are getting those sorts of directions from someone claiming to be your guide, stop and question just from where the instructions might really be coming.

Finding Your Spirit Guide

We all have a spirit guide, whether we are aware of it or not. Many Christians think in terms of a "guardian angel," perhaps even identifying it with one of the Christian angels or archangels, or one of the saints, and can accept the concept in those terms. As a Spiritualist and potential medium, it is a good idea to make contact with your guide. There is an easy way to do this, which is through a meditation journey.

Begin by making sure you are quite secure (unlikely to be interrupted), and sit in a comfortable, straight-backed, meditation chair. Go through the relaxation technique I gave above and then go on from there, on a psychic journey. There are two main ways you can take this journey. You can carefully read through what follows and get it firmly in your mind, then you can repeat it to yourself (it doesn't have to be word-for-word; just get the general feel of it) and follow through with the suggestions as you give them to yourself. Or you can first read the written journey on to a tape recorder and then, when you are ready, simply play it back and follow through on the suggestions. Either way can be effective. The choice is yours. Here is the journey:

> *You are walking along a country lane. The sun is shining down and you feel warm and happy. There's an open field on your left and a large woods on your right. You can hear birds singing in the trees and a gentle breeze wafts against your face. You see, ahead of you, a small path that leads off to the right, into the wood. Take that path. It leads at a slight downwards slope, winding in amongst the trees. You can see the sun up above, shining down through the branches and creating a wonderfully warm and comforting environment. Small animals, such as squirrels, rabbits, and chipmunks, peek out at you as you go on your way. You catch an occasional glimpse of a baby deer through the trees.*
>
> *The angle of descent gradually steepens, and you come to a cliff edge. You are not very high up; in fact, no higher than the tops of the trees on the ground below the cliff. You see that*

someone has cut large steps into the face of the cliff and these lead down to the wooded ground below. You go down these steps. It's an easy descent and you feel safe and secure as you go down. At the bottom you cross the short expanse of grass to go, once more, in amongst the trees.

As you move on, you soon become aware of the babbling of a brook. The sound gets louder as you approach it. As the path makes a turn to the right, you see the brook ahead of you; its busy waters rushing over and around small and large stones. The path you are on follows along the side of the brook and you walk along it, noticing how the water swirls and eddies as it goes on its journey. Other small streams come in to join it and gradually it swells until it becomes a small river. As you walk on, beside it, you enjoy occasional glimpses of fish in the river, and of a duck or two that lands on the water then takes off again.

A large tree has fallen and stretches across the river, its upper branches on the far bank. Take the opportunity to cross over; jump up onto the tree trunk and walk across. You feel firm and secure, knowing you will not slip or fall. On the other side, you notice a large number of wild flowers growing in amongst the trees and underbrush. There is another path—you were obviously not the first to cross by the fallen tree. Follow along the path and notice the flowers and, again, the animals and birds.

Ahead of you the trees start to thin and you come out of the wood into a field. Stop and stand with the wood behind you. Fields stretch away to the horizon ahead of you. Off to the left you can make out high mountains, and to the right you can see the wood curving around and off with more fields beyond. But in front of you, in the middle of the field at whose edge you stand, there is a circle of standing stones. Each stone stands nine or ten feet tall. There are a number of them forming this circle . . . great granite monoliths. They look older than time; as if they have stood here for century upon century. Count how many there are.

Move forward into the ring. You feel happy, warm, and comforted, as though the stones are guardians surrounding you and keeping out all negativity. Walk into the very center of the circle they form and sit down on the grass. You are aware of the warmth of the sun and the sound of the birds. Again you feel that gentle breeze on your cheeks. Close your eyes for a moment and breathe deeply. Breathe in the wonderful, positive energies of this sacred place.

As you sit there quietly, you become aware of another person joining you. Keep your eyes closed. This person has come up from behind you and now moves around to face you. It is a good presence; a comforting one. It is your personal guide. It is the doorkeeper who has watched over your progress for many years. Don't yet open your eyes, but stand up and reach out your hands and take those that are offered. Feel them. Feel the warmth and love that comes from them.

Now open your eyes and see your guide. Is it a man or a woman? Young or old? What is he or she wearing? Notice everything about this guide. Ask by what name you should call him or her and greet them appropriately. Ask if they have any special message for you.

Know that this stone circle is your "special place." You can come here at any time, knowing that you can meet with your guide, or anyone else you wish, and be perfectly safe and secure. You can ask all you wish to know of your guide. No one else can come here without your permission.

When you have finished speaking with your guide, bid him or her goodbye and say that you will meet again very soon. Then turn and walk out of the circle, back toward the woods.

Retrace your steps, going back to the river and across the fallen tree trunk. Follow back

> Q: What is the mission of the spirit-protector?
> A: That of a father towards his children—to lead the object of his protection into the right road, to aid him with his counsels, to console him in his afflictions, and to sustain his courage under the trials of his earthly life.
>
> Q: Is a spirit protector attached to an individual from his birth?
> A: From his birth to his death; and he often follows him after death in the spirit-life, and even in several successive corporeal existences; for these existences are but very short phases of his existence as a spirit.
>
> **Allan Kardec**

---

along the path until it parts company with the stream. Go up the steps in the cliff and head out of the wood again, back on to the country road. Know that you have had a unique journey, but that you can repeat it any time you wish.

Find yourself back in your meditation chair; breath deeply and relax, as you prepare to come back to your normal surroundings. Follow the steps I've previously given, for coming out of meditation. In other words, go through your body from the top of your head down to your toes, feeling your muscles awakening, feeling fresh and energized, ready for anything you want to tackle. Finish by opening your eyes and, after a couple of minutes of reorientation, stand up and feel good.

As I've said, you can return to your special place at any time you wish. If you wish to go straight there when entering meditation, without going on the long journey through the woods, then you may do so, though I do recommend taking the "long scenic route" for the first few times at least. Also, if you'd prefer a different destination—a different "special place"—then you can have it. I know of one person who ends up going into a cave to meet his guide. I know of another whose special place is high up in a room in an old stone tower, and one who meets her guide underneath a waterfall! If you prefer to be in a room in a house with relatively modern surroundings, that too is fine. Simply let your journey take you where you would feel most comfortable. On coming out of the woods, you may see an old castle that you enter, or you may cross the field and go into a house and then to a particular room. Whatever is the most comfortable place for you is the right place. If it is to be furnished, then furnish it as you will.

Exercises

Wherever you decide to go in your guided meditation, after first accessing it ask yourself some questions. What were your feelings on various stages of your journey? What animals did you see, and did you have any special feelings about them? Was there more to be seen than given by me in the general directions for the journey? If so, what? How did you feel when you first became aware of your guide being there? What did his or her hands feel like? What did he or she look like? What was the name? Was there any message?

There are no right or wrong answers to these questions. Simply study your answers and see if they have special meaning for you.

Examination Questions

1. How many guides does each person have? Is the idea of spirit guardians a relatively modern belief, perhaps born out of the episode of the Fox sisters in the nineteenth century?

2. Who is the "doorkeeper," or "gatekeeper"?

3. Why is it incorrect to refer to a guide as a "spirit control"?

4. Do all well-known mediums have doorkeepers?

5. What is the purpose of the doorkeeper?

Profile

Leonora E. Piper

Leonora E. Piper was born in 1857. At eight years of age, when playing in the garden, she felt a blow to the side of her head, on the right ear, which she said was accompanied by "a prolonged sibilant sound." This sound gradually became the letter *S,* which then was followed by the words: "Aunt Sara, not dead but with you still." Leonora was terrified. Her mother noted the time of day and a few days later they learned that Aunt Sara had indeed died at that very moment. Other childhood experiences for Leonora included bright lights seen in her bedroom at night and an unexplained rocking of the bed.

In 1881 Leonora married William Piper of Boston and a few short years after, in 1884, she discovered her psychic and mediumistic abilities. This came about when, because of a tumor, she visited Dr. J. R. Cocke, a blind healer and clairvoyant. Cocke went into trance but Piper also went into trance. While in that state she wrote down a message to a Judge Frost of Cambridge (another of Cocke's clients), from his dead son. Shortly after that a number of spirit guides made themselves known and, as word of her message to Judge Frost spread, she was talked into conducting her own séances. In trance she would undergo spasms and grind her teeth ferociously, though in later years this passed and she went smoothly into trance. Then she would speak with various voices; many of them deep men's voices. Her guides included a purportedly French "Dr. Phinuit" (pronounced "Finney"), who knew little French and less about medicine! There was also a Native American girl named Chlorine. Piper wasn't happy with this development and initially would only sit with relatives and close friends. But when Mrs. Gibbins—who happened to be Professor William James's mother-in-law—asked for a sitting, for some reason Leonora accepted her. The results were so amazing that Mrs. Gibbins reported them to her son-in-law. In turn Professor James, a founder of the American Society for Psychical Research, was so impressed by Piper's séances that he devoted the next eighteen months to carefully controlling everything she did, making all arrangements, and reporting (in *Proceedings,* Vol. vi): "I repeat again what I said before, that, taking everything that I know of Mrs. Piper into account, the result is to make me feel as absolutely certain as I am of any personal fact in the world that she knows things in her trances that she cannot possibly have heard in her waking state, and that the definite philosophy of her trances is yet to be found." Between 1885 and 1915 Leonora Piper became one of the most investigated mediums of all time.

William James examined her and after attending many séances (some with his wife) became convinced that Piper was "in possession of a power as yet unexplained." She was never found cheating. She was examined by James, by Dr. Hodgson, Professor Newbold, Dr. William Leaf, and Sir Oliver Lodge. James introduced her to Richard Hodgson, who had exposed a number of other mediums. Hodgson was stunned with the personal information that Piper provided about his own family. He tested her with other subjects only to get similar results. Her details about deceased persons were so accurate Hodgson hired private detectives to carry out surveillance to see if she actually obtained the information fraudulently. Then Hodgson decided to remove her from her surroundings. He sent her to England, where she arrived in November 1889 and was met by Sir Oliver Lodge. Lodge gave a glowing report on her mediumship after she had eighty-eight sittings between her arrival and February 1890. All sitters were introduced anonymously to Piper. Servants were changed in houses where she stayed. She wasn't even allowed to go shopping alone and couldn't see a newspaper for three days prior to a sitting.

In the end, on Leonora Piper's return to America, and after further testing by Dr. Hodgson, Hodgson reported (*Proceedings,* Vol. xiii, in 1897): "I cannot profess to have any doubt but that the 'chief communicators' . . . are veritably the personalities that they claim to be; that they have survived the change we call death, and that they have directly communicated with us whom we call living through Mrs. Piper's entranced organism. Having tried the hypothesis of telepathy from the living for several years, and the 'spirit' hypothesis also for several years, I have no hesitation in affirming with the most absolute assurance that the 'spirit' hypothesis is justified by its fruits and the other hypothesis is not."

On Hodgson's unexpected death in 1905, Professor Hyslop took over. The following year Piper went back to England and, with the later deaths of Myers, Gurney, and others, started producing cross-correspondences from their various spirits. Seventy-four sittings were held with her and other sittings with mediums Mrs. Verral and Mrs. Holland. The cross-correspondences were produced by the three mediums.

Since Leonora Piper never had any remembrance of what came through her in the trance state, she always remained unconvinced herself that she was a channel for spirits! But, as Sir Oliver Lodge pointed out, "Little value would be attached to her opinion . . . Mrs. Piper in fact is not in a more favorable, but even in a less favorable position for forming an opinion than those who sit with her, since she does not afterwards remember what passes while she is in trance."

In later years Leonora Piper's abilities faded, especially when she had to devote time to her ailing mother. Various controls took over, at different times. The French doctor was pushed out by the spirit of George Pelham, a deceased friend of Dr. Hodgson. Then a group known as the Imperator group took over, producing what was described as a "higher caliber" of spirits making contact. Piper's trance mediumship ended in 1911 and she then did mainly automatic writing. In October, 1924, Dr. Gardner Murphy conducted a series of sittings and from 1926 to 1927 the Boston Society for Psychical Research took over. Leonora Piper died in 1950, at age eighty-three.

LESSON SIX

Spirit Communication

How sincere are you in your desire to become a medium? This is a serious endeavor and should not be undertaken lightly. Do you want to channel for some reason of ego, or will you be doing it in a serious and dedicated manner, genuinely desiring positive results for the good of all concerned? It seems that those who don't have the true desire and the belief that it can be done, have a much harder time of it than others. To try it "just to see if it works" will not bring the same results as trying it in the sure knowledge that it can be done. There must be knowledge that contacting spirits is possible.

Start off by acknowledging to yourself that you do have a belief in the afterlife, and that our spirits live on at another, higher level of existence after physical death. Without this belief, you are certainly not going to get far in your attempts at mediumistic development. Having acknowledged this belief, then one of the first steps is to ask yourself the question: "Do I really want to become a medium?" and, if so, "Why do I want to become a medium?"

Is it simply to prove to yourself that there is a life after death, or to prove that to others? Is it a desire to communicate with specific departed loved ones? (If so, then perhaps you can do so without actually becoming a medium yourself.)

But perhaps there is more of the lure of achieving fame and fortune, and of flaunting your psychic abilities. Or perhaps there's just a desire to continue developing your already manifested psychic abilities. There are many possible answers to "Why do I want to become a medium?" and no single one of them is necessarily the right one. Conversely, none of them may be really "wrong." (Certainly many mediums in the past have achieved both fame and fortune. Some have certainly flaunted their abilities. Whether or not this is "approved" by others is something else and, perhaps, a moot point.)

Know that not all people work the same way. We are all individuals; we all develop differently, even on psychic levels. What works for one person may not work for another, so some experimentation may well be necessary. We also develop at different rates; some become strong channels in a very short time, while others work for years to achieve that same state. No one can guarantee that you will become a medium of any particular type within a certain specified period of time.

Exercises

To begin with, you have to know yourself. Who are you? What is your purpose in life? What path is it that you wish to tread and where, exactly, does that path lead? Do you have goals—both long term and short term? It's a good idea to sit down with a piece of paper and a pencil and address some of these questions. Ask yourself these, and similar questions, in all sincerity, and see what you come up with.

Affirmations

Affirmations are a good start and lead to more direct development. Indeed, affirmations can remain a very useful tool throughout your development and long after your psychic maturity. Affirmations are positive statements repeated by an individual, thereby establishing them in the subconscious mind and reinforcing the conscious mind. In other words, to repeat several times over, every morning, that you are (for example) growing more attractive and self-assured will actually work on your inner self to the point where not only will you sincerely believe that you are becoming more attractive and self-assured, but you actually will become more attractive and self-assured.

Affirmations can be composed for just about anything and are especially effective for psychic development. As Stuart Wilde says (*Affirmations* 1987):

> *An Affirmation of word will serve for almost anything—health, wealth, happiness—whatever you are concentrating on at the time.*

Wilde goes on to say that the affirmations you compose yourself are by far the most effective, and this is true. But to give you an idea of the type of composition, here are one or two you might use for starting mediumship. Write some more of your own.

1. Psychic powers are natural powers and I possess them strongly.
2. My natural psychic abilities are opening up and flowing.
3. By believing in my psychic power, I unveil my natural mediumship.
4. Every day, in every way, my mediumship develops and progresses.
5. The gateway to the world of spirit swings open wide for me.

It can be seen that affirmations can be slanted in any direction, depending on where you feel your greatest need(s) might be. You can take any affirmation—or two, or three (don't take too many though; you'll dilute your concentration)—and repeat it several times every day. A lot of people write out the affirmation and then post it up about their house/apartment. To get up in the morning and see your affirmation right there in front of you, stuck on the bathroom mirror, prompts you to say it there and then. On the refrigerator door is another good place, as is the edge of the screen of your computer.

Post them all over the place. Write them on colorful, eye-catching paper, or with brightly colored inks.

Say them and get into the habit of saying them. Say them . . . and believe them!

The Problem of Connecting

One of the questions often raised at the idea of spirit communication is, if it is truly possible, why aren't a lot more people doing it? Also, of the millions of people who die, why don't more come back through mediums?

The short answer to both these questions is that really good communicators are comparatively rare. There is the potential for a great many, as will be seen, but few take the time and trouble to develop themselves. And to further answer the second question, if there were a lot of good mediums, then many more people would be able to "come back" from the spirit world and many more potential mediums would be encouraged to develop.

In order to communicate you need both a "sender," who wants to communicate, together with a "receiver," who is also trying to make contact at that same time; one in each of the two separate levels of existence. Plus, you must have the medium of communication—the individual who is able to make the connection. A good simile might be to imagine a host of people in the United States wanting to speak to relatives in Europe, but with an extremely limited supply of telephone operators, no known phone numbers, and the relatives in Europe unaware that they are trying to be contacted!

To continue the simile, when a connection is made, there might very well be a bad line, and the operator may be unable to make a direct connection and have to relay everything back and forth . . . with the attendant problems of interpretation!

In the "here and now" it's not always easy to understand what someone is trying to say to you. In everyday life there is constant misunderstanding and misinterpretation. "What do you mean?" "What are you trying to say?" These are not uncommon expressions in the course of many "normal" conversations. Just listen to any conversation between a parent and a child—especially a teenager—and you'll see what I mean! It shouldn't come as a surprise, then, to find that communication with the spirit world can be even more difficult.

In the past there were many more mediums though, even then, really good mediums were never plentiful. In the earliest days of the Spiritualist movement, and the development of the Spiritualist Church, there were a lot of "home development circles" (see lesson sixteen). These were gatherings of people all equally interested in Spiritualism and all eager to develop their gifts of mediumship. With the advent of television and the development of radio and the movies, among other things, development circles quickly became a thing of the past. Today, therefore—especially with the added distractions of home computers, computer games, outdoor sports of an incredible variety, ease of travel, etc.—there are very few active mediums and only a tiny trickle under development. Yet to make contact with spirits of the dead, and to learn of the afterlife, must surely be far more exciting than any sport activity or television program!

Atmospherics

One of the difficulties that is often mentioned by spirits when they first make contact is that they become easily fatigued. They seem quickly to become exhausted and complain of feelings of suffocation, often necessitating breaking the connection for a short time. They will then later return, apparently refreshed. The reason for the fatigue is unknown, though some have suggested it has to do with the density of the medium's aura. Obviously there is a very delicate "attunement" that takes place between the spirit and the medium to bring about successful communication.

> I suffer much less. The music is so beautiful. . . . Listen, listen in the midst of all those voices I recognize my mother's!
>
> **Last words of Louis XVII**

> A medium, or sensitive, is a person who is able to feel and/or hear thoughts, voices, or mental impressions from the spirit world. Spirits also use telepathy. A medium is able to become completely receptive to the higher frequencies or energies on which spirit people vibrate.
>
> **James Van Praagh**

Another reason for difficult communication—with direct voice, automatic writing, and the like—is simply that the spirit is unused to the medium's body. All of us have certain mental and physical habits that we have formed over many years, making it easier for us to do certain things in certain ways peculiar to ourselves. If you were suddenly transplanted into someone else's body (especially someone of the opposite sex) you might well experience great difficulty trying to do the simplest things. So this is how it is with spirit trying to use a medium's body. With direct voice, just trying to adjust to the medium's vocal cords can take a while, let alone trying to use his or her finger, hand, and wrist muscles to hold a pencil and do automatic writing.

Dates, Names and Ideas

There are other difficulties of communication, other than just those of the mechanics of making the connection. For example, if a spirit is giving a message that is being received clairvoyantly or clairsentiently (see lesson ten), the medium can frequently pick up the general idea of the message without necessarily getting the exact wording. Yet if all that is being relayed is a name or a date, or some other abstract, there is no general "idea" that can be grasped. A spirit may be able to convey the feelings of love felt for the person with whom they are communicating, and this may be picked up and passed on by the medium. Or the word "table" will evince a particular picture in the mind of the medium. But how does one pick up the "feelings" of, say, May 27, 1963, or of the name "Fred"? This is one of the reasons why mediums who seem otherwise excellent may fall down on receiving accurate names, numbers, dates, etc.

Where dates are concerned there is the added factor that time, as we know it, is not a part of the world of spirit. Time is human-made. It is a convenience only (or inconvenience!).

Have you ever been away on vacation, perhaps just relaxing in the mountains or at the beach, and then suddenly had the thought "Hey! What day is it today?" With no need to keep note of the passing of time, with no pressing appointments to make or keep, it's easy to lose track of how many hours, days, or even weeks have gone by. And, to continue the idea of not having to make and keep appointments, why should you bother to keep track of how many hours, days, or weeks have gone by anyway? No reason at all!

So it may well be in the world of spirit. You can be where you want to be whenever you want to be; you can be with whomever you want whenever you want to be. Would it be any wonder that you would lose track of the passing of time, as it is recorded back here on earth?

> The Spiritualistic movement has rendered an incalculable service in bridging the gulf that used to separate the living from the dead. The fact of survival of bodily death has been established beyond any possible question by any reasonable person who will take the trouble to acquaint himself with the evidence.
>
> **Dion Fortune**

> D. Scott Rogo and Raymond Bayless, authors and psychic investigators of note, have found that every year hundreds of telephone calls are received in America alone which apparently come from the dead.
>
> **Harold Sherman**

> I'm not afraid to die. I just don't want to be there when it happens.
>
> **Woody Allen** (*Getting Even*)

Symbolism and Its Interpretation

A symbol is a sign; an expression to give the impression of something else. As Webster puts it, "Something concrete that represents or suggests another thing that cannot in itself be represented or visualized."

The only drawback with symbols is that they have to be interpreted. Certain symbols have become universal and are immediately recognized as representing specific things—traffic signs are a good example of this symbolism, whereas others are so infrequently used or so personal that someone unfamiliar with them would have a hard time interpreting them. This can often be the case in mediumship; something is presented in the form of a symbol that the medium may or may not correctly interpret.

Don't forget that we never actually see anything in the physical world as it really is! What we do is to realize, through our five senses, various aspects or qualities of the object. For example, if you are looking at an orange, your sense of sight tells you that it is an orange-colored sphere with an irregular, pockmarked surface. Your sense of touch tells you that it is round, smooth yet slightly rough, and cool. Your sense of smell supplies you with the information that it has a distinctive yet pleasant odor, which is confirmed by your sense of taste. In this particular instance your sense of hearing does not enter into describing it.

Now all these things that appeal to your senses are "qualities" of the orange rather than being the orange itself. The orange is always something different from all of these, and above and beyond them, and is more inclusive than any of these qualities and symbols.

So suppose you were to take away one of those symbols—the color, for example. The orange would immediately become invisible to you, and yet it would continue to exist. This shows that the symbols are very inadequate and imperfect representations of a vaster "something" lying behind them. They represent only a small fraction of the totality of the thing as it really exists.

Interpreting Actions

Interpreting actions seen clairvoyantly can especially become a problem in mediumship. When we communicate with one another on the physical plane, we do so by a pre-arranged code. We either use written symbols or we use our facial expressions, motions of the head and hands, together with vocal sounds. If we did not have these pre-arranged codes we would have great difficulty making ourselves understood.

> The nearest simile I can find to express the difficulties of sending a message is that I appear to be standing behind a sheet of frosted glass—which blurs sight and deadens sound—dictating feebly to a reluctant and somewhat obtuse secretary.
>
> **F. W. H. Myers, five years after his death,**
> **recorded through the automatic writing of a medium.**
> **Reported in Society of Psychical Research**
> **journal *Proceeding*, vol. xxi.**

> ". . . there's a whole other world going on right here, right at the same time our world is going on. There's a kind of church here. . . It's a tiny mission, a Spanish mission."
>
> "I certainly don't feel very happy sharing my office with a lot of dead people." (he said)
>
> "You've nothing to fear from them, really," she assured him.
>
> **Sylvia Browne,**
> **reading for a doctor moving into a new office.**

This can be seen when two people meet who do not speak the same language. Suppose you want to tell a Russian, who speaks no English, to get something—let's say a watch—from another room. It would be useless to say the word "watch." You would probably tap your wrist, go through the motions of winding a watch, setting the hands, etc., then point to him and then to the other room. If he didn't understand what you were trying to say you would have great difficulty getting what you wanted.

In *Amazing Secrets Of the Psychic World* (New York 1975), I gave an example of what might happen with a medium trying to interpret the actions of a spirit seen through clairvoyance:

> *He taps his stomach and looks at a spot over his left side. He seems to wish to convey the impression that he suffered much from bowel trouble, perhaps a cancer on the left side. Yes, he seems to be taking something away from the body; evidently they removed some growth. Now he is examining his hand. He is looking intently. Now he is doing something with his fingers. I can't see what it is; a little movement. Was he connected with machinery in life . . . ?*

In actual fact, dear dead Uncle Charles was trying to let you know that it really was him there by doing what he had always done, so many times, while alive: he had a favorite pocket watch that he would take out of his vest pocket, wind, and reset if necessary! He never had any stomach problems, cancer, or connection with machinery. So here, although the medium had made contact and had correctly seen Uncle Charles's actions, he had incorrectly interpreted what was seen to the point where the recipient could not believe there had even been any true contact!

This is a not uncommon problem. The answer to all this is simply, as a medium, to not interpret what you see; just describe it, exactly as you see it, and leave the actual interpretation to the sitter.

Triviality in Messages

A criticism often leveled at Spiritualism is that the messages received from the spirits are many times so trivial. "Why don't they tell me something important?" "Why are they wasting time talking about an incident in my childhood?" "Why don't they tell me what's coming up in the future?"

> It's analogous to a radio with very heavy static. You hear a voice, but it's not clear and you try to catch a word here or there. Other times the messages are very faint, like a whisper, or come and go incredibly fast. You catch it for a split second as it rushes by, like a train. And still other times it's like a voice that keeps breaking up.
>
> **John Edward**

> I think there is too much phenomena without philosophy. I am much more interested in the phenomena if it helps a person become a better person and to look deeper.
>
> **Rev. B. Anne Gehman**

In fact it is the very triviality of most messages that underscores their authenticity. If I were sitting with a medium and she (or he) claimed to have my grandfather come through, it would leave me quite cold to be told that he saw me becoming rich and famous. It would be nice to hear, perhaps, but I could hear the same thing from a carnival fortuneteller. How much more striking to be told that he was reminding me of a certain time when, as a child, I accompanied him to the banks of the River Thames and to tell me of what happened when we stood watching another young boy fishing. A "trivial" incident, yes. But an absolute confirmation that I was indeed in contact with my late grandfather.

Many, if not most, people sitting with mediums are doing so because they are looking for the comfort of knowing that there is a life after death and that their loved ones are still available to them. The so-called trivial details are the ones that give this assurance more than could anything else.

If you are a regular sitter, then you can go on beyond the trivia stage, by all means. And most people do. It is, however, the trivia that critics seem to dwell on, perhaps feeling that it makes Spiritualism an easy mark.

Names, Colors and Lights

As I have mentioned, names are not so easy to get across. Family names, however, can often be projected through symbolism. For example, if a medium describes an elderly man and then says something like, "He is showing me a field . . . a large green field . . . and now an inn. A field and an inn." The sitter might well immediately recognize that the spirit was giving the name "Fielding," a name well-known to the sitter. A man sitting sewing could be representative of the name "Taylor," and so on. There are many names that can be got across through this kind of symbolism. As a medium you need to be aware that this may be the sort of information that is being channeled.

There are also symbols that have almost become the universal symbols of Spiritualistic communication. They include the following:

Bells: wedding; celebration.

Black border: as on a letter, indicates a loss.

Cake with candles: birthday.

Clouds: if white, happiness; dark, misfortune; receding and fading away, indicates a journey.

Colors: these have various meanings, basically whatever you "feel" they mean to you (and you should here be consistent). Generally blue, lilac, and purple are associated with spirituality; red with passion and/or anger; yellow/orange with change; pink with love and health; green with envy and with money.

Cradle: a birth.

Diploma: graduation; promotion.

Key: success.

Letter: news coming.

Light: specks of light show good progress in spiritual and psychic development. A bright light is often a spirit trying to communicate.

Money: money coming, whether as an unexpected lump sum (inheritance, lottery win) or in the form of a pay raise.

Rainbow: happiness

Rose: pink—love; red—anniversary; yellow—friendship.

Wishbone: opportunity . . . make a wish!

There may be any number of symbols that become your own personal ones. For example, you may always see a large U-Haul whenever any sitter is going to relocate, or an airplane when they are to take a trip. Over the years you will come to recognize when a particular thing is a symbol rather than something integral to the specific sitter.

Examination Questions

1. What are some of the questions you need to ask yourself before trying to become a Spiritualist medium?

2. Is it wrong to seek fame and fortune through mediumship?

3. Why are there so few mediums these days?

4. How easy is it to make a "connection" with the other world and to talk to spirits?

5. Many mediums are thought to be poor at establishing the identity of the spirit they contact. What is a common reason for this?

6. With contact such as direct voice—the spirit actually speaking through the medium—there can be initial difficulties. What are they and why is that?

7. Why are so many messages received from the spirit world so trivial in nature?

8. What are the meanings of the universal symbols (a) key, (b) bells, (c) cradle? Do these symbols mean the same thing to all mediums?

9. How would you expect a spirit to try to indicate to a medium that his (the spirit's) name was Smith?

10. Is there any guarantee that you can become a direct voice medium?

Profile

Eileen Jeanette Garrett

In his introduction to Eileen Garrett's autobiography, Allan Angoff says: "Eileen Garrett holds no professional degrees and has no license to practice any of the healing arts, but she has helped and apparently cured hundreds of physicians, scientists, writers, editors, secretaries, psychiatrists, psychologists, bereaved parents and children, and the prime minister of a very large country."

Born on March 17, 1893, in County Meath, Ireland, Eileen Jeanette Vancho Lyttle showed psychic abilities from a very early age. Suffering from tuberculosis and bronchial asthma, she spent many long weeks confined to her bed. As a young child, she claimed that she was able to speak with the dead. Her mediumship started in earnest following the end of World War I. She came to be considered one of the greatest mediums the world has ever known.

During the war, and after a failed marriage to a young architect named Clive Barry, Eileen ran a hostel for wounded soldiers. She had precognitive visions of many of the men with whom she came into contact, often seeing them killed on returning to action. One of the soldiers she saw die in this way was a man who, as she nursed him, she agreed to marry. At the end of the war, in 1918, she married James William Garrett, another wounded soldier. Like her two previous marriages, this one did not last long. It ended in divorce and Garrett did not marry again.

One day Garrett joined a group of women who were doing table tipping. In the middle of the session she went into a trance, and started speaking of seeing dead relatives of the women around the table. The women were so surprised and startled that they shook her awake. Garret was persuaded to consult with a man who would help her understand this aspect of herself. When the man put her into a light hypnotic trance, a spirit "control" named Uvani came through and stated that Garrett would be active as a trance medium for the next several years. This turned out to be true. It took a while for her to come to terms with this new role, but eventually—through the agency of people like James H. McKenzie and the British College of Psychic Science—she accepted her gift.

Eileen Jeanette Garrett

Garrett came to work with people like Hereward Carrington, Nandor Fodor, Sir Arthur Conan Doyle, and Sir Oliver Lodge. In 1931 she was invited to visit the American Society for Psychical Research, which she did. While in America she also worked with other notable mediums, with Dr. J. B. Rhine, and with Dr. Anita Mühl. In 1938 she wrote a book titled *My Life As a Search for the Meaning of Mediumship* (Rider, London 1939) that was published and successful. Shortly after its appearance, she traveled to Europe; to Juan-les-Pins, in France. At the beginning of the World War II, she tried to remain in France to help orphaned children, but eventually had to leave.

On March 8, 1941, back in New York, Garrett was inspired by the name of the Life Extension Building to start a publishing company at its location on East Forty-Fourth Street. On impulse she rented two rooms on the eighteenth floor and planned to launch a magazine, to be called *Tomorrow,* which would deal with serious investigation of the paranormal. The proceeds, she decided, would go to the starving children of France. She actually started by publishing two books; one on *Nostradamus,* by Lee McCann, and one of her own called *Telepathy.* These were under the banner of her publishing company, Creative Age Press, though this name was later changed to Helix Press. The first issue of her magazine *Tomorrow* appeared on September 1, 1941. In 1947 Garrett became a U.S. citizen.

In 1951 Garrett founded the Parapsychology Foundation, to promote organized scientific research into parapsychology. The Foundation published the *International Journal of Parapsychology.* Garrett was always somewhat uncertain about psychism generally, and her own in particular, and allowed herself to be subjected to numerous tests at such institutions as Johns Hopkins University and the New York Psychiatric Institute.

Eileen Garrett died on September 15, 1970, in Nice, France. She had been ill for some years before that. She has been acclaimed as one of the world's greatest mediums.

LESSON SEVEN

Talking Boards

Many people experience their first brush with "the occult" through the talking board. This is an ancient form of communicating with spirits of the dead, used in China and in Greece from as early as 600 B.C.E. Today there are several commercially produced boards on the market, one of the originals being the "Ouija" board (from the French *oui* and the German *ja,* both meaning "yes") of William Fuld, first commercially produced in 1892 and more recently marketed by Parker Brothers. This is a smooth-surfaced, rectangular board with the letters of the alphabet written across it in two curving lines. Below the letters are the numbers one through nine, zero, and the words "Yes," "No," and "Goodbye." With the board comes a sliding pointer, or planchette, which rests on three felt-covered feet and has a circular, clear plastic window through which the letters of the board can be read as it slides around.

The modus operandi for this board is for two people to sit facing one another with the board resting between them, on their knees. At the outset the planchette sits in the center of the board and the participants each have their fingertips resting lightly on it. By gliding about the board and stopping over different letters, the planchette spells out messages and answers to questions put to it. It moves seemingly of its own volition, not from either person pushing it (at least not consciously).

Let's look at a typical case (based on an actual happening) of someone who had never used a talking board before.

Jim Waite had been invited to his first séance. He was seated opposite his hostess, Mary Wilson. After a few moments, in response to Mary's repeated "Is there any spirit present?" the planchette started sliding across the board to the word "Yes." It was quite a firm movement and Jim had no

Various examples of this divination tool have been used for centuries, one of the earliest forms being alectromancy, where a cockerel picks up pieces of corn or wheat placed alongside letters of the alphabet arranged in a circle, thereby spelling out words in answer to questions asked by the diviner. In ancient Greece and in Rome, a small table on wheels moved about, to point to answers to questions, while in China, c. 550 B.C.E., similar tools were used to communicate with the dead. The Ouija is not unlike the squdilatc boards used by various Native American tribes, to obtain spiritual information and to locate lost people and objects.

Raymond Buckland
The Fortune-Telling Book

Mediumship is much more common and diverse than people think. It extends to automatic writing, bibliomancy, divination, and direct-voice phenomena, as well as the Ouija board. All of these forms are communication by words or symbols, the same way we communicate our mental thoughts in our normal everyday consciousness.

Barbara Honegger

Using a talking board

doubt that it was Mary Wilson who was causing it—he was sure she was pushing it.

"Do you have any message for any person here?" asked Mary of the board.

"Yes," repeated the planchette. It then proceeded to slide around to point directly at *J, I,* and *M* . . . JIM! Jim himself, however, remained unimpressed. So he remained until the planchette, continuing on its way, spelled out a message: "LOOK ONE MORE TIME BUTCH." Suddenly he became very much interested. "Butch" was the nickname of a favorite uncle who had recently died. Mary knew nothing of either the uncle or his nickname. Not only that, but the message itself made a lot of sense. After Uncle Butch had died Jim had spent many hours going through his uncle's effects looking for a particular book that had been promised him. Jim had been unable to find it and had virtually given up the search. Now here was a message that fit that situation and something of which Mary Wilson could have no knowledge.

Can we now, then, assume that the message came from Jim's dead Uncle Butch? No . . . at least, not yet. The message obviously clears Mary of pushing the planchette, but it doesn't clear Jim himself. Obviously he was not consciously pushing it, but he might have been doing so unconsciously. At the back of his mind was the frustration of the search for the book. He might even have had some vague thought of Uncle Butch coming through at the séance to tell him where the book was. So long as the information received is known to at least one person present, then you can never rule out extrasensory perception rather than spiritual contact. What would have clinched it, in this case, would have been if the board had gone on to tell Jim exactly where the book was hidden. (It didn't do that, though it did inspire him to look one more time and, as it happens, Jim did find the book in that final search.)

As with automatic writing, it is the muscle power of the participants that actually causes the movement of the planchette. The question is, what is the source of the intelligence directing that use of the muscle power? The short answer seems to be, in many cases, spirits of the dead. A great deal of interesting research can be done with a talking board. Additionally a lot of fun may be had.

Commercial Faults

With the commercially produced boards there are, in my opinion, two faults. One is but a slight inconvenience, and that is when the planchette goes to the extremities of the board, one foot of the planchette may slip over the edge. You then must lift it back onto the board before you can continue. This is merely an aggravation, though it does interfere with the smooth run from letter to letter.

The second fault is more serious. It is in the design of the planchette. The instructions given (with the Ouija board) say: "The mysterious message indicator (planchette) will commence to move . . . as it passes over Ouija talking board each letter of a message is received as it appears through the transparent window covered by the message indicator." This is not strictly true. Sometimes you receive a string of letters that seem to make no sense whatsoever—until it is realized that the planchette is no longer showing the relevant letters through its plastic "window" on the one line, but is pointing to the letters on the line above with its tapered end! Consequently you must often watch, and note, two sets of letters rather than one! To overcome this drawback, I suggest covering over the "window" and going solely by where the pointed end of the planchette indicates. Some other talking boards

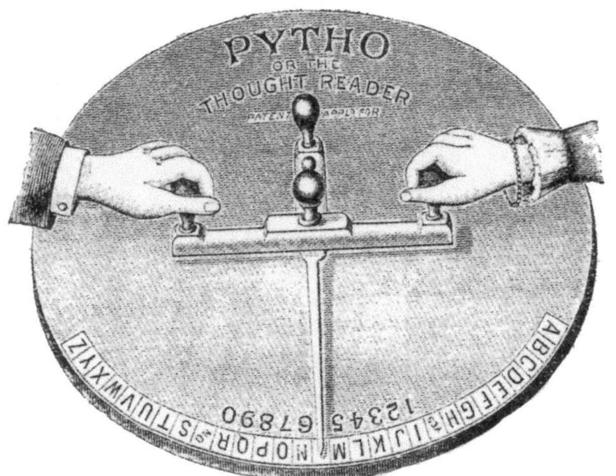

Pytho talking board

I'm not a Spiritualist! I'm a Presbyterian. I built this factory on Ouija's advice, but I haven't consulted the board since. Things have been moving along so well I didn't want to start anything.

William Fuld (first promoter of the Ouija Board)

The nature of the Ouija phenomenon is controversial; so too are its roots. No one person or culture can take credit for its development. Ouija origins are multiple and ancient, having been independently reinvented and rediscovered in a wide variety of locations.

Stoker Hunt

(and the original Fuld design) do not have the "window"—they are just a solid, heart-shaped pointer—and so it is a simple matter to see what letters are indicated.

The indication in the instructions that only two people may operate the board at any one time is also incorrect. The board should be placed in the center of a small table and a number of people (four, five, or even six) can then sit around and each place a fingertip on the edge of the planchette. In this way you will give far more energy to the board and receive back much more energetic responses.

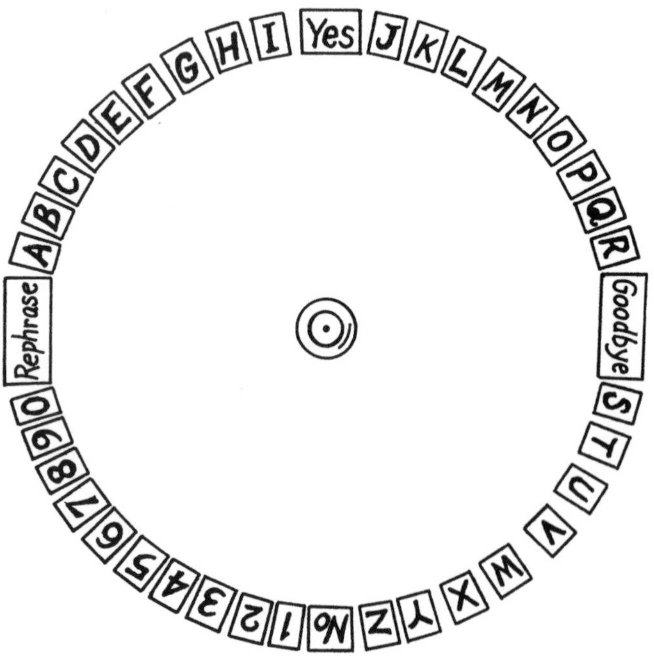

Homemade talking board

Do-It-Yourself Talking Board

An older way of using the board is not to have an actual board at all. Simply print the letters of the alphabet on pieces of paper or cardboard (index cards are good for this) and lay them in a circle around the edge of a table. Include in the circle the words "Yes" and "No." "Goodbye" and "Rephrase" are also two useful things to include. Now upturn a wineglass in the center and use that as your planchette, resting fingertips on the rim of its upturned base. You will find that the wineglass will glide around the tabletop and stop at letters working just as well, if not better, than a commercial board.

"Goodbye" is nice to have included, since it is only polite to bid farewell to the spirits at the conclusion of the evening, and they also like to be able to say goodbye to you. "Rephrase" can be useful. Sometimes you will ask a question and get no response. It might be that the question you have asked is ambiguous and you haven't realized it. If the wineglass goes to "Rephrase" then you can do just that; put the question another way.

Cross-correspondences stand today among the very best evidences we have of the survival of the human personality, in intimate and recognizable form, beyond the experience we call death . . . the new science of parapsychology accepts the cross-correspondences, and rates them with the best evidence we have for the survival of the individual human personality beyond the grave.

Alson J. Smith

You will have nothing to fear from "evil spirits" if you have nothing to fear from yourself.

Gladys Osborne Leonard

I am inclined to believe that the Ouija board may take honorable place with Sir Isaac Newton's apple, Watt's tea kettle, Benjamin Franklin's kite, and other historic playthings which have led to many great results.

Stewart Edward White

Record Keeping and a Spokesperson

Record keeping is one of the most important aspects of all forms of psychic research, and of Spiritualism especially. Appoint a secretary; someone to take notes. Let that person not be in on touching the planchette but concentrate on writing down everything asked and noting all the letters indicated in responses. The human memory is notoriously unreliable, so write down everything. An additional safeguard might be to also have a tape recorder running. (Certainly use a tape if there are only two of you present.)

One person, and one person only, should act as spokesperson. If anyone else has a question, let them give it to the spokesperson to ask. Different people asking different questions, sometimes more than one trying to speak at the same time, can be very confusing, even in everyday life! You can certainly make a change to a different spokesperson after a time, but the changeover should be definite and announced to the spirits. In fact it is a good idea to try different people in the position, for some seem to have more success and draw better response than do others. But don't make the changeovers too frequently; give each person a reasonable amount of time in the position.

It's also a good idea to prepare a list of questions before the sitting. This way there will be no long pause while everyone racks their brains to think of what to ask. This helps the secretary, if all he or she has to do is fill in the answers and not have to also write out long questions as they are thought of and asked.

Procedure and Verification

There is no need to work in subdued light. Start your séance by creating a harmonious atmosphere. Establish a protective barrier, and simply relax and enjoy it. Everyone should have their feet flat on the floor with hands loosely in their laps. Breathe deeply and calm yourself. Then, as you breathe, imagine you are breathing in the soft, positive, white or blue light of protection. Feel it filling your body and driving out any negativity. As you continue to breathe it in, see it expanding to fill the circle of friends about the board. Continue to breathe deeply until the light expands to fill the whole room in which you all sit. If you feel so inclined you may all say a prayer. Many

The Ouija board "began its career with no taint of evil. The reason for this is that it emerged in a cultural context (in China and then ancient Greece) in which many gods were respected, and in which good and evil were intermingled freely and considered equally necessary parts of reality, expressed in the flow of seasons and in the cycles of decay and renewal, death and birth, that are acted out by all that lives."

Gina Covina

The Brazilian book *Evolution In Two Worlds* was initially written one chapter at a time, with automatic writing, by medium Francisco Candido Xavier. It seemed to make little sense when finished. Then Xavier's spirit guide told him that other, alternate chapters had been channeled to Waldo Vieira, a doctor living two hundred and fifty miles from Xavier. When the two documents were put together, they fitted and made absolute sense. This was the first of seventeen books to be produced by cross-correspondence by the two mediums.

Sue Leonard

Spiritualists sing a song together to help create a pleasant, happy atmosphere. This should certainly be a light, happy song. (It doesn't have to be a hymn or anything religious . . . so many Christian hymns are heavy and depressing, anyway!) The purpose of the singing is simply to help attune the sitters to one another and to create a pleasant atmosphere into which you may invite the spirit.

As everyone places their fingers on the planchette, the spokesperson starts by asking, in a normal voice, "Is there anybody there?" The question is repeated until the glass, or planchette, starts to glide across to the answer "Yes." It should then return to the center. If it doesn't return, simply ask it to: "Thank you. Will you please return to the center?"

For this initial movement it may be that you will have to sit and wait, asking if anyone is there, for five or ten minutes. This is especially so when you haven't used a board before. How quickly you get a response, and the "power" of that response, will depend on many factors, including the attunement of the sitters, their acceptance, the willingness of the spirits to communicate, and their ability to do so.

At no time should anyone present attempt to push the planchette. This is most important. It shouldn't be necessary to say this but it seems that often there's someone present who is tempted to interfere. Certainly it's easy to do, without anyone knowing. You can get a few laughs at the expense of your friends . . . but what's the point? It is so easy to do that it's certainly not "clever." You can, and should, approach the whole talking board experience with a sense of enjoyment—of pleasure. But at the same time, it should be a serious approach in that you don't want to be wasting your time and you do want to receive appropriate material.

When you first start using a board you are bound to think, at some point, that someone is pushing it, as shown in the example I gave, above, of Jim Waite and Mary Wilson. It is a natural suspicion, but try to get it behind you and you'll soon find it allayed.

After establishing contact, the sitting may proceed on lines such as the following:

"Is there anybody there, please?"

YES.

"Are you willing to speak with us?"

YES.

"Do you have a message for anyone here?"

YES.

"Would you please give the name or initials of that person?"

J. B. D.

"Is the message for John?"

YES.

"Please spell out the message."

WAIT FOR THE SMUMRF.

"Would you please repeat the last word?"

SUMMER.

"Thank you. Carry on with the message."

NOW IS TOSOON.

"Do you mean, 'Now is too soon'?"

YES.

"Is there more to the message?"

NO.

This is typical of the way the communication can go. Once in a while the letters may get a little jumbled and you will need to break in to straighten them out. Don't hesitate to ask questions if the incoming message is not clear. If there is any doubt about anything, simply ask for a repeat. In the above example where "WAIT FOR THE SMUMRF" appears, not only are the letters of the last word jumbled but there is an *F* given instead of an *E*. It could have been that the pointer moved too close to one letter rather than to the one next to it, or it might have stopped between the two. If that happens, and the secretary is unsure which is meant, the spokesperson should be asked to clarify it.

It can also happen that the spirit mistakes a letter. We don't know just how clearly it is possible to see from one level to another but it is easy to mistake between the letters *H, K,* and *N,* for example; or *C, G, O,* and *Q* or *D, P, R,* and *B* . . . just try reading an eyechart!

When a long message is being spelled out, it can sometimes help your understanding of it by having the pointer pause briefly, in the center, to indicate the end of a sentence. In fact I have used the technique of asking the spirit to move the planchette all around the circle, once, at the end of a word and three times at the end of each sentence, to be quite sure. There have been times when the spirit has seemed impatient to get on with the message and the glass has absolutely raced around that circle!

As with so much of psychical research, it is the followup—the verification after the séance—that can be most interesting. Did the spirit really live at the time claimed and is its body buried where it stated? Can a grave be found? Check burial records, church records, public records, newspaper reports, and obituaries; anything that might help. Was the spirit ever in the army or navy? Check military records.

Cross Correspondence

If you have a sufficient number of people interested in talking boards to form two groups—this can be done with a minimum of four people; two sets of two—you can experiment in what is known as "cross correspondence." Let's call our two groups "A" and "B." Let's also appoint an unbiased coordinator.

Start with each group advising its particular spirit contact of what they wish to do. This can be done in this fashion:

Spokesperson: "We want to do a cross-correspondence with our other group. They are meeting at Michelle's house, 115 Main Street, tomorrow night at 9:00 P.M. During our sitting here tonight please start a message that you will continue with them."

Then somewhere within the material that each group receives will be part of a message. On the face of it there will be nothing unusual. It may blend in with whatever else is received. Each group should send the record of its sitting to the coordinator. He or she should be an intelligent, fairly learned person. The coordinator's job is to search through both sets of material and find a total message. Let me give you an example to clarify this.

Let's suppose that among the many pages of group A's material the coordinator finds this:

"What sort of place are you in now?"

It is very pleasant, as though the winter is past, the rain is over and gone, and everything is nice and fresh again—almost a rebirth.

Something suddenly strikes the coordinator as sounding vaguely familiar. Very carefully going through group B's equally lengthy material, this is discovered:

"Was there anything you knew on this level that you miss?"

No.

"Can everything be experienced where you are, then?"

Yes.

"The different seasons?"

Oh, yes, even when the flowers appear on earth, the time of the singing of birds, gamboling of lambs—everything really.

Now the coordinator recognizes the whole phrase. It is a quotation from The Song of Solomon (ii. 11,12): "For lo, the winter is past, the rain is over and gone; the flowers appear on the earth; the time of the singing of birds is come, and the voice of the turtle is heard in our land."

Such a cross-correspondence could be continued for a number of sessions. The main point with such an experiment is that neither group should see the other's notes and neither, of course, know what quotation to expect.

The coordinator can select a quotation beforehand, and the spokespersons would then ask that "the continuing message be the one being thought of by Terry Meister, our coordinator." This makes his or her job a lot easier when searching through the materials. In this case, however, there is always the possibility of unconscious ESP between the coordinator and someone in each of the groups, rather than it being actual spirit contact. To have no one know what the quotation will be, beforehand—though much tougher on the coordinator—is much more convincing.

Solitary Use

A common question is "Can the talking board be used by just one person, or does it have to have two participants or more?" Certainly to start with you need at least two. I would even suggest your very first encounters be with four, five, or six people around it. You'll generate far more energy to the spirit trying to come through and get more satisfying results, as I've already mentioned.

But when you've dealt with it as a group for a while, and have a good feel for what is happening, there's no reason why you shouldn't cut down the number of participants. Some people seem to naturally work well together. If you find you are in wonderful harmony with a particular person, certainly try some talking board work with just the two of you. If this goes well, then you can each try working alone. But ease into this. After you've been sitting at the board together for a while, one of you sit back and leave the other to handle the planchette alone. You can even lead up to this by having one person gently lift their fingers from the planchette as it is moving, leaving just the other person's fingers there. Many times this will cause the board to immediately stop. If so, replace the missing hand and continue before trying again later.

Eventually there will come a point where the planchette, although it may slow considerably, will still keep moving with only the one hand on it. Keep on with this and you'll find—just like first starting with a group—the board will seem to gain confidence, and power, and build up speed once more. Then you can continue from that point working alone, right from the start of a sitting.

Pencil Planchette

There is a way of using the planchette as a platform for automatic writing (which I will be dealing with more fully in the next lesson). Instead of having a leg, or support, under the pointed end of the moving platform, drill a hole through and insert a pencil, or ballpoint pen. The point of the pen or pencil serves as the third foot for the planchette. With the platform resting on a large sheet of paper, any movement of it will cause the pen to leave a line on that paper. With a group of people sitting around the table, resting their fingers on the planchette in the center as with the talking board, it is possible to get the pen to literally write out its messages as it moves around.

This arrangement especially lends itself to one-person operation. With just one hand resting lightly on the platform, the planchette will move around and spell out messages, or "converse" with you. It's interesting to use the opposite hand from your normal writing hand for this; you will notice it makes no difference to the writing. You'll also notice that the "handwriting" can and will change with different spirits coming through.

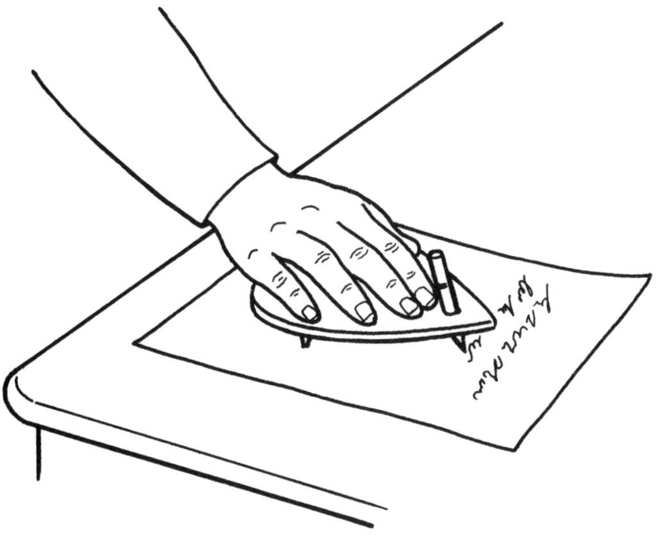

Pencil planchette

More on automatic writing in the next lesson, lesson eight.

Caution

Some books on the subject of talking boards take a rather sensational approach, telling dire tales of people—usually very young or very old people—who have been sadly led astray by the messages received. They tell of young teenagers who have asked the board when they will die, only to be told that it will happen that following year! Needless to say, this can have a terrible psychological effect on the recipient of such news. But this only points up the fact that the talking board is not a toy; it is a tool.

There are certain precautions that you need to take when using this, as with any tool. First of all, if you start getting a lot of negative messages—particularly messages telling you to do certain things that go against your grain, which you would not normally consider doing—then stop using the board! It's as simple as that.

If "the board" tells you to give away all your worldly wealth, for example—stop and think about it! Who is telling you to do this, and why? It may be a spirit claiming to be Jesus or one of the angels . . . but what is the likelihood? And why, if they are who they claim to be, would they tell you to do something that would leave you in dire straits? Don't quit your job on the advice of a long-dead relative, or a character from hundreds of years ago. What would they know about today's labor market? How conversant would your great-grandfather be with, say, modern computer science?

In other words, use your head. Don't run to the talking board expecting to get answers to all of life's problems. The spirits don't necessarily have the answers—they can't necessarily see into the future, and they may be the last persons to give you good advice.

In marketing the Ouija board, the phrase "Mystifying Oracle" is used. This implies that the board is able to divine the future. Here is where that teenager put so much store in the misinformation that she was soon to die. The board is not an oracle; it cannot tell you of the future. But use it with common sense; use it taking the precautions that I have outlined; use it and don't abuse it . . . and you will have no problems. Far from it, you will gain a lot of enjoyment.

Examination Questions

1. How old is the Ouija board?

2. Since the board is sold in toy stores, does that mean it's a toy?

3. How many people can use a talking board at one time?

4. Is the board evil?

5. There is a problem with the design of the Ouija (commercial) planchette. What is the problem and how can it be overcome?

6. What makes the planchette move around the board?

7. Why should you not push the planchette, to get it to move or to go to a specific letter?

8. What is a cross-correspondence and what is its purpose?

9. What is a pencil planchette and what is it used for?

10. Should you always follow the advice given you through a talking board?

Profile

Rosemary Brown

For several decades Rosemary Brown received spiritual messages, in the form of music from deceased composers. Brown claimed that since her childhood she has been in contact with such people as Chopin, Liszt, and Beethoven. Liszt first came to her when she was seven years old. She saw him only as a white-haired old man. It wasn't until ten years later that she saw a picture of Liszt and recognized him as that old man. All of these composers dictated new compositions to Brown, who dutifully copied them down. Brown's mother was supposed to have been a psychic.

In 1964 Brown had suffered injuries, including broken ribs, in an automobile accident. She spent some large part of her recuperation sitting at the piano. She had not played for at least twelve years before that, and had little formal musical training, but suddenly she found herself playing. She claims she felt the spirit of Liszt guiding her hands. Liszt went on to introduced to her Bach, Beethoven, Berlioz, Brahms, Chopin, Debussy, Grieg, Monteverdi, Rachmaninov, Schubert, Schumann, and Stravinsky. She said that she would chat with the composers while they worked. Rachmaninov wrote a special piece just for Leonard Bernstein and asked Brown to give it to him specifically. Bernstein was quite impressed.

Brown is not alone in her association with dead composers. Clifford Enticknap and British concert pianist John Lill have both experienced spirit contact. In the case of Enticknap it was Handel who came through, while Lill claims he actually saw the figure of Beethoven and spoke with him.

On April 14, 1970, CBS television's *Sixty Minutes* carried a segment on Rosemary Brown. A number of notable musicians—among them André Previn and Virgil Thomson—were impressed with the material that Brown had produced. Previn stated

Rosemary Brown

that it would require someone with a great deal of musical knowledge and technique to fake that kind of music, though he added that he felt the quality of the compositions was far below the usual standards of the attributed composers. Others have acknowledged that the works are in the style of the claimed composers, but say they lack the quality of the masters. Hephzibah Menuhin said: "I look at these manuscripts with immense respect. Each piece is distinctly in the composer's style."

Some critics said that what they heard from Brown was simply reworkings of the composers' known works, but they admitted that it would take a person of considerable musical knowledge and ability to pull off such a feat. Brown did not have that ability. In fact, she had great difficulty playing the compositions she wrote down.

In *Time* magazine for July 6, 1970, British composer Richard Rodney commented "If she is a fake, she is a brilliant one and must have had years of training . . . I couldn't have faked the Beethoven."

As word spread about her mediumship, Brown started to give public performances. She received more than four hundred compositions from the various dead composers. She issued a recording of some of the works in 1970, under the title *Rosemary Brown's Music.* She also authored three books: *Unfinished Symphonies, Immortals By My Side,* and *Look Beyond Today.*

An interesting story is given by Jenny Randles and Peter Hough, in *The Afterlife: an Investigation into the Mysteries of Life after Death.* They say that a skeptical German reporter interviewing Rosemary Brown suddenly spoke a few sentences in German when she claimed Liszt was present in the room. Brown neither spoke nor understood German. She told the journalist that Liszt had left the room then, a moment or two later, said that he had returned with a woman. She described the woman. As Randles and Hough put it: "The color drained from the sceptical photo-journalist's face. Seemingly she had just given a perfect description of the complete stranger's dead mother. He had just asked Liszt to go and bring her—but in words Mrs. Brown claims she had no way of comprehending."

The late conductor Sir Donald Tovey communicated with Brown and (again according to Randles and Hough) said: "It is the implications relevant to this phenomenon which we hope will stimulate sensible and sensitive interest and stir many who are intelligent and impartial to consider and explore the unknown of man's mind and psyche."

LESSON EIGHT

Automatic Writing and Spirit Photography

The Hand that Writes by Itself

Automatic writing is that which is performed without the use of the conscious mind. That is, writing that is performed using the unconscious muscular energies of the hand and arm. Yet, you cannot use those muscles to write without some direction governing what is being written. The "director" of automatic writing—the one whose brain is being used—is the spirit with whom you are in contact.

In practice, what happens is that you take up a pen or pencil and hold it over a large sheet of paper as you direct your attention elsewhere. In a short time your hand will start to make small movements, seemingly of its own volition. These movements will cause marks to be made on the paper. As time goes on these marks become more and more consistent and consecutive, beginning to form circles, hooks, etc. Gradually letters, then words, and finally whole sentences, are written out.

One of the joys of automatic writing is that it can be done virtually anywhere. It can be done while reading a book, watching television, or even while talking to someone on the telephone. Just seat yourself comfortably, where you can have a sheet of paper beside you, with your hand and pen resting on the paper. I would suggest first doing your cleansing and protection exercises, to set up your barriers. You can even go so far as to make contact with your guide and ask him or her to invite in spirits to make contact with you through writing.

Then get into whatever it is you will be doing: reading, watching television, or whatever. And here is one form of spiritual contact where you do want to be absorbed in something else entirely, at least for the first dozen or so times you do this. You see, if you just sit and concentrate on your

Francisco Candido (Chico) Xavier from the town of Pedro Leopoldo, in the state of Minas Gerais . . . is held in such high esteem in his country that he has even featured on a series of Brazilian postage stamps. Xavier spent at least five hours a day for fifty years allowing dead authors to write through him while in a trance. Having had only an elementary schooling, much of what he writes is beyond Xavier's understanding.

Sue Leonard

The popular view of the sceptic is that the mind is a largely untapped source of information, and that if one puts the body into a state of reverie—idling and submitting conscious control to a back seat—strange things can happen. Indeed, we all have evidence of doing this ourselves in our day-to-day existence. If we had to think about the process of breathing we probably would not be able to do it. It is a complex affair which requires the control of many muscles and processes that have simply become automatic. We go from minute to minute never giving it any thought and yet doing it all of the time thanks to the systems built into our subconscious. Is that how automatic writing works? Do we simply let these hidden skills come to the fore and control the hand muscles and transcribe what is pouring freely from within the mind? If so, what is the source of the material that emerges? Is it imagination, as skeptics would believe, or can our minds at this deep inner level tap into the consciousness of others—even after death?

Jenny Randles & Peter Hough

---

hand and pen, your own conscious mind will come into play. You may start to write but you are just as likely to be writing something that you are directing, rather than allowing a spirit to come in and communicate. So better by far to project your attention elsewhere and leave the spirit to its own devices for a while.

Try to forget that you are holding the pen. Once your hand starts to move, you'll have an almost irresistible urge to look down and see what's being written. But do resist it. Get absorbed in whatever you are doing and let your hand do its thing. You'll find that it will move very slowly at first but will gradually travel faster. Once the spirit has adjusted to your muscle power, the hand will start to move very rapidly. In fact, once you get going your hand will just fly across the page, writing far faster than you would be able to do normally. For this reason I suggest using a large sheet, or pad, of paper. When you get to the bottom of the page you will certainly need to glance down enough to turn the page of the pad. What I have done in the past, and found to be very useful, is to sit at a table and have a large sheet

Automatic writing while engaged in conversation

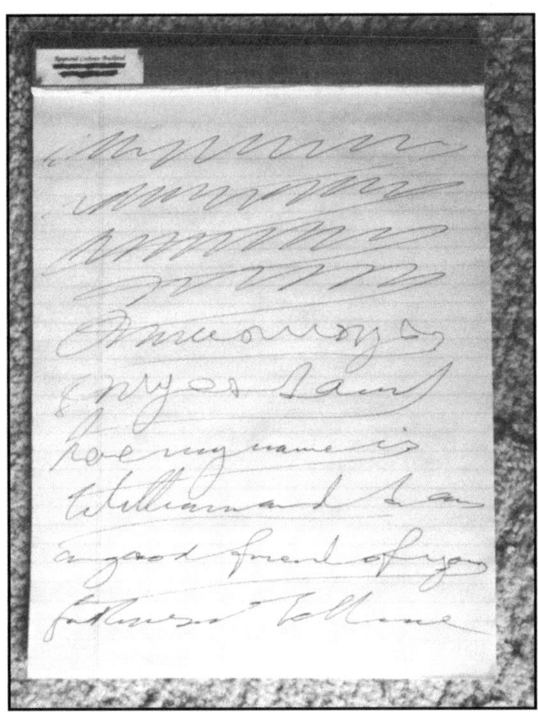

Sample of automatic writing

of artist's paper (the back of rolls of wallpaper is ideal, too) spread out so that I can write a tremendous amount without having to pause to turn a page, or interfere in any way.

You may find that it helps to hold your arm clear of the table. That is, so that neither the wrist nor elbow touches it. In this way a certain amount of fatigue will occur, which seems to help induce the writing.

Don't Try to Direct

Be careful to separate your mind from the actions of your hand and arm. Don't in any way try to direct what's being written. If you had the discipline you could certainly sit and just let the spirit take charge and write, and you could watch what was being written as it happened. (In fact I will talk about doing just that a little later on.) But, for now, few of us have that much discipline that we can sit and not influence what is produced. You would see something and think—however briefly perhaps—"Oh, it's going to write such-and-such." Sure enough it would write "such-and-such" . . . but it might do so simply because of your influence. Perhaps it had been about to write something quite different. So—at least until you really get used to the action of automatic writing, and can really keep your own mind apart—just absorb yourself in some other activity so that the spirit can have free rein.

Some people obtain the writing more easily if they hold the pen or pencil between the first and second fingers, like a cigarette. This is different from the normal way of holding a writing instrument and helps in not forcing the writing in any way. But you don't have to hold it like this. Do whatever feels most comfortable and allows you to temporarily forget that you are holding anything.

You will sometimes find that to start with you are not really getting writing, in the sense of actual letters and words. Sometimes the pen will go scribbling across the page, line after line, and when you later study it you find there's nothing there but scribble. This may even happen for the first two or three times you try automatic writing. Don't be discouraged. Eventually the scribble will form into words. What is happening is that the spirit communicating is simply getting the feel of your muscles and familiarizing him or herself enough to be able to write. Usually when there's this long preliminary to the actual writing, then when the writing finally comes it's especially striking, both in its content and its length.

Types of Messages

What sort of things will be written? One automatist read what had been written and found it was by a man calling himself James Valentine, who said that he had just recently (a few hours earlier) been killed in a railroad accident. He gave the details: time and place. On later checking, the automatist found everything to be accurate; a James Valentine had indeed been killed at the time and place stated. The man had been driving his car across an unguarded railroad crossing when the vehicle stalled out. He sat there and tried to restart the car, thinking he could make it before the oncoming locomotive reached him.

It's not common to make immediate contact with a newly dead person. You are far more likely to be contacted by a deceased relative or friend. Or by someone whom you didn't know when alive but who has a special interest in you.

One of the especially interesting things that can happen is that you will find the handwriting is not your own! In fact, when you get messages from a number of different spirits you will frequently find that each has his or her own handwriting, as they had when alive. A Mrs. Grace Rosher worked with a pen propped lightly against her fingers and soon found herself getting long communications in a strange hand. The spirit signed the messages "William Crookes." It was later verified that the handwriting was in fact that of the late Sir William Crookes, the pioneer parapsychologist!

Check What You Receive

As with all spiritual contact, carefully check the material you receive. Make note of all names, dates, and places. Try to verify what you are told. Only in this way will you be able to assure yourself (let alone anyone else) that you are indeed in contact with the spirit world; the second level.

When you've been receiving for a while—about a dozen or so separate occasions, at least—then you can start to respond directly to what you are receiving. You can read what has been written and then, consciously writing yourself, write out a question. Giving up control again, wait for the answer to come from spirit. In this way you can get into a conversation with the spirit. The trick, of course, is to be able to give up conscious control and let the arm/hand/pen go free, so that you get unadulterated responses to your questions.

Either Hand

Another way to ensure that what you get is not coming from you, is to use the other hand from the one you normally use for writing. If you are normally right-handed, hold the pen in your left hand for automatic writing, and vice versa. In fact, when you get into "conversation," you can have your left hand write for the spirit and ask your questions through your normal right hand! It will take longer for the spirits to adjust to writing through you this way, however. The reason is simply that you are not used to moving your hand and manipulating your wrist for writing with that hand and so spirit will have to work harder to get it as supple as the hand you normally use. But, again, persevere and you'll get great results.

William Stainton Moses

William Stainton Moses (1839–1892), born at Donnington, Lincolnshire, probably became the greatest physical medium after Daniel Douglas Home. He initially distrusted Spiritualism but went on to demonstrate levitation, apports, and eventually produced a great number of automatic writings. These latter, from various spirits, were published under the title *Spirit Teachings.* Of his writing, Moses said:

> *At first the writing was slow and it was necessary for me to follow it with my eye, but even then the thoughts were not my thoughts. Very soon all the messages assumed a character of which I had no doubt whatever that the thought opposed my own. But I cultivated the power of occupying my mind with other things during the time that the writing was going on, and was able to read an abstruse*

I have been familiar with the phenomenon of Psychography, and have observed in a vast number of cases, both with recognized Psychics known to the public, and with ladies and gentlemen in private, who possess the power and readily procure the result. In the course of these observations I have seen psychographs obtained in closed and locked boxes . . . ; on paper previously marked and placed in a special position, from which it was not moved; on paper marked and put under a table, so as to get the assistance of darkness; on paper on which my elbow rested, and on paper covered by my hand; on paper inclosed in a sealed envelope; and on slates securely tied together. I have found such writing to be almost instantaneously produced.

W. Stainton Moses

---

book and follow out a line of close reasoning, while the message was written with unbroken regularity. Messages so written extended over many pages and in their course there is no correction, no fault in composition, and often a sustained vigour and beauty of style.

William T. Stead (1849-1912) was another excellent automatist. He was a British journalist in the late nineteenth century who became interested in automatic writing and received many messages from the spirits of dead friends. Later he went on to another unique aspect of automatic writing . . . he started receiving messages from living friends! He would write out a question addressed to someone he knew and after a few moments his hand would write out the response. In this way he came into possession of a great deal of information not previously known to him yet vouched for by the friends who "wrote" it! An interesting sidelight on William Stead is that he had repeated dreams and visions of a giant ocean liner being sunk by an iceberg in the Atlantic Ocean. He wrote about this and about the number of lives that could be lost if there was a shortage of lifeboats. Twenty-six years later he was himself to go down with the *Titanic.*

Character of the Messages Received

Many of the messages you receive, especially at first, will seem incoherent and disconnected; almost like dreams. In fact they may be dreams. When you first start you may be able to disassociate your mind from the page, yet your unconscious may still be tenaciously clinging to the point where it intrudes on what is written . . . it may be your dream consciousness (or subconscious) that is originating the messages. The only way to work this out is through your meditation before you start, by aids such as affirmations, and by engrossing yourself as deeply as possible in some other activity right from the start. Working a crossword puzzle or solving mathematical equations, rather than just watching television, are good, deep-rooting activities to start with, if you feel your unconscious is intruding.

Some people find it helps—as with many types of spirit communication—to sit in a darkened room when first trying automatic writing. If you have no luck in full light then certainly try this in varying degrees of darkness.

Patience Worth

In the earlier part of the twentieth century, a St. Louis housewife encountered a spirit named Patience Worth. Mrs. Pearl Curran was persuaded by a friend, Emily Hutchinson, to use a Ouija board. Although not particularly interested, Mrs. Curran agreed and worked the board with her friend a number of times. On the evening of July 8, 1913, the planchette started spelling out a message that read: "Many moons ago I lived. Again I come; Patience Worth my name."

The spirit identified herself as a seventeenth-century Englishwoman who had lived in the county of Dorset. She said that she was a spinster and that she later immmigrated to America and was finally killed by Indians. The two women, Curran and Hutchinson, started speaking with Patience Worth on a regular basis. Then they found that Mrs. Curran could contact her by herself, whereas Mrs. Hutchinson had no luck alone.

From the Ouija board, Pearl Curran went on to automatic writing and, through that, ended up producing twenty-five hundred poems, short stories, plays, allegories, and six full-length novels—all authored by Patience Worth! She produced a total of over four million words within a period of five years.

What is especially interesting about the Patience Worth case is that Pearl Curran had dropped out of school at the age of fourteen and had virtually no knowledge of life in the mid-1600s, either in England or in the American colonies. Yet experts have examined the writings produced, have not found a single anachronism, and have found revealed an amazing insight into the life and times of that period. The vocabulary had an incredibly high percentage of old English in it—90 percent. This is probably one of the best recorded examples ever of spirit contact. The writings continued through from 1913 to the late 1920s. Mrs. Pearl Curran died in 1937.

Inspirational Writing

Another form of automatic writing, known as inspirational writing, is where you study what you are writing as you write it. Although you do not set out to write anything in particular, you find that the words form in your head, rather than directly onto the paper, and you write what seems to be "inspired." This can be a form of spirit communication in that the spirit may be coming through your head, rather than directly to the muscles of your arm. It is far more likely, however, that what you write is influenced by your own thoughts and feelings. It is not "pure" spiritual writing; or is unlikely to be. What you produce is probably a mixture coming from your own unconscious and from your higher self.

Typewriters and Computers

Some automatists have gone on from handwriting to typing automatically. Jane Roberts, who channeled the entity known as Seth, wrote most of the material he dictated by typing it directly as she received it. Others have done the same, both for automatic writing and for inspirational writing. These days the use of a computer will work. So long as you are able to disconnect yourself from the composing aspect—by directing your attention elsewhere, or however—then you can use whatever means you prefer to record the information being received. I feel, however, there is far more of an impact felt when you can actually see the handwriting itself that belongs to a departed entity. The elaborate penmanship that can materialize from a spirit who left this earth over a hundred years ago is worth far more—to me—than the convenience of having the material neatly typeset.

Great Composers Return

In 1964 Rosemary Brown, a widowed housewife in Balham, London, struggling to bring up two children, began to write music that she claimed was actually written through her by the spirits of Liszt, Schubert, Chopin, Brahms, Bach, Rachmaninoff, Debussy, Stravinsky, and Beethoven. She didn't play the piano well enough to play most of the music she was receiving, yet she had been observed writing out the manuscripts at a tremendous speed. Pianist Hephzibah Menuhin said, "I look at these manuscripts with immense respect. Each piece is distinctly in the composer's style."

Composer Richard Rodney Bennet said, "A lot of people can improvise, but you can't fake music like this without years of training."

> People are in a new readiness. Look at what Shirley MacLaine has done. There is more of a need for channels today because there are more people questioning; there are more people asking for answers. For everyone who asks a question, there has got to be someone out there they can come to.
>
> **Patricia Hayes**

> (Spirit photography) is a physical phase of mediumship and gives to one the power to produce faces and forms of spirit loved ones who have passed on, on a sensitive plate or film, thus producing a spirit picture.
>
> **Zolar**

> Spirit photography is used by some ghost hunters in their investigations of haunted sites. When the film is developed, the photographer looks for anomalous lights, shadows, and shapes that were not visible to the naked eye.
>
> **Rosemary Ellen Guiley**

In 1970 a recording was issued (*Rosemary Brown's Music*) with Rosemary Brown struggling through some of the pieces on one side of the record and, on the other side, concert pianist Peter Katin playing the more difficult pieces.

Automatic Art

Although automatic writing is the best known, and most common, of the automatisms, there are also many instances of pictures being drawn and paintings being painted by mediums. A housewife in Michigan, with no artistic training, suddenly started drawing and painting beautiful pictures. Her unusual method was to start at one side of the paper or canvas and work her way across to the other side, doing all the details of the picture as she went. It was like peeling back a top cover to reveal the picture beneath. She claimed that it was dead artists who worked through her.

In 1905 another untrained artist, Frederic Thompson, started painting in the style of the dead painter Robert Swain Gifford. Professor James Hyslop, the psychical researcher, was so impressed he reported the case in his book *Contact With the Other World* (New York 1919).

But perhaps the most amazing examples of automatic, or spiritual, art are the paintings of the Bangs sisters. Elizabeth (Lizzie) S. and May E. Bangs—known collectively as the Bangs sisters—of South Elizabeth Street, Chicago, Illinois, were extraordinary Spiritualist mediums. They were able to produce amazing spirit portraits in full color. They also did

Automatic art

> Several photographs spring to mind which remain puzzling to this day. A figure unknowingly captured on film in Arundel church in West Sussex (England) is clearly not a fault. Better still is the unambiguous image of a ten-foot-tall hooded figure, which appeared in a photograph taken by the vicar of Newby in Yorkshire near the altar of his church. The picture has been scientifically examined and yet no rational explanation can be suggested. Another remarkable photograph, clearly showing a figure, was unwittingly produced by another clergyman.
>
> **Jenny Randles and Peter Hough**

---

slate writing. Everything they did, they did in broad daylight and invariably were very carefully observed and investigated. Their production of phenomena had started when they were extremely young children, with the falling of coal from the ceiling of their parents' home and the moving of heavy furniture. The production of spirit portraits did not begin until the fall of 1894.

Initially two blank paper "canvases" (mounted on frames) were placed, face to face and standing on a table, leaning up against a window. The sitter would sit beside the table, holding the edge of the canvases with one hand. The Bangs sisters would be on the other side of the table, not touching the canvases. Curtains would be drawn across the window on either side, up to the edges of the canvases, and a blind pulled down to the tops. This then ensured that the only light coming into the room filtered in through the paper canvas. After a while, shadows would seem to appear on the translucent surface, as

William Mervin spirit painting by the Bangs sisters

Clara spirit painting by the Bangs sisters

Fox sisters spirit painting by the Bangs sisters

Mrs. Caldwell spirit painting by the Bangs sisters

Nora spirit painting by the Cambell brothers

> At around four-thirty the police phoned to say the alarms were going off. We came down to the club but there was no sign of a forced entry, so the police came in with us to check the interior. Everything was okay. The alarms had been triggered from inside the cash office, but this was still securely locked and there was no one inside. When we checked the video, we found we had filmed someone coming down the corridor, who turned and walked through the closed cash office door. The door was shut; indeed the video showed it shut, yet the figure seems to go through the door.
>
> **Cameron Walsh-Balshaw, manager,**
> **Butterflies nightclub, Oldham, Lancashire.**

---

though an artist was doing preliminary sketches. Then color would be seen, which would rapidly cover the canvas. When the canvases were separated, there would be a beautiful portrait on one, with no smudges of paint on the other still plain one. The portrait would be of a deceased relative of the sitter and be extremely lifelike.

Later the portraits were produced in full daylight, often on a stage with a single canvas propped up facing the audience. The sitter (who might be picked at random from the audience) would sit on one side, not touching the table, and the Bang sister or sisters on the other side, some distance from the table and canvas and never touching or even approaching them. The painting would then manifest, fairly quickly, much like a Polaroid photograph develops, and be of a relative of the randomly chosen audience member.

Art experts have examined the portraits and cannot explain the media used. It is not paint, ink, pastel, nor any known substance. It looks as though it has been applied with a modern airbrush and has the consistency of the powder on butterfly wings. Admiral W. Usborne Moore, in *Glimpses of the Next State* (Watts & Co, London 1911), said, "The stuff of which the picture is composed is damp, and rubs off at the slightest touch, like soot, it comes off on the finger, a smutty oily substance." The portraits were produced in a matter of minutes when artists who have studied them have stated they should have taken many hours, if not days, to complete. Some sitters would mentally request that such an item as a flower in the hair be added, and it would appear. Eyes in the portraits would often be closed and open later.

In the early 1900s the Bangs sisters also produced amazing spirit writing, which was scrutinized and analyzed by Sir William Crookes, the physicist. Many frauds tried, unsuccessfully, to duplicate the performances of the Bangs sisters and many skeptics tried to explain away the phenomena, but without success. Indeed, some of the "explanations" were ludicrous!

Examples are to be seen at the Lily Dale Museum—where historian Ron Nagy is probably the country's leading expert on the phenomena—and in Lily Dale's Maplewood Hotel and elsewhere.

If you feel so inclined, you can ask your spirit guide to bring artists through you in automatic communication. Let your hand roam freely as you sketch; have colors available to paint; just let it happen. But, as with writing, check as far as you are able to find out who is coming through you. The artist may sign his or her work or you may have to haunt galleries and dig through art books to find the originator.

Spirit Photography

Unexpected Visitors

Mr. and Mrs. Chinnery, of Ipswich, England, went to visit the grave of Mrs. Chinnery's mother. They laid some flowers there and turned to leave. As Mabel Chinnery lingered a moment, her husband got into their car. She turned and, on an impulse, took a photograph of her husband looking at her out of the car window. Then she, too, got into the car and they left. Some few days later Mabel Chinnery picked up the developed photographs from the store and took them home. Imagine her surprise when, on looking at the picture of her husband in the car, she saw her deceased mother sitting in the back seat! This happened in 1959. *The London Sunday Pictorial* newspaper published the photograph, declaring it genuine after their photographic expert had examined it.

Can spirits of the dead be photographed? Obviously, from the above, they can. There are certainly many examples of ghosts—disembodied spirits—that have been photographed. One of the most frequently pictured is Dorothy Walpole, the so-called Brown Lady of Raynham Hall, in Norfolk, England. She appears from time to time descending the staircase of the hall. She has been photographed on several occasions.

Around the turn of the century there were any number of professed "spirit photographs" produced. They were usually pictures of sitters with an image of a deceased family member hovering in the background. It seems probable that virtually all of these were fraudulently produced, by double exposure or similar means. In those early days of photography there was also a lot of unconscious fraud brought about by poor developing, incorrect chemicals, light streaks, and the like. One or two were very carefully examined by photographic experts, however, and proclaimed genuine.

William Mumler was the first to produce spirit photographs. He was an engraver who lived in Boston. In 1862 he tried to take a photograph of himself by focusing his camera on a chair, uncapping the lens, and then leaping into the picture to pose in the chair! Waiting a little too long, his first picture just

Spirit photograph of subject's mother

Spirit photograph

showed the chair; the second the chair . . . and a young girl sitting in it! The figure was transparent and the girl seemed to fade away from the waist down. Mumler recognized her as a cousin who had died nearly twelve years before.

Some reports say that actually Mumler was photographing a Dr. Gardner when the figure of the girl appeared on one of the plates. Be that as it may, Mumler went on to make a name for himself as a spirit photographer, though most of his later pictures were of the fraudulent variety. On one occasion, however, Mary Todd Lincoln, the president's widow, went to him under an assumed name. There was no way that Mumler could have known who she was, yet the developed photograph of her showed the late president standing at her side.

British Experiments

Spirit photography appeared in Britain a decade after it had stirred the hearts of Spiritualists in America. A number of British mediums tried to get results without success. Finally two respected mediums, Mr. and Mrs. Samuel Guppy, hired a photographer named Hudson and asked him to take pictures. Hudson took a picture of Samuel Guppy and the photograph revealed a faint, draped, spirit-like form in the background. Further pictures showed other figures.

Hudson soon became very popular as a spirit photographer, and was intensively investigated by the Spiritualist community. Thomas Slater, an optician by profession, and another professional photographer named Beattie—an out-and-out skeptic where

Newby Church ghost

spirit photography was concerned—gave Hudson a thorough examination. They subsequently issued the following statement:

> *They (the photographs) were not made by double exposure, nor by figures projected in space in any way; they were not the result of mirrors; they were not produced by any machinery in the background, behind it, above it, or below it, or by any contrivance connected with the bath, the camera, or the camera-slide.*

The editor of the *British Journal of Photography,* Traill Taylor, added that "at no time during the preparation, exposure, or development of the pictures was Mr. Hudson within ten feet of the camera or the darkroom."

Repeatable Phenomena

It was not until 1962 that anyone seemed able to produce repeatable phenomena, and then it was in the form of thought photographs, rather than specifically spirit photographs. Using a Polaroid camera, Ted Serios produced an amazing array of pictures of anything he thought of. He would concentrate on a particular building, for example, point the camera at himself, and click the shutter. The photograph that came out was of that building!

Serios would use anybody's camera, not just his own. He was thoroughly investigated, with people carefully marking their film before it was used and giving him the subject on which to concentrate. Curtis Fuller, president of the Illinois Society for Psychic Research, was the first man to bring Serios's achievements to the public eye. Dr. Jule Eisenbud did extensive studies over a period of four years, eventually writing a book on the subject (*The World of Ted Serios,* Morrow, 1967). Not every single one of Ted Serios' pictures came out. Many were blank or just showed what the camera aimed at. But a tremendous number showed houses, people, street scenes, famous buildings . . . an incredible variety of verifiable pictures produced by his concentration alone.

Your Own Spirit Photographs

To preclude conscious fraud, the best thing is to take photographs yourself. And the best place to take them is right in the room you use for your séances.

Set up a camera on a tripod, far enough back that it can take in the whole scene of you and your friends around the table. Start as you normally do by establishing harmony, visualizing light, and then "grounding" through singing and/or prayer. Then continue with either table tipping or a talking board, or whatever method you prefer to contact spirits. (If you want to do everything alone, then do your meditation and move on to contacting your guide and then the spirits.) When in contact, ask the spirit if he or she would be willing to appear in a photograph. Of course, willingness is no guarantee of appearance. You may take many photographs before you actually get an appearance. But, as with so much in spirit communication, perseverance is the keyword.

When the spirit agrees, move across to the camera and take the picture. Do not use flash. Use a fast speed film; I would recommend at least 400 ASA. You can get 1600 or even 2000 ASA film, if you hunt a little. This is ideal for use in very low light situations. And if you want to experiment a little more, get hold of some infrared film and take your pictures in the dark or near dark. You will probably go through a number of rolls of film, but there's no reason why you shouldn't be successful.

From here go on to more direct portraiture. Get one member of your circle to sit in a chair, ready to be photographed. Again, ask your spirit to participate. Then simply take a picture of the person in the chair. There is a chance that you will find a second figure in the developed photograph.

The use of a Polaroid camera can give you immediate results, but a roll of 35mm or similar film is less expensive, since you will be taking a lot of pictures. (These days perhaps the better alternative is a digital camera.) Use as slow a shutter speed as you can. It seems that too fast a shutter speed doesn't always allow the spirit time to materialize on the film, though why that should be I don't know. I would recommend a speed of no faster than 1/30 second.

If one of your circle is able to go into trance, then photograph him or her that way. (Again let me stress, no flash.) Many of the earlier pictures of spirits were taken with the camera focused on an entranced medium.

Photographs Without a Camera

An experiment was carried out in 1932 in Los Angeles. A number of scientists were present and were subsequently able to reproduce the results. They gathered together in a photographic darkroom. The only light was the red safelight, normally used in the darkroom. To double-check that there was no light intrusion of any sort, sheets of unexposed photographic paper were put down on the floor all around the room. If there was any extraneous light it would afterward show up on one or more of those.

Sheets of similarly sensitized photographic paper were cut into strips about two inches wide and passed out to the scientists. They were instructed to hold the strip by the ends, across their foreheads, bowed out so that it did not actually contact the skin. The sensitive side was toward them. Holding the strips of paper in this fashion, the scientists then concentrated their thoughts on various objects of their own choosing. For example, one would concentrate on a person, another on a building, another on a flower or bird. After a period of this intense concentration, all the paper was gathered up and processed.

None of the photographic sheets scattered around the floor produced anything, showing that there was no light seepage of any sort. But of the strips, several developed actual pictures corresponding to the image that the holder had thought of at the time.

Exercises

You might try a variation on the above. In a darkroom you could load up squares of photographic paper in small light-restricting envelopes (or wrap them carefully in aluminum foil). Then bring them out into the séance room and pass them out to the sitters, where they could hold them to their foreheads. This would save everyone from having to squeeze into a darkroom.

Another variation would be for everyone to concentrate their thoughts (of the same object) on to one square of paper in the center of the table. Or, hold hands around the table and ask the spirit to cause its image to appear on the sheet lying on the table.

Put up a movie/slide projection screen and have everyone concentrate their thoughts—projecting an image onto that screen—all thinking of the same thing, of course. Then take a photograph of the blank screen.

Try the same thing but using a dark sheet, rather than the white screen. Sometimes it seems it is easier for the spirits to come through on one type of background and sometimes on another. Remember to try both regular film and infrared.

Do not forget to keep notes on everything you try. This is especially important with photography, so that you might duplicate what is successful. Note the type of film used, its ASA rating, the aperture and speed, and the type and amount of lighting you had. Note also the number of people both present and concentrating, proportion of males to females, positions, and distances from camera/screen.

Examination Questions

1. You have a limited amount of time. You want to read more of a book you are in the middle of yet you very much want to try automatic writing. Which should you do?

2. Why is it important to separate your mind from what you are writing when doing automatic writing?

3. Who was (a) William Stainton Moses? (b) William T. Stead? (c) Patience Worth?

4. What is the difference between automatic writing and inspirational writing? Where do music and art fit into this category of mediumistic phenomena?

5. What are the pros and cons of directly typing what you receive (or entering it on a computer)?

6. Who was the first photographer to capture images of departed spirits on film? Had he set out to do this?

7. Who was Ted Serios and how did he work?

8. Is it possible to take spirit photographs yourself and, if so, what is the recommended type of film? What type of film would you use for photographing in complete darkness?

9. How is it possible to take "photographs" without a camera? (Give at least one method.)

10. Would it be possible to capture the image of a spirit with a modern digital movie camera?

Profile

Allan Kardec

Hypolyte Leon Denizard Rivail was born on October 4, 1804, in Lyons, France. His was an old family of Bourg-en-Bresse; from generations distinguished as magistrates. His father, like his grandfather, was a barrister. His mother—described by many as a very beautiful woman—was adored by both her husband and her son.

Rivail was educated at the Institution of Pestalozzi, at Yverdun (Canton de Vaud), and it was there he developed an inquisitiveness and desire for investigation that lasted his whole life. He enjoyed teaching and even at the age of fourteen directed the studies of his fellow students, helping students who struggled. His big interest was in botany and he would often walk as many as twenty miles or more in a day, searching for specimens. Despite his young age, he spent a lot of time meditating on a means to bring about a unity of the Catholic and Protestant elements in his country.

Rivail returned to Lyons in 1824, intending to devote himself to law. Various acts of religious intolerance that he witnessed, however, led him to move to Paris, where he translated French books into German for younger readers. In 1828 he purchased a large and flourishing school for boys and devoted himself to teaching, for which he was very well suited. Two years later he also rented a large hall in the rue de Sèvres and offered free lectures on chemistry, physics, astronomy, and comparative anatomy. These free lectures he continued for ten years. He invented an ingenious method of computation and constructed a mnemotechnic table of French history that could help students remember important events and dates. He published a number of works, including *A Plan for the Improvement of Public Instruction* (1828), *A Course of Practical and Theoretical Arithmetic* (1829), *A Classical Grammar of the French Tongue* (1831), and many more. He was also a member of several learned societies, including the Royal Society of Arras, the Phrenological Society of Paris, and the Society of Magnetism. This latter lead to his investigation of somnambulism, trance, clairvoyance, and similar phenomena.

In 1850 the phenomenon of table tipping came to France. Rivail saw it as an important step in the communication between the worlds of the living and the dead. The two daughters of a friend and neighbor became mediums, though much of the information they produced seemed of a frivolous nature. But when Rivail sat with them the messages became much more serious. The spirits told Rivail—when he asked—that it was because "spirits of a much higher order than those who habitually communicated through the two young mediums came expressly for him." Rivail tested this by drawing up a list of questions on life and the universe, and worked with the two sisters for over two years. In 1856 Rivail was introduced, by Victorien Sardou, to the séances of Celina (Bequet) Japhet, where further research was conducted.

Ravail was not himself a medium and so had to rely on others for all of his information. But he amassed a lot of it. During the course of his work he was encouraged (by the spirits) to publish his findings and to do so using the name Allan Kardec. Allan was a family name he had had in one of his previous incarnations, as was the name Kardec. The two names were combined for his nom de plume. The title given to his first book of spirit teachings (again on the advice of the spirits themselves) was *Le Livre des Esprits,* or *The Spirits' Book* (1857). The book sold extremely well throughout France and across the Continent. The name Allan Kardec quickly became a household name. Shortly after publication of the book, Kardec founded the Parisian Society of Psychologic Studies and put out a monthly magazine *La Revue Spirite.*

One of the teachings received by Kardec was the acknowledgement of reincarnation as a fact. This was—as it still is with Spiritualists—a controversial subject. Kardec made a point of publishing only views that agreed with his acceptance of reincarnation. He also dismissed such things as physical phenomena in Spiritualism (he totally ignored such famous physical mediums as D. D. Home, for example). The other great Spiritualist pioneer in France was M. Pierart, who disbelieved in reincarnation. Pierart published the rival magazine *La Revue Spiritualiste.* For years there was intense rivalry between the two camps. From later material, Kardec published *The Mediums' Book* (1861), which came to rank right alongside its precursor.

Over the years Kardec's influence came to fade in his native France, but it flourished in South America—especially Brazil—and, to a lesser extent, in the Philippines. Kardec had adopted the terms "Spiritism" and "Spiritist" for his version of Spiritualism. These terms were used in South America along with the term "Kardecism" (Kardecismo). Today, in Brazil, there are Kardecist psychiatric hospitals in operation and fully accepted. The Instituto Brasileiro de Pesquisas Psicobiofisic, or the Brazilian Institute of Psycho-Biophysical Research, collects and studies Spiritist works.

Allan Kardec died on March 31, 1869.

LESSON NINE

Trance Work

I WOULD FIRST say that it's not necessary to go into a trance in order to be a Spiritualist medium. Many top mediums do not. John Edward is a good example; a person who operates in full consciousness (and in full light) and is extremely effective in his spiritual contact. But there are others who do go into trance. And for some phenomena—mostly physical—it does seem to be essential.

Levels of Brainwave Activity

There are four different levels of brainwave activity that prescribe altered states of consciousness. These are designated beta, alpha, theta, and delta. Normal wide-awake consciousness is the beta state, with brainwaves ranging from 14 to 27 cycles per second. The next level down is the alpha level, and this is characterized by brainwaves of 8 to 13 cycles per second. Below this is theta at 4 to 8 cycles per second, and delta operates at 0 to 4 cycles per second.

Beta, then, is our usual wide-awake mode; though during this mode we actually spend up to 75 percent of our consciousness monitoring physical functions. The next step down, alpha, is achieved in meditation. It is also used when we are daydreaming and when in the hypnagogic state (just prior to falling asleep at night) and the hypnapompic state (just as we are coming out of sleep in the morning). Alpha would be a "light trance" state.

The theta state is the equivalent of a light sleep, where we are generally unaware of what is going on around us. It is possible to achieve this state when in deep meditation. Delta, the deepest level, is where we are absolutely

It wasn't until I was a teenager, after an encounter with a psychic named Lydia Clar, that I began to explore what was going on inside my head, and by college I was spending my free time as a psychic medium. But I never considered "psychic medium" as a viable career choice. It never even entered my mind. Imagine putting that on your tax return.

John Edward

You will find that spirits have interesting ways of making their presence known. Sometimes communication announcements are subtle, such as a touch, a tickle on the cheek, a tap on the shoulder or arm, or the feeling of a hand resting on the shoulder. For the very blessed, spirit will manifest in the physical, right before your eyes. Spirits may also appear as if we are seeing them "in our head." Sensing the presence of spirit teachers is an announcement of their arrival and hearing spirit voices is yet another.

Elizabeth Owens

---

sound asleep, with no knowledge whatsoever of what is happening about us. It's the equivalent of somnambulism in hypnosis.

Spontaneous Trance

Many mediums go into trance, either intentionally or spontaneously. This might be just a light trance or one of the deeper variety. In the lighter trance, the medium invariably has full memory, after the event, of all that transpired. In the deeper states, the medium has no knowledge of what took place the whole time he or she was in the altered state.

Sometimes a medium is not even aware of being in trance, because it is such a light one. For example, most mediums and psychics would swear they are not entranced when doing something like psychometry (see lesson eleven) or simple clairvoyance (see lesson ten), yet they have invariably slipped from the beta state into the beginnings of alpha.

Although, as you'll see, mediumistic trance can be induced hypnotically, it is essentially different from plain hypnotic trance. When a hypnotist places a subject under hypnosis, that subject remains in rapport with the hypnotist, a living person. In a mediumistic trance, the medium loses all contact with the living and attunes to the spiritual realm, to the point where it is almost as though the spirit guide is the "hypnotist."

Trance Experience

William Stainton Moses (1839–1892), the nineteenth-century English medium and religious teacher mentioned in lesson eight, described a trance of Daniel Dunglas Home, which he witnessed:

> *By degrees Mr. Home's hands and arms began to twitch and move involuntarily. I should say that he has been partly paralyzed, drags one of his legs, moves with difficultly, stoops and can endure very little physical exertion. As he passed into the trance state he drew power from the circle by extending his arms to them and mesmerizing himself. All these acts are involuntary. He gradually passed into the trance state, and rose from the table, erect and a different man from what he was. He walked firmly, dashed out his arms and legs with great power . . .*

Very few spirit contacts occur without some type of altered state shaping the consciousness of the person who sees or hears the spirits . . . Altered states of awareness are common human facilities. There is nothing supernatural or bizarre about them, other than that they are not the style of consciousness in which we go through most of our daily activities.

Tom Cowan

Although it's best to make the acquaintance of a spirit companion while in deep meditation, with your outer eyes closed, the relationship obviously becomes more practical as you learn to interact with your guide when your eyes are open . . . open-eyed, routine activities tend to induce mild trance states in which you can reach your guide and your guide can reach you.

Laeh Maggie Garfield & Jack Grant

Mrs. Leonora Piper (1859–1950), the Boston medium, who has been described as "the foremost trance medium in the history of psychical research," (*Encyclopedia of Occultism and Parapsychology,* New York, 1973) described her own trance thus:

I feel as if something were passing over my brain, making it numb; a sensation similar to that experienced when I was etherised, only the unpleasant odour of the ether is absent. I feel a little cold, too, not very, just a little, as a cold breeze passed over me, and people and objects become smaller until they finally disappear; then, I know nothing more until I wake up, when the first thing I am conscious of is a bright, a very bright light, and then darkness, such darkness. My hands and arms begin to tingle just as one's foot tingles after it has been "asleep," and I see, as if from a great distance, objects and people in the room; but they are very small and very black.

Nandor Fodor, speaking of Leonora Piper's trance, reported that:

On awakening from trance Mrs. Piper often pronounced names and fragments of sentences that appeared to have been the last impressions on her brain. After that she resumed the conversation at the point where it was broken off before she fell into trance.

In the earlier days of mediumship the act of going into trance frequently seemed a painful one; mediums would grimace and contort their faces and bodies, some even tearing out their hair! Thankfully the process today seems much easier, with the medium slipping into unconsciousness as one slips into sleep.

The Best Way to Enter Trance

Many would-be mediums will find that they can pass easily into trance from the meditative state. Indeed, if you follow the instructions I've already given for finding your spirit guide (lesson five), you can simply continue from there, speaking with your guide and having him or her go immediately into contact with other spirits.

But it might be preferable to keep your special place as just that, a special place—where only those you invite may enter. So, having made contact with your guide and, over a number of get-togethers, having established a good rapport, you may go on

Trance

to arranging with him or her to act as go-between in bringing those in the world of spirit through to you (or through you to others) whenever you desire. You may, of course, wish to arrange another "special place," or setting, always to be used for just this purpose. Your guide will then take the initiative. Should you want to go into trance for purposes of mediumship (and don't forget that trance is not necessary for all forms of mediumship), he or she will facilitate the inducement and will be ready and waiting for you on the other side.

But many mediums have started their mediumship by having their trance induced by a second party: a hypnotist. As you read in lesson three, Andrew Jackson Davis started that way. If you plan to take this route, make sure that the person who is to hypnotize you is trained. Don't just go along with someone who "has read a couple of books on the subject"! There are certain inherent dangers in hypnotism; not so much in the state itself but in the reaction (or nonreaction) of the hypnotist to control situations. In other words, the hypnotist must be competent to handle anything that may arise.

For induction, many hypnotists will go through similar steps to the ones I gave you for meditation. They will go through the parts of your body, having you relax them and sink down deeper and deeper into relaxation and into hypnosis. The advantage of having a trained hypnotist take you down is that he can give certain tests, at various stages, to see how well you are responding and can determine just how deeply into trance you have progressed. He can monitor your progress every step of the way. Have the hypnotist give you instructions, while in trance, on how you can self-induce the state in the future. In this way you can then later get away from relying on that second party.

One method of inducing trance yourself I gave in *Amazing Secrets Of the Psychic World* (New York, 1975).

Begin by gazing for some time at a bright object, such as reflected light coming from a mirror, crystal ball, etc. This will tend to tire the eyes and nerves slightly and bring about a dazed condition, which is usually the beginning of trance. While looking at the bright object, breathe deeply and regularly through the nose and from the diaphragm. You must not let this distract your attention, however, as all the bodily processes should be unconscious. If you have already practiced deep breathing you should by this time be so far advanced that you can do so at will without consciously thinking of it.

While looking at the bright object do not concentrate or think of anything in particular beyond keeping yourself conscious and remembering all the time that you are "yourself," that you are not leaving your body, and that you are not going to become totally unconscious. During this process the room should be as quiet as possible, though some monotonous sound, such as the ticking of a large clock, might assist matters. Do not listen to this consciously, however; abolish all feelings of fear and all anxiety, as such mental states will effectually prevent you from entering the trance condition. "Let yourself go" and develop as far as possible.

> . . . the kind most popularized by the media is what is called full-trance mediumship. The medium or channel appears to go unconscious or into trance, and someone or something else appears to occupy the brain and body and use it for speaking, writing, or moving about. Usually, when a trance channeling session is over and the individual regains normal consciousness, he or she cannot remember anything that occurred during the session. Occasionally, however, a channel remembers an out-of-body experience of floating near the ceiling and watching his or her body being used by another.
>
> **Jon Klimo**

> As a light trance channel, I remain fully conscious when I channel. Light-trance channels can listen to the information that passes through them and continue to experience the external environment as they channel. However, like all channels, they have temporarily turned away from the outer world and turned into the inner world—where the five physical senses have less prominence.
>
> **Kathryn Ridall**

When you feel you are in a good, relatively deep, trance state, give yourself a suggestion that will help bring about that same state on any future occasion. Give yourself a key word or phrase. For example, while in trance say to yourself, "Anytime in the future, when I want to go into trance for mediumistic purposes, I have only to relax, breathe deeply, and say to myself the word 'Spirit-state' and I will immediately be in a deep state of trance, even deeper than the one I am now in." (You can, of course, choose any word or make up one of your own. I would suggest a word that you would not be likely to use in everyday conversation . . . you don't want to accidentally put yourself out when standing around at a cocktail party !)

Exercise

A popular way of going into trance involves gazing at a candle flame. It's basically a variation on the method of gazing at a bright object that I described above, and you may find that it works better for you than the gradual relaxation technique. You can be sitting or lying down. Soft music playing in the background may or may not help . . . some people are simply distracted by the music. Have a lit candle at eye level or below. Any other light in the room should be low.

Gaze steadily at the candle flame. Take a number of slow, deep breaths and start to give yourself suggestions of relaxation. Such suggestions as: "I am feeling completely comfortable and at peace. I am totally relaxed. As I look into this candle flame my eyelids become heavier and heavier and want to close." You will find that your eyelids do indeed become heavier and want to close. Let them close. And when they do, continue with the suggestions that you are comfortable and secure. Go on to say that you are drifting down deeper and deeper into relaxation and into a state of trance. From there you can go on to meet with your guide or contact the spirits. For some people the candle flame is more effective than any other method. Try it and see if it is for you.

Early Symptoms of Mediumship

Many mediums will tell you that they passed through a period, when starting out, when either they thought themselves to be in great danger, or they thought they were losing their minds! This, fear, however, passes off as you progress. You will certainly find it easier, and much more reassuring, to be able to sit with another experienced medium when you are first developing. Unfortunately, of course, other mediums are not easy to find.

The oncoming of trance is sometimes signified by certain physical and psychical manifestations that should not alarm you when and if they appear. Cramps, sudden pains (often abdominal), nausea, even hiccoughs—these and other manifestations can be signs of developing mediumship. You may see flashes of light, become suddenly faint, or feel that everything is rushing in upon you. These are some of the symptoms you may experience when you first start sitting. And I do say *may* experience, for certainly not everyone goes through this. But if you do, go with it. Keep sitting, knowing that these are signs that trance and spirit contact are making themselves felt.

As a contrast to the unpleasant signs, you may go to the other extreme and have the sensation of warmth and beautiful flower scents and perfumes wafting about you. You may have the sensation of falling slowly backward and descending on a white cloud, hearing beautiful music and seeing wonderful sunrises and sunsets.

Return from Trance

There seems to be a consensus regarding the medium's feelings on returning from trance. There is a general feeling of sorrow at having to leave the spirit level and return to the "ugliness" of the earth plane. Even on a bright, sunny day the medium may feel that he or she is returning to somewhere dark and dingy. There have also been occasional comments from some mediums about coming back "on a silver cord" of the type familiar in astral projection.

Ivy Northage says of trance work:

> *The medium's mind is taken over to a greater or lesser degree by the controlling spirit. In my own case this was a gradual process of complete withdrawal on my part and an increasing command on Chan's (her spirit guide). Its purpose in psychic and spiritual terms is to extend the power of spiritual influence to reach and obtain more positive response in communication with the other world. Many would-be mediums believe trance work will automatically separate them from subconscious interference, but this is not so. Its first essential is a loose etheric body, together with a mental confidence in their own purpose and the ability of the guides who work with them. It is never a substitute for positive mediumship, but can reduce obstruction to spirit activity by creating a real dependence upon the guide, thus enabling him to work more freely. This must depend upon the depth of trance and the ability of the medium to control his own thoughts and emotions.*

Trance, in the Spiritualistic sense is, then, the freeing of the spiritual perception; the freeing of those faculties that belong to the spiritual being thereby suspending the physical being. As the physical senses become dormant there is a sinking sensation (or, depending on the individual, it can be a soaring sensation). It is a sensation of freedom; of leaving the earthly restrictions on the physical body. Most mediums say that it helps to be working in a circle of like-minded people. Whether or not they are all holding hands, there is a concentration of energies that can be enormously beneficial to the medium in passing into trance and establishing contact with the second level.

Rules For Development

There are three basic rules that professional mediums suggest. You should try to follow them.

> The moments when you feel deep love for a friend, awe as you look at a beautiful sunrise, appreciation for the beauty of a flower, or the reverence of deep prayer all contain elements of this state of consciousness. When a very clear internal voice tells you things that seem to come from a higher level than your normal thoughts, when you are teaching others and suddenly feel inspired, when you feel an impulse to say unexpected and wise things or touch in unusual and healing ways, you may be experiencing elements of how trance state feels.
>
> **Sanaya Roman & Duane Packer**

---

1. Your mental and physical health must be good. If you feel depleted, exhausted, or rundown physically; if you are suffering from any disease or are full of fear, apprehension and doubts; or if anger rages, you may anticipate a difficult time in your development and unpleasant experiences throughout the slow process. Good diet and deep breathing exercises are wonderful aids to psychic development.

2. You should be careful to keep your conscious mind alert when first entering trance. Don't give up completely at the very beginning. Always keep in the background of your mind the thought: "I am myself; I am (name). I will remain in my body. I will not be influenced negatively. I will not be influenced against my will. I can always return to myself whenever I wish." It's not easy to keep thoughts going in your mind while, at the same time, becoming passive in all other ways, but do it.

3. Assure yourself, repeatedly, that you have a guide, a guardian angel, or however you wish to think of him or her. Reassure yourself that you have a whole band of spirits on the next level who are ready and anxious to help you.

Physical Conditions and Development Exercises

There are many books on Spiritualism that say you must work in darkness, or near darkness. This is not so. Many very successful mediums (John Edward is a good example) not only work in the complete light of day, but insist on doing so. It's true that darkness seems to aid such physical phenomena as materializations, but for most work—clairvoyance, clairaudience, clairsentience, psychometry, automatism, etc.—there's no reason not to work in an open room, in daylight, or full artificial light. Make sure there is a good supply of fresh air in the room. (No smoking!)

Soft, unobtrusive music seems to be a positive stimulant. "Unobtrusive" is the keyword; it can be classical, pop, or even rock, so long as it does not become obtrusive. Flowers in the room are also most welcome. Personally I like to burn a little (very little) incense to add to the vibrations. Dried sage, in the Amerindian style, is good. But this latter would be very definitely a personal preference.

Make sure you have everything ready before you go into trance. If you are going to need, or might need, pencils and paper (for automatic writing, perhaps), see that they are there.

A good practice in developing trance mediumship is to cultivate the habit of analyzing your "falling asleep" process. Try to catch yourself as you fall asleep and hold onto yourself in this semisleeping condition—what is known as the hypnagogic state—for as long as you can before actually dropping off to sleep. It won't be easy to do, but you will master it in time.

Remember that you are probably not going to develop into a great medium overnight! Spiritual progress is an individual thing, but many if not most mediums spent years in development. This doesn't mean you won't be able to "do anything" in all of that time, it just means that it may take a while for you to be able to make spirit contact at all, to do so reliably and consistently, and to get used to mastering the difficulties of communication, interpretation, symbolism, etc., as I have spoken about them. But keep at it. You wouldn't expect to be able to pick up a violin and play it expertly if you had never handled one before. Look upon your spiritual gifts in a similar way to musical gifts; they will take time to develop and will need lots and lots of practice.

Examination Questions

1. How many levels of brainwave activity are there and what are their names?

2. Is a medium always aware of being in trance? Is it a painful experience? Is it necessary for a medium to go into trance?

3. Is going into a trance a feeling of restriction or of freedom? What do many mediums find helpful, when going into a trance?

4. How does hypnotism relate to entering the Spiritualist trance state? How does hypnotic trance differ from mediumistic trance?

5. What are the three basic rules suggested by professional mediums, regarding trance development?

Profile

Sir Arthur Conan Doyle

Born in Edinburgh, Scotland, on May 22, 1859, Arthur Ignatius Conan Doyle was the third child and eldest son of ten siblings born to Charles Altamont Doyle and Mary (Foley) Doyle. Arthur became best known as a novelist and as the creator of Sherlock Holmes. Much of his life, however, was spent involved with Spiritualism, which he adopted as his religion in 1918.

Holmes was educated at Hodder College, Stonyhurst College, and at Feldkirch College (Austria), before going on to Edinburgh University to study medicine. From February to September of 1880 Doyle served as a surgeon on the Greenland whaler *Hope,* and in 1881–1882 on the steamer *Mayumba* to West Africa. In June of 1882 he moved to Southsea, near Portsmouth, in the south of England, where he stayed until 1891. After writing a number of short stories and nonfictional articles, Doyle wrote and had published *A Study in Scarlet,* in 1887. In that year he moved to Upper Wimpole Street, off Harley Street, London, where he set up as an eye specialist. The first six Sherlock Holmes stories appeared in the Strand Magazine in 1891 and *The White Company,* a historical novel, was also published that year.

In 1885 Doyle married Louise Hawkins, sister of one of his patients. From 1885 through 1888 Doyle took part in table tipping experiments at the house of General Drayson, a patient of his and a teacher at the Greenwich Naval Academy. These séances prompted Doyle to become a member of the Society for Psychical Research and to carry out an investigation of the medium Mrs. Ball. In 1906 Doyle's wife died of tuberculosis. The death affected Doyle deeply though a year later he married Jean Leckie.

Although Doyle hadn't arrived at a definite conclusion regarding survival by the time he met Sir Oliver Lodge, he was very much impressed by F. W. H. Myers's book *Human Personality and Its Survival of Bodily Death.* It has been suggested that one of

Sir Arthur Conan Doyle

the factors contributing to Doyle's conversion to Spiritualism was the death of his young son Captain Alleyne Kingsley Conan Doyle, from influenza aggravated by wounds incurred in World War I. Doyle denied this, since he had proclaimed himself a Spiritualist in April, before his son's death. From early in 1918, he and his wife started traveling, visiting Australia, New Zealand, America, and Canada, and speaking on Spiritualism. He first toured Great Britain, going to all the principle cities. He was in America in 1922 and South Africa in 1928. By the end of 1923, he had traveled fifty thousand miles and addressed nearly a quarter million people.

Doyle's wife Jean became a medium and delivered many messages through her Arab guide, Phineas. Some years after the death of Kingsley, Doyle attended a séance with a Welsh medium and his son came through, giving a great deal of information know only to Kingsley and his father. At a different séance, with another medium, Doyle's mother and his nephew materialized "as plainly as ever I saw them in life," according to Doyle. In 1925 a Spiritualist novel written by Doyle, titled *The Land of Mist* and featuring Professor Challenger (of *The Lost World*), began serialization in *The Strand* magazine. It was published in book form the following year.

In 1922 Doyle had a falling-out with the Society for Psychical Research and he eventually resigned from that body, widening the gulf between the S.P.R. and Spiritualists. Other members followed Doyle's lead. In 1924 he wrote and published, at his own expense, *The History of Spiritualism* (dedicated to Sir Oliver Lodge) and actually opened a Spiritualistic bookstore. He said he wrote the book "to give man the strongest of all reasons to believe in spiritual immortality of the soul, to break down the barrier of death, to found the grand religion of the future." In 1925 he was elected honorary president of the International Spiritualist Congress in Paris and later that year trounced Sir Arthur Keith in a public discussion on Spiritualism held in London.

Doyle was president of the London Spiritualist Alliance when one of its mediums, a Mrs. Cantlon, was charged with fortunetelling. He wrote a stirring letter to *The Times* against what he saw as persecution of Spiritualists and Spiritualism and began a drive to modify the Fortune Telling Act. Doyle led a deputation to the Home Secretary on July 1, 1930, but six days later he died at his home in Crowborough.

LESSON TEN

Spirit Sights, Sounds, and Sensing

Clear Seeing

"Clairvoyance" is derived from two French words: *clair* meaning "clear" and *voir* meaning "to see." In Spiritualism, however, it means far more than that. It is used to cover, if not explain, a large number of different phenomena. It is, perhaps, the best known of psychic faculties.

Types of clairvoyance include the medium being able to see people and things on the second level; the spirit world. It also includes being able to see within the human body, and thereby diagnose disease (this is sometimes called "medical clairvoyance"). To see into closed areas, such as closets, boxes, safes, etc., is sometimes termed "x-ray clairvoyance." This would also cover the reading of sealed letters or billets (which we'll look at later).

An extension of clairvoyance is the ability to see persons and objects in the future, which actually connects with precognition ("to know before"), and retrocognition ("to know the past"). Psychometry and scrying (crystal gazing) could also come under the general heading of clairvoyance. Seeing the spirit world does not necessarily include being able to hear it, or hear those who appear. This is where the problems of interpretation arise, as I described in lesson six.

Many psychics and mediums say that the psychic center for clairvoyance is situated at the position of the third eye—between and slightly above the two eyebrows. Other mediums, however, claim that the center is at the solar plexus, while still others say at the heart center. It is probably a personal matter . . . certain individuals work better through one particular center rather than another.

> It is more common, though, for people to be in a meditative state viewing images with closed eyes, termed "seeing" with the third eye. This is subjective clairvoyance. Colors are usually the first experience a beginning student will encounter, followed by symbols, before they experience the image of a spirit. The spirit may appear hazy in form, in full figure, or perhaps only the face or hands will be seen.
>
> **Elizabeth Owens**

> Clairaudience comes to us through the ability of developing the inner spiritual ear to the point where it can catch these higher vibrations of sound which are inaudible to the physical ear. It seems that we cannot all of us develop that ability any more than we can all develop the physical phases. I believe that each human soul has some one phase of mediumship in which she or he excels, and it is that phase that she or he should seek to bring out the strongest.
>
> **Zolar**

In the early stages of medium development it may not always be easy to tell the difference between true clairvoyant pictures and hallucinations. As with many other forms of psychic development, only later follow-up and verification can distinguish the truth from that which is apparent. For example, a medium might say, "I see an elderly couple. They appear to be in their eighties. The woman is short—about five feet two inches—the man tall and thin. Both are white-haired. Her hair is pulled back in a bun, while his is brushed straight back and is showing signs of thinning on top. He wears glasses and has a drooping moustache . . ." and so on. The sitter might have absolutely no recollection of any such couple. To all intents and purposes it could well be that the medium was hallucinating, letting his or her imagination get in the way, was in touch with the wrong spirits, or was completely wrong for whatever reason. Yet later, on checking old family photo albums, the sitter may well find just such a couple revealed, albeit distantly related. It always pays to follow up on spiritual readings. Mediums who have been practicing for some years invariably know that what they are seeing is from the second level. It's amusing to watch John Edward, for example, insist to a sitter that what he sees is correct, no matter how vehemently the sitters deny it!

Clear Hearing and Sensing

Clairaudience, or "clear hearing," is similar to clairvoyance; it is the ability to hear sounds and voices on the other level. Many times a medium will seem to hear a voice whispering in his or her ear. To the medium this is quite distinct, as though someone is standing there beside him or her. Other times the words seem to come from inside the head. The classic example of this was, perhaps, Joan of Arc who, in the fifteenth century, followed the advice of her "voices" and led the French army against that of England. Joan had been hearing, and listening to, her voices since she was thirteen years old.

Clairsentience is neither actually seeing nor hearing, but simply "sensing" in some way. "I get the feeling of such-and-such . . ." is the way the medium might say what she or he is picking up on the second level. The medium might feel hot or cold; might feel something of the pain experienced by the deceased; might sense the loneliness, the longing, the joy of the communicating spirit. All these could be sensed without ever actually seeing the spirit or hearing what they have to say.

The Other "Clairs"

There are also such terms as clairalience and clairhambience. The former is clear smelling and the latter clear tasting. The smelling (clairalience—also known as clairgustance) is the more common of these two. Sometimes at a séance one or even all of the sitters will smell, for example, the scent of roses, or some other flower. Or it might be the scent of a particular tobacco or a cigar that was smoked by the spirit when in physical form. The medium invariably receives the smell but quite often the sitter(s) will also get it.

Clear tasting (clairhambience) is less common. This is when a medium will get a very specific taste in his or her mouth, which is associated with the contacting spirit. Perhaps the visitor always sucked on peppermints in life. Such a taste, relayed to the sitter by the medium, would be a definite confirmation of contact with that spirit.

Developing Clairvoyance

As I've said, clairvoyance is probably the most common and best known of psychic faculties. This is because we use our eyes more than any of our other organs of sense. The sight centers in the brain are used more than any others. In dreams, we "see" things more than we hear them. Our memory consists mainly of visual symbols—when remembering, we pull up pictures of people and things more than we do sounds, smells, etc. Since these parts of the mind and brain are so active, it's only an extension of this faculty of inducing memory images that enables us to see figures and objects in clairvoyance.

Exercises

Concentration is probably the most important part of clairvoyance. You must be able to concentrate on one particular object for several minutes without allowing anything else to enter your mind. As an exercise, take a simple object, such as an apple or a flower. Look at it and concentrate on it for five minutes. When you first do this you will find that after only a minute or so your mind will start to wander from the object. Don't let it. Really concentrate and review every part of the object. Then close your eyes and continue to see the object. As soon as the image starts to fade, open your eyes to refresh your memory, then close them again.

Next, move on to photographs. Concentrate on someone's photograph. Let it be the photograph of just one person standing alone; preferably a head shot. Be able to continue seeing the person with your eyes closed. Now, still with your eyes closed, see them slowly turn their head. Be able to see all the details of the head from these new angles.

If you have a friend who is willing to sit quietly (without talking) and let you concentrate on him or her, this is even better than a photograph. It also, of course, allows you to verify your "seeing" of the other angles of their head after you have mentally turned them.

From here proceed to actual events. Think of some particularly striking event that took place during the day. A small event—not too complex, with only two or three people involved. Recreate that event in your mind, with your eyes closed. See everything that happened. Really concentrate on it and pick up all the details. You will surprise yourself by noticing things that you didn't even realize you had noticed at the time.

Here is where you can make use of a modern tool —the VCR, or video recorder. Find, or make, a tape of some small but significant scene. (Any historical scene from a public television miniseries could be good.) Don't let it be too long; just a couple of minutes to start. Turn down the sound and watch the scene. Watch it several times over. Then close your eyes and recreate the scene in your mind. See if you can pick up all the small details. The great thing here is that you can go back and replay the tape as often as necessary to check on what you see.

Scrying, or Crystal Gazing

Crystal gazing, otherwise known as scrying (or skrying), is a good way of getting into clairvoyance. A possible problem, however, is coming to rely on the crystal and not being able to make contact without it. This is because you are externalizing the visions rather than producing/receiving them inside your own head. But we'll look at that problem in just a moment.

The crystal or glass ball you use should be of about three to four inches in diameter and as clear as possible (i.e., free of bubbles or other defects). If you cannot obtain a ball, you can do this exercise using a tumbler of water, filled to the brim. Let this be a clear, unpatterned glass. Ball or water glass, stand it on a piece of black cloth (velvet is best) so that when you look down into it there is nothing immediately around that will draw your attention and distract you.

As with all psychic development exercises, sit in a quiet room where you will not be disturbed, and do your preliminary breathing and relaxation. Have the crystal ball on a table in front of you, at a comfortable height. If you prefer you may hold it in the palm of your hand, though I recommend using the table at least to start with. With this form of clairvoyance it is a good idea to start by working in a semidarkened room, any light being behind you as you sit.

Close your eyes and try to make your mind blank. Then open them, and gaze into the crystal. Still try to keep the mind blank (not easy!). Try to look into the center of the ball rather than the surface. One of two things will eventually happen. You may immediately see someone or something in the ball or you may see the ball seemingly start to fill with white smoke. If it is the latter, the smoke will fill the ball then will gradually dissipate and leave a scene of a person or thing. The smoke filling the ball is known as "clouding." If in your case the smoke should be gray, or even black, don't panic—the color is not significant.

Don't be concerned if you get nothing at all the first time you try this. Keep looking for about ten minutes. If you spend much longer than that you will merely be straining your eyes, so give up and try again the next day. Some people see images right away but many more have to try for days (or even weeks) before getting results. The secret—if secret there is—is as with so much in psychic development: do not strain to get results, just relax and let it happen. Don't try to keep the eyes unblinking; just blink naturally when necessary.

The scene that you see will be like looking at a miniature television screen. It will usually be in color (though a few people do see only in black and

Scrying

> Our first lesson . . . is to possess a totally open mind and enter this work with a sense of humility and love. When we open ourselves up to the spiritual realms, we must enter into the work with as much knowledge as is available. The more aware and certain we are of the techniques, the etiquette involved, and the natural spiritual laws, the more effective the mediumship can be, and the clearer and more precise are the results.
>
> **James Van Praagh**

> Clairsentience . . . can take a variety of forms. It's how spirits convey emotions they felt or are feeling, as well as physical feelings to show me what they were feeling prior to death and after. This sometimes includes "sympathetic pain," where I "feel" what parts of their physical bodies were the focus of whatever problems they had.
>
> **John Edward**

---

white), and may be a still picture but is more likely to be moving. What you see can be anything. To start with you probably won't have much control over what comes. But as you progress, start out by meditating on what you want to see, then do your mind-clearing and go into the gazing. Then you will probably see what or whom you had mentally asked for. As in all mediumship exercises, it's a good plan to try to contact your guide before you try any scrying.

Clairvoyant Exercises

Before you start, sit comfortably in a chair that has good back support and, preferably, has arms on which to rest your own arms. If the chair is without arms, then let your hands rest loosely on your upper thighs, palms upwards. Feet flat on the floor, close your eyes and breathe deeply several times, doing your relaxation exercises and then your cleansing exercise—breathing in the white light and breathing out any negativity.

Exercise 1

Picture a large tube, like a cardboard mailing tube, standing on its end on the floor in front of you. The ends of the tube are open. See yourself pick up the tube and look through it. "See" (with your eyes still closed) the wall of the room where you sit. Move the far end of the tube around and see the different objects in the room, the pictures on the wall, and the furniture. Open your eyes and verify.

Exercise 2

Now imagine that the tube is no longer simply rigid cardboard but is infinitely elastic—able to stretch away into the far distance. No matter how far it stretches, or how many turns and twists it makes, you are still able to see through it and clearly see what is at the far end.

Mentally direct the end of the tube to the house of a friend or relative. See the outside of the house and notice all the detail. Then take the tube inside the house. Take it to various rooms and see them in all their detail. See if there is anyone in the house. Who is it? What are they doing? After this exercise, when you have returned to normalcy, as it were, telephone your friend or relative and find out if what you saw them doing was correct. You may be surprised to find that it was! If it was not, however, don't be discouraged. Keep practicing, going to various locations and observing a number of different places, people, and actions.

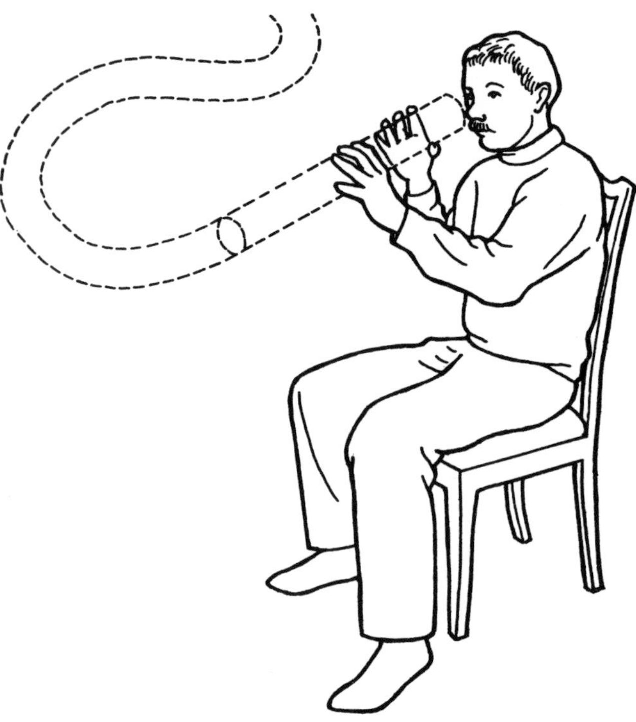

Using the visualization tube

Exercise 3

The tube is now about a hundred yards long. At the end of it, see the face of a friend. See the face just as clearly as you possibly can. Adjust the tube like a telescope, to bring the face into full focus or to enlarge any particular detail(s). Now gradually shorten the length of the tube, drawing in the face toward you as the tube shortens. Bring it in till the tube is only inches long and the face is right there before you. Practice drawing in various people's faces, objects, and scenes, so that you can see them at close range.

Exercise 4

Extend your tube and focus on the face of a deceased relative. Again draw that face toward you and enlarge it; be able to examine it clearly from every angle. Readjust to a good comfortable length, as though the person were there in the room with you. Mentally ask how the person is and listen for any response. Ask if the person has any message for you, or for anyone else, and again listen carefully for a response.

You can see that exercise 4 has led you into mediumship itself. In fact many mediums start exactly this way, with the mental tube, and for quite some time always work with it to bring themselves into contact with the second level. You don't really need the tube to make contact, of course, but it can be a very useful tool to get started.

You might want to insert another intermediate step between exercise 3 and exercise 4: focus your tube on your guide or doorkeeper. Bring him or her into focus and communicate. Then the guide can bring the spirits to the end of the tube (actually cutting out exercise 4).

There is yet another variation you might like to try, especially if you have difficulty getting either your guide or a spirit to appear. Simply extend the tube and see, at the far end, the color green. Focus the tube and see that the green is actually green grass. Now open up the view—like a zoom lens on a camera opening to include a full scene—and see that it is a field with a person, or several people, standing on the grass. Now focus in on one or more of the people.

Alternatively, let the green that you see turn out to be the green fabric of an armchair. As you pull back, you are looking at the back of a chair and someone is sitting in it. Then, slowly, bring the end of the tube around the chair (or have the chair turn) so that you are able to see who is sitting in it.

There are many ways, such as these, to "sneak up on" the person you wish to see when you have difficulty simply zooming straight in on them.

A miracle is a manifestation of power new to experience and counter to the current thought of the time. Miracles are therefore always in order. They always happen.

Claude Bragdon

The thought of death leaves me in perfect peace, for I have a firm conviction that our spirit is a being of indestructible nature.

Johann Wolfgang von Goethe

There is no hard-and-fast limit to man's power of response to either etheric or aerial vibrations, but that some among us already have that power to a wider extent than others; and it will even be found that the same man's capacity varies on different occasions. It is therefore not difficult for us to imagine that it might be possible for a man to develop his power, and thus in time to learn to see much that is invisible to his fellow-men, and hear much that is inaudible to them, since we know perfectly well that enormous numbers of these additional vibrations do exist, and are simply, as it were, awaiting recognition.

C. W. Leadbeater

Clairaudience Exercises

Exercise 1—Conch Shell

Most of us, as children, have held up a seashell to our ears and heard the "sounds of the sea." A similar practice can lead to the development of clairaudience.

Obtain a good size conch shell and hold it to your ear. You will again hear that distant roaring sound, as of the ocean. It is probably due to the air within the cavities of the shell and the resounding properties of the various inner curves of its surfaces. If you use two shells, and hold one to each ear, the experience will be doubled but may be extended even more than that.

If you sit quietly and do your lead-in exercise—head exercises plus deep breathing—then close your eyes and take up the shells, you can pick up sounds other than those of which I've just spoken. Many psychics can hear distant voices. By concentrating, you can frequently hear your own name being called. Once again, you need to try to clear your mind as much as possible, thinking of nothing in particular. Just sit and listen. Starting with hearing their own name, many psychics then go on to distinguish other words and even to distinguish particular voices. Clairaudient messages can eventually come through.

What you hear may be merely the externalizing of your own thoughts and auditory messages from the unconscious mind. But it may also be more than that, being telepathic or premonitory messages that are actual spirit communication. Much depends on the content of the message, of course. And, as with the above-mentioned exercises, everything should be checked out so far as you are able. If you obtain a jumble of nonsense it is probably your own subconscious activity and may be disregarded. But if you obtain a characteristic and direct message, check it out to see if there is validity to it. As in so much of spiritual contact, you must use your own judgment as to the value of what you receive.

Shell hearing is an easy way of easing into clairaudience and can be very pleasant. The voices may emerge from a confused babble or from a mishmash of sound, or they may come through loud and clear by themselves. You may immediately recognize the voices you pick up or you may not. If you do recognize them then, obviously, it will help prove their authenticity.

You may also pick up the sound of music from the shell. Sometimes this is significant insofar as it may be music especially associated with a particular spirit.

Exercise 2–Psychic Telephone

A variation on the shells is to imagine a telephone. Start as with the clairvoyant tube (above), but instead of the tube, imagine a telephone sitting on a small table in front of you. Know that when it rings there will be someone from the spirit world on the other end of the line. Then, hear it ring. Mentally pick up the receiver and put it to your ear. Again, you should hear someone call you by name and you may proceed from there. You can, of course, do this exercise with an actual (disconnected) telephone. Some people prefer this since, as with the shells, it gives them an actual physical object to hold. This can help strengthen an otherwise weaker imagination. Again as with the tube, you can get a "phone call" from your guide first, who will then bring others to the phone to talk to you.

One word of warning: if, after stopping listening to the shell(s) or telephone, you continue to hear voices, immediately stop all such experiments, at least for several days. You are probably just straining too hard to capture something. Don't—either in this or the above clairvoyant experiments—try too hard. Concentrate, yes, but don't strain. The phenomena should happen fairly easily, gradually easing into your awareness. Spiritual contact should not be a strain nor in any way be distressful.

Examination Questions

1. What is the literal meaning of (a) clairvoyance, (b) clairaudience, (c) clairsentience?

2. When a medium sees things in the spirit world, does he or she also hear what is being said by the spirits?

3. How is it best to differentiate between what is actually true, in a medium's reading, and what may be simply hallucination on his or her part?

4. A medium describes a man in military uniform sitting astride a horse, and feels, strongly that he is a relative on the sitter's father's side. The sitter insists that there were no military men in the family. Who is right?

5. What is the most important part of clair-voyant development?

6. Name two real or imaginary tools that can be used in the development of clairvoyance and clairaudience.

7. Is there any significance to the "sound of the sea" that is heard when holding a seashell to your ear?

8. If a sitter at a séance smells smoke, does this mean (a) there is a fire in the building, (b) the medium is a smoker, or (c) there is some significance to the smell connected to the spirit world?

9. What should you look for when buying a crystal ball? Is the size of the ball important?

10. You have been gazing into a crystal ball for fifteen minutes, without result. What should you do?

Profile

Emanuel Swedenborg

Emanuel Swedenborg was a Swedish engineer, philosopher, and mystic. He was a military engineer who turned the fortunes of a campaign for Charles XII of Sweden. He was an authority on astronomy and physics, and on the tides and latitudes. He was a zoologist and anatomist. He was a Spiritualist before there was such a term.

Regarded as one of the greatest and most learned men of his country, Swedenborg was born in Stockholm on January 29, 1688. He was the second son of Jesper Swedberg, a Lutheran pastor who was later appointed bishop of Skara. Emanuel assumed the name Swedenborg when he was elevated to the nobility by Queen Ulrica, in 1719.

Swedenborg was educated at Uppsala University. After graduating, in 1710, he traveled about Europe for five years, until 1714, pursuing scientific and mechanical knowledge. In 1716, back home, he started the publication of a scientific periodical called *Dædalus Hyperboreus.* Charles XII of Sweden, who was interested in the publication, appointed Swedenborg Assessor Extraordinary to the Royal College of Mines, a position to which Swedenborg devoted thirty years of his life. He finally resigned to devote the rest of his life to the spreading of the spiritual enlightenment for which he believed himself to have been especially chosen. Although he accepted the Bible as the work of God, he said that its true meaning was quite different from its seeming meaning and that only he, Emanuel Swedenborg—with the help of the angels—could give its true meaning.

In 1734 Swedenborg published an important work: *Opera Philosophica et Mineralia* about the formation of the planets and, in the same year, *Prodomus Philosophiæ Ratiocinantrio de Infinte* on the relationship between the finite and the infinite and between the soul and the body. He followed these with other major works on anatomy, geology, and mineralogy.

Swedenborg believed he was in direct communication with heavenly spirits and in his books recorded conversations he had with them. He was an established clairvoyant. At one time—through astral projection or, as it was then known, "traveling clairvoyance"—he was able to describe a fire that was taking place in Stockholm, more than two hundred and fifty miles away from where he was. This was attested to by the philosopher Kant, who was present when Swedenborg described the fire and who followed up on it to check the facts. Swedenborg had shown similar psychic ability as a child.

Swedenborg had his first vision in 1744, at the age of fifty-six. Describing it, he said he saw "a kind of vapor steaming from the pores of my body. It was a most visible watery vapor and fell downwards to the ground upon the carpet." This, to a modern-day Spiritualist, is an apt description of ectoplasm. His later descriptions of the world beyond death included details of a number of spheres, "representing various shades of luminosity and happiness," according to Conan Doyle. He said that in these spheres the scenery and conditions of this present plane were closely reproduced; there were houses and temples, halls for assemblies, and palaces for rulers. Possibly because his views were tinged by his theological background, he spoke of angels and devils, though he did say that both such were the spirits of those who had previously lived on earth and were either highly developed souls or undeveloped souls. He gave many views of the afterlife, all in great detail. Many of his ideas have been absorbed into Spiritualist beliefs.

At the death of his friend Polhern, Swedenborg reported, "He died on Monday and spoke with me on Thursday. I was invited to the funeral. He saw the hearse and saw them let down the coffin into the grave. He conversed with me as it was going on, asking why they had buried him when he was still alive." Sir Arthur Conan Doyle suggests that every Spiritualist should honor Swedenborg and that his bust should be in every Spiritualist temple.

The Swedenborg Church, also known as the Church of the New Jerusalem, was founded after his death in 1772. Many of his ideas influenced the later Spiritualist movement. Sir Arthur Conan Doyle suggested that it may have been the spirit of Swedenborg that influenced Andrew Jackson Davis.

LESSON ELEVEN

Touching the Past

From the Greek words *psyche* ("soul") and *metron* ("measure") we get the word "psychometry." To psychometrize an object is to hold it and, from its vibrations, to sense a part, or the whole, of the object's history. To help explain it, Hereward Carrington related the story of a Professor Denton, a minerologist. Denton's wife was a gifted psychometrist. When he gave her a specimen to hold, from a carboniferous formation, she closed her eyes and immediately started describing swamps, trees with tufted heads and scaled trunks, and great frog-like creatures that lived in that age. He then gave her lava from a Hawaiian volcanic eruption. She held it and described a "boiling ocean"; a "cataract of golden lava." Denton's mother, who didn't believe in psychometry, was given a meteorite to hold. She said: "I seem to be traveling away, away through nothing—I see what looks like stars and mist." Denton's wife gave a similar description, adding that she saw a revolving tail of sparks.

Another good example is of a psychometrist who, as a test on British television some years ago, was handed a sealed package. After holding it for a moment he said that he felt he was in a very small room that either had no windows or whose windows seemed painted over with white paint. He felt extreme anxiety. He went on to say that the package he was holding contained a green-covered book that could explain his feelings. When it was opened, the package was found to contain a green-bound book that was the logbook from a small boat that used to travel regularly between England and Ireland. The last entry in the log was written by the captain as he strained to see out through the windows of the enclosed bridge and through a thick fog that enveloped the ship. Needless to say, the captain was feeling very worried, situated as he was in a busy shipping lane.

Psychometry is something that most people possess, and can be brought out with just a little practice. Experiments have shown that it is especially strong in one out of every ten men who try it, and in one out of every four women. It can be a useful tool for the medium. To be able to pick up a bracelet, a ring, a brooch, or a watch, for example, which once belonged to someone, is to be able to "tune in" on that person almost immediately. It can be a way to make the necessary contact with the spirit for communication. Many mediums will ask to hold some personal object when starting to do a reading.

Psychometry Exercises

Every object gives off certain emanations, or vibrations. With practice you can develop the sense to pick up on these vibrations. Gather together a selection of objects, such as small pieces of wood, metal, and stone; bits of cloth, fabric, and leather. Choose some that are of similar size and texture, such as pieces of cloth, fur, and leather, or bits of wood, stone, and metal.

Sitting quietly, take each of the objects in your hands, one at a time, and concentrate on it. Feel its texture. Think of its origins. See the tree from which the wood came; see the animal whose fur you handle, and so on. Spend as long as feels comfortable with each piece. You'll probably be able to concentrate best by closing your eyes as you work. Do this as an exercise at least once a day for several days. You will gradually come to receive your impressions almost as soon as you touch the object.

Then start keeping your eyes closed so that you don't really know which object you are picking up. Sure, you'll be able to feel the difference between, say, a piece of metal and a piece of felt, but what about between bamboo and oak, or tin and copper? To further keep your physical senses out of it, next place each sample in an envelope. Pick up the envelope on the palm of one hand and gently close the palm of the other over it. In this way you shouldn't be able to "guess" what you are holding but have to depend more on your psychic impressions.

Keep a record of your exercises in a notebook. Number the envelopes and make up a list of the different objects, together with the number or letter assigned to each, in a column down the left side of the first page:

Actual	Envelope	Impressions
Cotton	A	
Silk	B	
Velvet	C	
Snakeskin	D	
Seashell	E	
Wool	F	
Ivory	G	
Clay	H	
Iron	I	
Bamboo	J	
Oak	K	
Feather	L	

Draw a number of columns, vertically, down the page, headed "Impressions" and numbered 1, 2, 3, etc. (see page 135). Lay the envelopes, numbered side down, on the table and pick them up one at a time and try to connect with the contents, to find out what it is. You might "see" the object itself or you might simply pick up its background—you might see the small piece of wood or you might see a single tree or a whole forest of oak trees, for example. On another piece of paper, write down your impression—number 1: "Oak." Place the envelope to one side and pick up another. Work at that, record your impression, and place the envelope to the right of the first. Work through them all, being careful to lay them down in the order in which you worked with them.

When you have finished, look at your results. Let's say that your first impression was of oak. Turn over the first envelope and see what its number is. Perhaps it's E—seashell. In your column of "Impressions"

Actual Content	Envelope letter	Impressions 1	2	3	4	5	6	7
Cotton	A	silk	cotton	silk	wool	cotton	cotton	cotton
Silk	B	cotton	silk	velvet	silk	silk	cotton	silk
Velvet	C	wool	feather	bamboo	velvet	wool	velvet	oak
Snakeskin	D	ivory	feather	snakeskin	oak	feather	snakeskin	feather
Seashell	E	oak	ivory	shell	ivory	shell	shell	ivory
Wool	F	shell	oak	velvet	wool	wool	iron	wool
Ivory	G	feather	shell	ivory	ivory	ivory	shell	shell
Clay	H	iron	iron	clay	velvet	feather	clay	clay
Iron	I	velvet	snakeskin	ivory	iron	silk	bamboo	iron
Bamboo	J	oak	velvet	bamboo	oak	bamboo	oak	oak
Oak	K	oak	wool	oak	oak	oak	bamboo	bamboo
Feather	L	clay	wool	cotton	velvet	snakeskin	feather	feather

under "1" write "Oak" alongside seashell. Recording all your guesses will give you something that looks like the table above.

You can see that although you only got one right (Oak) you got several very close (A, B, C, J). Repeat the exercise a number of times. After a while you will find that your impressions are getting better; you are at least picking up the woods as woods and the cloth as cloth, with several "right on the money."

You can see that there is a very definite pattern emerging. The more you practice, the higher rate of accuracy you will achieve. With several absolutely right, there are also several that are very close, with certain similar types often confused. Keep on practicing over a number of days or even weeks. You will find that you will eventually be able to score correctly most of the time.

Now take the next step. Place various photographs of people in different envelopes (each photograph being of just one person). You will find, in fact, that this is easier than working with the objects. You will find that you pick up not only the physical appearance of the person whose photograph you are working with, but also a variety of facts about them—their likes and dislikes, residence, habits, employment, hobbies, etc. Keep records and see how you progress.

Psychometry

> Psychometry is also on the emotional level. It can be defined as sensory perception. It is the ability to experience the nature and history of an article held in the hand. Everything has its own auric emanations. Psychometry is the means by which, in the hands of a sensitive, these emanations are tapped and interpreted. All matter absorbs atmosphere and stores this on its own auric note. The medium is able to "read" these emanations on the level of their own attunement.
>
> **Ivy Northage**

> It is true that there is no instrument, electrical or otherwise, which can reproduce for us the sights and sounds, the emotions, passions and thoughts which have been recorded upon material objects. Certain people, however, appear to have a kind of "sixth sense" which enables them to pick up these hidden vibrations and impressions, and bring them into their waking consciousness. Such people are called 'psychometrists'.
>
> **W. E. Butler**

From there, borrow small objects from friends. If they are all similar objects, such as all rings, you probably won't need to place them in envelopes (though don't confuse whose is whose when you go to return them). Ask yourself questions other than "To whom does this belong?" For example, ask yourself, "How long has this person had this item?" "Where did it come from?" "Was it a gift and, if so, from whom?" "How old is it?" See if you can get the history of the piece and then, also, more details of the person who owns it. Of course, you will need to verify with the owner what you receive telepathically.

The final step is to borrow objects that have belonged to the deceased relatives or friends of your acquaintances. Here you certainly will not need to place the object in an envelope. You can simply hold it in your hand while the friend is present . . . as you will do when working as a medium.

Spirit Speaks First

Relay everything you pick up from the object. Talk about its previous owner and all that you can get connected with that person. Again, get as much verified as possible. I cannot stress too strongly that you mustn't be afraid to say what you feel. No matter how "silly" or "stupid" it seems, logically, to state something about an object you are holding, go ahead and say it. It has been said that the spirit speaks first and you speak second. In other words, the first impression you get is invariably the correct one, coming from spirit. The second impression is coming more from your conscious or unconscious reasoning and logic, and may not be correct at all. So, no matter how it sounds, speak up with the very first impression(s) you get.

After that first impression has been received, analyze your sensations and emotions as best you can. See what you feel or experience within yourself. Then express this in words, to the best of your ability. These emotions often express, in that form, facts that couldn't be expressed in any other way, though they apparently have no connection whatsoever with the object you are holding. For example, if you are holding a bracelet and you get, in connection with it, a feeling of deep depression followed by sudden difficulty breathing and sensations of water, of suffocating and drowning, say all of this. State it as fully as you are able. It may be that

> When reading geological specimens, the great peculiarity was that sensitives seemed, for the moment, to live amid the flora and fauna of the time, and were able to describe types of vegetation peculiar to the period. Often, their amazement at finding themselves in a world so entirely different from the normal, lent a zest and interest to their discoveries which transformed indifferent psychometrists into studious evolutionists.
>
> **Harry Boddington**

> The images faded, leaving the ring only a chilly piece of metal in my hand. I had experienced the feelings, emotions and surroundings of a woman dead for perhaps a hundred years or more.
>
> **Beverly C. Jaegers**

---

the person who owned the bracelet drowned herself in a fit of melancholy! In this way the emotions you recognize are fully in accordance with the sensations that you receive from the object.

Side Benefits

You will find that there's a side benefit to developing your psychometry. You'll find that when you meet people for the first time, you will pick up on them and on their feelings and emotions simply by shaking hands with them. Rather like "Counselor Troi" of the popular television series *Star Trek: The Next Generation,* you will become something of an empath. Though, unlike Troi, you will need to make physical contact with the person in order to pick up on him or her.

Different Readings for Different Mediums

Don't be surprised if you and another medium both read from the same object and get different stories. An object that has been around for a while may pass through many hands. What one medium tunes into may be from a totally different period from that tuned into by another medium. Even from an object that has had only one owner, what you tune into may be from one aspect, or one period, of the owner's life while the other medium may pick up on a quite different phase or interest of that same owner.

It may be claimed that the deceased had owned a particular object for many, many years. Yet—perhaps unbeknownst to the living relative—the object may well have belonged to someone else at some point; perhaps someone with particularly strong emanations that really pervade the object. To give a physical parallel, it is a little like a chair that started out painted in a dark green but was subsequently painted over with bright yellow paint. Outwardly the chair is, then, yellow and everyone may remember it as only being yellow. Yet to someone with a sensitive eye, the green paint still shows through.

Psychometry as a Tool in Spirit Communication

What is the place of psychometry in spirit communication? From what I have said it would seem that there's no necessary connection between the object being read and the spirit of that owner who now "exists" on the second level. We can learn about the deceased as they were, when alive and owning the object, but that doesn't necessarily help make a connection with their spirit.

But in practice it seems it does help make the connection—especially if the object is one that was

> An interesting variant of this class of psychics is the man who is able to psychometrize persons only, and not inanimate objects as is more usual. In most cases this faculty shows itself erratically, so that such a psychic will, when introduced to a stranger, often see in a flash some prominent event in that stranger's earlier life, but on similar occasions will receive no special impression.
>
> **Swami Panchadasi**

---

dear to the deceased. By virtue of holding that object and concentrating upon it, by aligning with its vibrations, you frequently do also tune to the wavelength, as it were, of the owner. He or she may not be making a point of staying close to the object, yet there is some sort of an emotional thread, or wavelength, that is still intact. Simply by practicing psychometry on an object we can often tune-in more easily to the deceased.

Billets and Billet Reading

Billet reading is sometimes done by mediums on public platforms and by Spiritualist ministers in Spiritualist churches. *Billet* is the French word for a "letter." In the Spiritualist sense it is a written note, usually on a piece of paper about the size of a playing card. Sometimes the person is asked to just write a name on the piece of paper—the name of the deceased, perhaps—and sometimes they are asked to write a question. The paper is then folded up and collected. The medium will go on to name the name (and, perhaps, contact the spirit of the person named) or answer the question. This is done without the medium opening the folded billet.

Billet reading is a development of psychometry, for you are picking up the feelings of the person from the paper. You will find that by practicing your psychometry it will not be difficult to pick up the writing on a small piece of paper, even if it's folded up. A good exercise, for practice, is to take a number of pieces of paper, all the same size. On each one write a different letter of the alphabet.

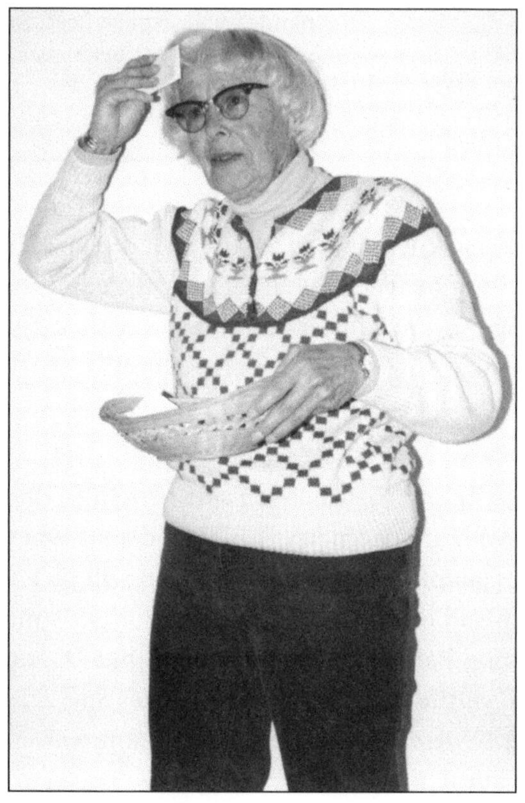

Billet reading

Fold the paper in half, then in half again. Place the folded pieces of paper in a hat, basket, or other container, and thoroughly mix them up. Take out one billet at a time, hold it and concentrate on it, and try to pick up in your mind what letter is written on it. When you have decided (I will not say "guessed" because you should not be guessing; you are picking it up by psychometry), open the paper and see if you're correct. Record your answers and see how many you get right.

You can proceed from there with names written on the pieces of paper. Write the names of different people whom you know to be in spirit. Again, fold them and mix them. If you have someone to work with, have them write down the names. Working in a group or Development Circle, each write a name and then pass the billets around so that each has one to work with. The last step, of course, is to work with questions. Have someone write short questions and see if you can pick up what is written and then answer the question. Again, in a group each write a question, fold the papers, and distribute them.

Flower Reading

Some mediums—Chris Meredith of San Diego, is an example—do flower readings. The sitters each bring a flower and place it in the center of the Circle. It can be any sort of flower, though if there happen to be more than one of a type (two red roses, for example) then you will need to tie on a piece of thread, or something similar, to tell one from the other.

The medium should not know who has brought which flower but will take them up one at a time and concentrate on them. He or she will be able to say who brought the particular flower and, through it, reach that person's spirit contact. You can practice this in your Circle by each person bringing a flower and, after they have been placed together and mixed, each drawing a flower.

Look for other exercises you can do to hone your skills as a medium. There are many, and there are certainly variations on the ones I have given. Remember, practice makes perfect.

Examination Questions

1. A woman visiting an antique store picks up a ring. She immediately gets a mental impression of an old lady wearing the ring, with many details about the lady. What sort of mediumship is the woman (unintentionally) practicing?

2. Is psychometric ability more prevalent in men or in women, or is it found equally in both sexes?

3. You are handling an object belonging to someone else and immediately get the impression that it is connected with Shirley Temple. On reflection, however, you seem to realize that what is meant is that the object belonged to the owner when she was a little girl. Would this last be the correct interpretation?

4. How can you pick up information about a person you meet without actually handling something that belongs to them?

5. Three different mediums—two male and one female—get three different stories about one object, as they take turns in holding it. Which one has the correct story?

6. Can psychometry relate to spirit communication? If so, how?

Profile

Arthur Ford

Arthur Augustus Ford was born on January 8, 1897, in Titusville, Florida. At that time it was a tiny town with a population of about three hundred. He was born into a Southern Baptist family and had three siblings. His father was a steamboat captain and was actually an Episcopalian (though seldom attended church) while his mother was the ardent Baptist. As a child, Arthur Ford grew increasingly skeptical of the church teachings—especially on Heaven and Hell—his independent thinking fired by meetings and discussions with a number of Unitarians. Eventually, at age sixteen, he was excommunicated from the Baptist church. Despite this, he decided he wanted to become a minister and studied for that at Transylvania College in Lexington, Kentucky. Ford's chosen affiliation was with the Disciples of Christ. But his studies were interrupted by World War I. In 1917 he was stationed at Camp Grant, in Sheridan, Illinois.

In 1918 a great flu epidemic raged across the country and struck the Camp Grant area especially hard. Every night soldiers died of influenza. One night, Ford dreamed that he had been handed a sheet of paper on which were written the names of those who were to die that night. The names were written in large, clear letters. The following morning the daily camp bulletin list of dead matched Ford's. This continued for several days to the point where his buddies shunned him as a harbinger of death! He quickly learned to keep his knowledge to himself.

After the war, when Ford returned to his studies, he was able to review these dreams with a friendly professor, Dr. Elmer Snoddy. Snoddy told Ford of the many studies then ongoing, both in America and England, by such people as Henry Sidgwick, Sir Oliver Lodge, Dr. William James, and Frederick Myers. Obviously, the professor assured him, he was one of the rare gifted ones who was a medium. He encouraged Ford to develop his gifts and use them for beneficial purposes to help others. Ford actively sought out people whom he felt might be able to help him. He went to New York in 1921, and spoke with the secretary of the American Society for Psychical Research, Gertrude Tubby. She arranged for him to meet with Dr. Franklin Pierce and with other more practiced mediums.

In 1922, at twenty-five years of age, Ford became an ordained minister and was appointed to a church in Barbourville, Kentucky. That year he also married Sallie Stewart. Shortly after, Ford was approached by Dr. Paul Pearson, who was personally acquainted with Sir Arthur Conan Doyle. Pearson persuaded Ford to give a series of lectures in New England, during 1924. This was to be the start of his career as a platform medium. The lectures were a great success and Ford went on to travel further on the lecture circuit. His young wife Sallie did not go with him and eventually they became estranged and divorced.

It was in 1924 that his spirit guide, Fletcher, made himself known. Ford became acquainted, and was advised by, swami Paramahansa Yogananda, who had great influence on the budding medium. Gradually, Ford increased his public readings and was soon traveling the globe. He especially impressed Sir Arthur Conan Doyle, when Ford visited England.

Ford is perhaps best known for his breaking of the "Houdini code." When Harry (Weiss) Houdini died he left a message with his wife, Beatrice. Houdini spent many years unmasking fraudulent mediums and told Beatrice that only a true medium would be able to give her his message. Many tried but it wasn't until Arthur Ford came along that there was success. Ford gave Beatrice the message "Rosabelle, believe," which was done in the long, complicated code that the two Houdinis had used in a vaudeville act they had done many years before. This made Ford world famous.

Ford was involved in an auto accident in 1930, which killed his sister and a friend. Ford was hospitalized with slim chance of recovery. The attending physician gave injudicious amounts of morphine to him, so much so that when he finally recovered from the accident, many months later, he found he was addicted. Going "cold turkey," Ford managed to break the habit only to get hooked on alcohol, when he was persuaded to use that as a way of relieving tension that would build up in him. In 1938 Ford married his second wife, Valerie McKeown, an English widow. They settled in Hollywood, California.

With the alcoholism, Ford began to miss lecture appointments and even his guide, Fletcher, disappeared. His health deteriorated and finally Valerie divorced him. In 1949 Ford had a breakdown, but was finally able to recover through Alcoholics Anonymous. Despite this, he never fully gave up drinking. The following year, however, in 1950, Fletcher did return and Ford was able to resume his mediumship. It was in 1967 that he held a televised séance with Bishop James A. Pike, whose twenty-year-old son had committed suicide the previous year, and provided what seemed to be evidence of contact with the son.

For the last twenty years of his life, before his death on January 4, 1971, Ford suffered several heart attacks. Each time, until the last, it seemed that there was someone on hand—or inexplicably drawn to the scene—who was able to summon the necessary help. Ford founded several organizations, among them Spiritual Frontiers Fellowship that he started in 1956.

LESSON TWELVE

Physical Mediumship

In mental mediumship the medium communicates through clairvoyance, clairaudience, clairsentience, psychometry, scrying, and so on, as we have seen. Physical mediums are those who levitate, who bring apports, create rappings, produce the sound of bells and musical instruments, move objects, exhibit transfiguration and, in short, interfere with a physical, material object without using any part of their body in a way that would normally explain the interference.

If a heavy table, on the far side of the room from where the medium and everyone else is sitting, should slowly rise up off the floor, hang suspended for a few moments, then gently settle down again, this would be classed as a physical phenomenon. And it has been known to happen!

Physical Spiritualist phenomena are of the sort that we have been taught, all our lives, cannot happen . . . it seems to go against the laws of physics. It also goes, frequently, against the law of gravity. Yet what we should really be saying is that all this goes against these laws as we know them today. It is, perhaps, presumptuous of us to believe that we know all there is to know. Obviously if we did, we would have no further need for scientists of any sort.

Perhaps the best introduction to physical mediumship is to look closely at one of the greatest physical mediums of all times, and what she could achieve. Her name was Eusapia Paladino; she was certainly one of the greats, and she has been mentioned earlier in this book. It is worth noting that she was caught in fraud a number of times, which will be addressed.

Eusapia Paladino

Eusapia was a rough, young, peasant woman from southern Italy. She was crude, chthonic, and uneducated, and never tried in the least to become cultured or genteel, often to the embarrassment of her sponsors and investigators. She was illiterate, yet she had a great understanding of human nature. In *The Unknown—Is It Nearer?* (Signet Books, 1956) authors Dingwall and Langdon-Davies say of her:

> *She cheated whenever she could. She cheated in England and she cheated in America. Whenever she found herself investigated by men so incompetent at their job that cheating was easy, she cheated. In England she was detested for her bad manners and worse morals, and in America the ballyhoo atmosphere was such that no genuine psi phenomena could have been expected. Eusapia quite bluntly paid her hosts out in both countries for grossly mismanaging their duties as serious researchers into paranormal phenomena.*

Yet when subjected to stringent controls by researchers who knew their job, Eusapia was a psychic investigator's dream. A wonderful example is to be found in the investigation conducted by three researchers from the Society of Psychical Research in London. Those men were Hereward Carrington, W. W. Baggally, and Everard Feilding. To again quote Dingwall and Langdon-Davies:

> *. . . (the) investigation was carried out by men so competent that we have to accept their word for what they saw, and what they saw was inexplicable in terms of fraud.*

Eusapia Paladino

Carrington had spent many years exposing fraudulent mediums and probably knew every trick in the book. He was a prolific writer on parapsychology and became the founder of the American Psychical Institute and Laboratory. Baggally did not believe in psychic phenomena at all and more of a skeptic would have been hard to find. Yet he had been puzzled and fascinated by some of Eusapia's previous demonstrations and very much wanted to investigate further. Both Carrington and Baggally, as well as being competent investigators, were also accomplished amateur conjurers fully versed in most mediumistic-type tricks. Feilding was the Honorary Secretary of the Society for Psychical Research. He had done an exhaustive investigation of the materialization medium Florence Cook.

The three investigators started by hanging two thin, black curtains across a corner of the room, at Eusapia's request. This formed what is generally known as a "cabinet" for the medium and is a common requisite. Some mediums actually sit inside this cabinet, though others sit just outside it. Behind this curtain was placed a small round table with various objects on it: a trumpet, a bell, tambourine, toy piano, whistle, and other odds and ends. The medium didn't look behind the curtain and had no way of knowing exactly what was there.

With the three investigators, Eusapia sat at a small oblong table, her back to the cabinet and about two feet from it. There was an investigator on either side of her holding her hands and controlling her feet and legs, by keeping their feet on hers and their legs pressed against hers. Additionally, the third investigator would sometimes actually get down on the floor underneath the table to make sure she was not cheating in any way. There was low light but it was, as Feilding reported, "bright enough to enable us to read small print."

The phenomena Eusapia produced included the levitation of the oblong table, which would rise up in the air a good two feet, remain suspended for a few moments, and then settle back down again. Frequently her hands were held by the others at a distance from the table, so that she was not in contact with it in any way. These levitations occurred in full light. The table would also rock upward, to stand on two legs. The men would press down on it but it would pop up again as though suspended on elastic cords.

When in lower light, although the men carefully kept hold of the medium, they felt themselves frequently being touched on the arms, shoulders, and head. Then, apparently living hands—they could feel the fingers and even the nails—would grasp at them through the curtains. It was the sort of thing that they would have thought could only have been done with an accomplice behind the curtains . . . yet there was no one else in the room and certainly no space for anyone behind the curtains!

Suddenly the small table inside the cabinet was projected out, through the curtains, and landed with its top against the oblong table, its legs pointing back toward the cabinet. Again in Feilding's words:

> *It would appear to hang there and try to climb on our table, which it never succeeded in doing.*
>
> *Then the objects that had been on the small table all came rushing out. The Flageolet tapped me on the head, the tambourine jumped on my lap, the teabell was rung and presently appeared, ringing, over Eusapia's head, carried by a hand that attached it quickly to her hair, reappeared, detached the bell itself, rang it again over Eusapia's head and threw it onto the séance table.*

While all this was occurring, Feilding was holding one of Eusapia's hands close to his face and Baggally was holding the other. Apparently there was sufficient light for a secretary, also present and sitting about eight feet away, to take notes in shorthand. A stool started to move and the secretary passed his hands around it but found no hidden strings or wires. It still continued to move.

Such were the phenomena produced by an extremely accomplished physical medium when she really got serious about it.

An equally accomplished physical medium was Daniel Dunglas Home, whom I mentioned in lesson four. Home was also examined on a great many occasions, by investigators whose credentials were impeccable, and found to be authentic. Unlike Eusapia, Home was never caught cheating.

But, sadly, for every Paladino and Home there were, and are, hundreds of frauds. So much so that physical mediums as a whole have a terrible reputation and are seldom taken seriously. Perhaps this is why there are so few of them around today.

Spirits Take Charge

The phenomena produced by the likes of Eusapia Paladino are certainly impressive, but what bearing do they have on spirit communication and the survival of bodily death?

At most séances where a physical medium is present, there is a tie-in between what is produced, by way of phenomena, and contact with the second level. It is usually a spirit who has been contacted who is responsible for the movement of the objects, or the touching of hands, etc. Such a séance usually starts in the normal way, with contact being made

The material seemed to emerge from a medium's body, usually from the mouth and nose. One Canadian medium called Mary M. was known for producing ectoplasm in which human faces appeared. It was taboo to touch ectoplasm, but those who dared said it felt like chiffon cloth.

Sue Leonard

The table rises off its four feet. Monsieur Guerronnan has time to take a photograph of it, but he fears that it may not be good. We beg Eusapia to begin again. She consents with good grace. The table is again lifted off its four feet . . . the dazzling magnesium light enables us all to verify the reality of the phenomenon.

Camille Flammarion

Séance

with the medium's guide and then contact with a sought-after deceased relative or friend of one of the sitters. The difference between the mental and physical medium then shows itself in that, rather than the medium relaying the spirit's words and actions, the spirit actually takes charge and produces evidence of being present.

One of the most common tools of the physical medium is the trumpet. This is a light, metal cone much like a megaphone. Frequently it is painted with luminous paint, either entirely or just around the rim of the mouthpiece and the bell. This way any movement of the trumpet can be observed, even in a darkened séance room.

The trumpet is placed in the center of the circle. At some point it rises up and floats around the circle. It will eventually stop in front of one of the sitters and the voice of the spirit may be heard coming out of it. Usually the voice is of such volume and quality that the sitter has no trouble in recognizing who is speaking. Apparently the trumpet can in this way serve to amplify the spirit's voice—that may otherwise be faint and weak—to the point where it can be heard directly by the sitter.

Tiny spots of light are also frequently seen floating about the circle and dancing around the sitters. These are often associated with the deceased, as their way of showing that they are indeed present.

Transfiguration

Sometimes when the spirit speaks through the medium, not only will its voice be quite recognizable but the medium's face will assume the characteristics of the spirit's face. A young female medium may suddenly assume the appearance of an old man; a clean-shaven older man may seem to get younger and grow a moustache! A very notable transfiguration can take place with a good physical medium. I have personally seen an older woman shed all the little lines, the "crow's feet," and bags under the eyes, to look like a young woman of about eighteen. It is striking the first time you see it.

On the other hand, I have also seen an older male medium who professed to change into about fifteen different characters. He worked in a red light, which was set down on the ground. In this way, by simply tipping back his head slightly a shadow was produced on his upper lip that gave the appearance of a moustache! For the rest, I'll just say it was unimpressive and there was no way I would have believed the spirits were present. Yet, it's amazing how gullible people can be; how very much some people want to believe. Of the sitters who were present with this particular medium, the majority were totally caught up in what they saw as incredible transformations. Some even saw extra characters, including John F. Kennedy and other notables! Perhaps I was at fault . . . perhaps they really were there but I didn't see them.

Ectoplasm and Materialization

Another of the psychic "tools," if I can call them that, of the physical medium is a strange substance known as ectoplasm (from the Greek *ektos* and *plasma;* "exteriorized substance"). This is white matter that exudes from the various bodily orifices of the medium. It varies in intensity from a fine mist to a solidity that can be felt and that can move objects. It has an odor peculiar to itself, which has been described by sitters as reminding them of ozone.

According to Foster Damon, of Harvard University, the philosopher Vaughan described ectoplasm back in the seventeenth century, though he referred to it then as "first matter" drawn from the body.

Ectoplasm is sensitive to light so few photographs had been taken of it until recently, with the use of infrared film. There are some excellent photos of the British medium Jack Webber, taken at a séance in the 1930s. They show lengths of ectoplasm coming from his mouth and from his navel.

Mediums usually said their apports were brought to a séance as gifts from the spirits. Other theories proposed that the medium pulled objects from other dimensions through sheer willpower and some sort of psychic magnetism, or that the medium somehow took existing objects in other locations, disintegrated them, then transported and reassembled them.

Rosemary Ellen Guiley

At 11:44 P.M. there commenced a short series of touches on both sitters given in different places in immediate response to requests, the medium's head being visible, her hands visible and held, and her feet tied. Whatever it was that produced the touches remained, however, unseen.

Everard Feilding

Jack Webber exuding ectoplasm

Each supports a trumpet in midair. Webber himself is seated in a chair with his arms and legs tied securely to those of the chair. Other pictures show a table being lifted by an ectoplasmic rod coming from the medium.

Ectoplasm will form into the likeness of spirits' faces, even full figures. Sometimes it becomes a hand and the hand is felt by the sitters. Gustav Geley, the distinguished modern psychic researcher, described how a misty column of the substance formed beside him at one séance then, out of the middle of it, came a hand that gradually became more and more solid. Finally the hand reached out and touched him on the arm. He described it as a friendly pat and the hand as being icy cold.

The fascinating, and nonprofessional, medium Elizabeth d'Esperance (1855–1919) produced some amazing materializations out of ectoplasm. Once, when at the house of a professor and circle of friends, an extremely beautiful young woman materialized. Elizabeth d'Esperance was sitting in the open, outside the cabinet, when it happened. The young figure dipped her hand into a paraffin bucket and left an impression that was later cast as a plaster mold. It was described as a hand of "rare beauty." What was especially surprising was that an expert claimed it to be normally impossible to extricate one's hand from the paraffin without ruining the mold. While materialized, the beautiful young woman wrote in a notebook provided by one of the sitters. What she wrote no one present could read. It turned out to be in ancient Greek and, when translated, said: "I am Nepenthes thy friend; when thy soul is oppressed by too much pain, call on me, Nepenthes, and I will come at once to relieve thy trouble."

> I accurately balanced the weight of medium, chair on which she was sitting, and drawing-board. The medium sitting perfectly still, I asked the operators to levitate the table . . . Immediately on request the table rose about eight inches into the air . . . The levitation was as nearly perfect as could be, and time was not a factor, as I had concluded my observations and there were no signs of the table descending. I had, in fact, to inform the operators that I had finished and to ask them to drop the table, which they did suddenly, so that it reached the floor with a crash.
>
> **W. J. Crawford, DSc**

Many were the fraudulent mediums who tried to hoodwink the public by producing "ectoplasm," which turned out to be gauze or cheesecloth, sometimes wadded up and held in the medium's mouth. None could duplicate some of the exudations photographed (sometimes without the medium's knowledge) by infrared, however, where the ectoplasm is seen emerging from the ears, nose, navel, breasts, etc., of the medium. Then, having emerged and been used to show contact with the spirit(s), the substance retracts back into the medium's body. Some mediums have been weighed, or placed on a scale throughout the séance. It has been found that, when producing ectoplasm, they can lose as much as 50 percent of their weight!

I have mentioned that ectoplasm is sensitive to light. Many mediums have been injured when there has been a sudden flash of light, unexpected and unannounced. It is as though the ectoplasm "snaps back" into the medium, like a rubber band. Franek Kluski, the Polish medium, was badly cut from such a sudden, unexpected retraction; Evan Powell, in London, at the British College of Psychic Science, suffered a bad chest injury; George Valiantine had a large bruise for several days after a flash of light caused his ectoplasm to spring back.

Apports

Sometimes the spirits wish to bring a gift to a sitter and an actual, physical object will materialize in the séance room. This is known as an apport (from the French *apporter,* "to bring"). It might be something as small and seemingly insignificant as a tiny pebble, or it might be a flower, or an expensive piece of jewelry, or statuary. Size and weight seem not to matter. Huge blocks of ice have been apported, as have tremendously big sunflowers, complete with clumped soil around the roots. I feel, personally, that the fact the object has materialized from out of thin air, as it were, is sensational enough whatever its form.

Sometimes the apport comes flying through the air and hits the face of the sitter before falling onto the table. Sometimes it strikes the table first, with force. Other times it simply appears there. Apports as strange as live lobsters have appeared in séance rooms! One of the most common forms of apports is for all the sitters to be sprayed with perfume.

Apports can be animate or inanimate. There have been innumerable instances of birds appearing. One famous case occurred in Boston in the early years of American Spiritualism. "The Olive Branch of Peace Circle" had been advised, by spirit, that there would be such an apport. To safeguard against fraud, the séance room was hermetically sealed for twenty-four hours before the séance. Yet, on cue, a white dove appeared and flew quietly around the room.

The opposite of an apport is an asport; when an object disappears from the séance room and is sent to a destination outside.

The two main theories regarding apports are that the object is brought from a fourth dimension, or that it is somehow disintegrated where it previously existed and reintegrated into the séance room, as in the "transporter" of *Star Trek* fame. This latter theory seems to be supported by the fact that many apports are hot to the touch when they first arrive, and a thermic reaction would certainly be expected with the law of transmutation of energy. A spirit guide named White Hawk explained the phenomenon this way: "I speed up the atomic vibrations until the (objects) are disintegrated. Then they are brought here and I slow down the vibrations until they become solid again."

The most interesting, and possibly most humorous, case of an apport was that of Mrs. Samuel Guppy, which occurred on June 3, 1871. Mrs. Guppy was herself famous for her apports, but in this instance she became an apport! The séance was being held by two mediums: Charles Williams and Frank Herne, at 69 Lamb's Conduit Street, in London. There were eight sitters present. The circle was in contact with a Katie King (who claimed to be the famous guide, by that name, of medium Florence Cook). When the spirit offered to bring an apport one of the sitters, jokingly, suggested she bring Mrs. Guppy . . . Mrs. Guppy was a very large lady! Everyone was laughing at the suggestion when, with a loud thump, the figure of a woman appeared in the middle of the table. It was Mrs. Guppy! She was dressed in a morning robe and wearing slippers. She seemed to be in a light trance when she first arrived.

Mrs. Guppy lived more than three miles away, in Highbury. Witnesses attested to the fact that she was sitting in her study doing her accounts. Indeed, when she arrived on the séance table, looking very puzzled, she was holding a pen still wet with ink! One of the sitters at this séance was the editor of *The Spiritualist* magazine. He and two others accompanied Mrs. Guppy back home, where there were assured by members of her household that only recently the lady had been seen working in her study.

Developing Physical Mediumship

The development of physical mediumship is usually much slower than that of mental mediumship. It requires a lot of patience. It's also something that lends itself more to personal, solitary development, whereas mental mediumship can readily flourish in a group setting and through circle development (see lesson sixteen).

Several physical mediums have spoken of feeling a "cobwebby" sensation, like very fine threads, when physical phenomena are about to materialize. Elizabeth d'Esperance said, "My first impression is of being covered with spider webs. . . . It seemed that I could feel fine threads being drawn out of the pores of my skin." You might also feel the sensation of being touched on various parts of your body. These are signs of physical power being present and can occur when you are meditating or doing affirmations.

When you speak with your guide you should ask that you be able to bring out any physical power, if you are inclined that way. Then, look for it; try to be aware of it if it comes. Don't let yourself be totally distracted from whatever else you are doing—clairvoyance, scrying, billet reading—but, should you become aware of the "cobwebby" feeling, let it come through.

This isn't to say that you are necessarily going to produce ectoplasm—few mediums seem to have developed that capability today. But you may well be led into direct voice, psychokinesis (moving objects without physical contact), apports, or the like. Direct voice and transfiguration seem the most common of the physical phenomena.

If you are doing clairvoyance and clairaudience, and can see your spirit contact clearly and can see/hear what they have to say, ask them if they will try to speak through you in direct voice. One way for this to happen is for the spirit to actually use your voice box. Another way is for them to construct a voice box out of ectoplasm, and speak using that.

Always have a trumpet in your circle, whether you feel you can produce direct voice or not. You can buy plastic megaphones that work well, though metal ones do seem preferable and certainly are more traditional. These can be made fairly easily, by bending a piece of tin or aluminum into a cone shape. Just stand the trumpet in the middle of the circle—on the floor or the table—and forget it. It may be there every time you meet and never get used, but one day you just may be surprised when it is used.

Examination Questions

1. What sort of phenomena are produced by physical mediums? Why are there so few such mediums operating today?

2. Was Eusapia Paladino ever caught cheating? Did she ever produce any apparently genuine phenomena?

3. Hereward Carrington and W. W. Baggally were very competent investigators of physical mediums. What was it that gave them an edge over other investigators?

4. What is a "cabinet?" Does a physical medium sit inside or outside this cabinet?

5. What is a "trumpet?" How might it be painted? What is it used for? Should you have one in your circle?

6. Do physical mediums ever change their appearance whilst in trance?

7. What is the name of the substance sometimes exuded by physical mediums? Does this substance have any strength? Where does it come from and where does it go at the end of the séance?

8. What does ectoplasm look like? Can it be photographed and, if so, how?

9. What is the name of an object that suddenly appears in the séance room? What sort of object would it be (give examples)?

10. What sort of physical sensation might a medium feel with the oncoming of physical mediumship? Is this something of which to be afraid?

Profile

Edgar Cayce

Known as "the Sleeping Prophet," from the fact that he delivered his predictions while in trance, Edgar Cayce is one of America's most famous psychics and seers. He was actually a photographer by profession, though when his psychic abilities developed fully they left him with little time to pursue that career.

Cayce was born on March 18, 1877, near Hopkinsville, Kentucky. With four sisters, he grew up surrounded by uncles, aunts, and other relatives, all of whom lived close by. From the family background and atmosphere, Cayce developed an early interest in the Bible, an interest which remained with him throughout his life. At the age of six, he told his parents that he was able to see visions and even talk with the spirits of dead relatives. His parents didn't believe him. At thirteen, he had a vision of being visited by a goddess-type figure who asked him what he most wanted in life. He replied that he wanted to help others; in particular he wanted to aid sick children.

For a short period Cayce demonstrated a special talent of being able to absorb knowledge by sleeping on books, papers, etc. He would sleep with his head on a book and, on waking, be able to tell everything about the material in the book, even repeating whole passages word for word.

When the family moved from their farm into the city of Hopkinsville, Cayce found employment in a bookstore. There he met and fell in love with Gertrude Evans, and the two became engaged in March of 1897. For a short while he moved to Louisville, in search of a better job, but returned to Hopkinsville by the end of 1899. There he formed a partnership with his father, who was an insurance agent. Cayce started traveling, selling insurance, and supplemented this with the sale of books and stationery. This job of salesman ended when Cayce developed a severe case of laryngitis; so severe that it lasted for months, despite attention from a number of doctors. Having to give up the insurance salesman job, he took a position as assistant to a photographer, where he wouldn't have to try to speak to anyone.

A traveling entertainer named Hart hypnotized Cayce and found that, under hypnosis, the young man's voice could be normal. But when out of a trance, Cayce's laryngitis returned. Hart moved on but a local hypnotist named Al Layne took over. Cayce put himself into trance, and had Layne give him suggestions. Layne asked Cayce what was wrong with his throat and Cayce responded with a full and detailed diagnosis. He further urged Layne to give the suggestion that the throat return to normal. When Cayce woke up, everyone was amazed to find that he now spoke normally, for the first time in almost a year. The date was March 31, 1901. This was Cayce's first diagnosis whilst in trance.

Al Layne, the hypnotist, had himself long been bothered with a stomach problem. Inspired by Cayce's recovery, he prevailed upon the young man to go into trance and diagnose for him. Reluctantly Cayce did so, and prescribed a dietary and exercise regimen to solve Layne's problem. Within a week it had worked; again after a number of doctors had been unsuccessful.

Although Cayce's personal desire was to be left alone to be a photographer and raise a family, he reluctantly gave in to pressure from his father, Layne, and others, and continued to give trance readings for people in need. He cured a five-year-old girl named Aime Dietrich, who had been seriously ill for three years. Cayce didn't understand how it worked, having no medical knowledge and frequently, on waking, not remembering what he had said while asleep. But the cures continued.

On June 17, 1903, he and Gertrude got married and moved to Bowling Green, Kentucky, where he opened a photographic studio. Later, a disastrous fire wiped out everything and he and his wife, now with a son, returned to Hopkinsville. An association began with a Dr. Wesley Ketchum, a homeopath, which eventually led to Dr. Ketchum reading a paper about Cayce's abilities to the American Society of Clinical Research. The *New York Times* picked up on this and featured an article: "Illiterate man becomes doctor when hypnotized." Soon Cayce was swamped with readings. He had earlier found that the person for whom he was reading didn't have to be physically present; all Cayce needed was a name and the location of the person and he could focus on that person and the problem.

In the late summer of 1911 Gertrude contracted tuberculosis and almost died. Cayce's diagnosis, and recommendation of revolutionary treatment, brought about her complete recovery by the end of the year. He was able to perform a similar service for his son, Hugh Lynn, some time later. The family had moved to Selma and Cayce had a new photographic studio. Hugh was playing with flash powder when it exploded in his face. Doctors said that he had severely burned his eyes and recommended removing one of them. Cayce thought otherwise and, from trance, prescribed for his son. Two weeks later Hugh could see again.

As Cayce's reputation grew, so did a problem with treating people. Doctors were reluctant to follow the diagnoses that the "Sleeping Prophet" recommended. Cayce began to dream of having a hospital, fully staffed with doctors and nurses, who would work solely on the cases he prescribed. He attempted to use his psychic talents to make the money to establish such a hospital, but very quickly it was made clear to him that he could not use his gift for making money.

In 1923 he had to hire a secretary, Gladys Davis, to write down all the information he was producing in his readings. His wife Gertrude was, by this time, conducting the readings and asking him the necessary questions. About this time a man who had received successful readings for two of his nieces, asked Cayce for a "horoscope reading." In the course of it, Cayce made mention of a past life that the man had once had. This opened the door to a whole new field of psychic investigation; however Cayce's personal attachment to Christianity (he read the Bible and taught Sunday school) made him uneasy. Rereading the Bible, in its entirety, he finally realized that the concept of reincarnation was not incompatible with any religion and actually followed his own ideas of what it meant to be a good Christian. So began what became known as the "Life Readings"—trance readings that looked at a person's past lives and the relationship to the present life. In time this further expanded into mental and spiritual counseling, philosophy, dream interpretation, and so on.

Finally, and very reluctantly, Cayce had to give up his photographic career, for lack of time. He also began to accept donations toward the hospital he still wanted to build. Readings that he gave indicated that it needed to be established at Virginia Beach, Virginia. In September of 1925 the Cayce family, with Gladys Davis the secretary, moved to that location and two years later the Association of National Investigators was formed to research the information that was now rapidly growing in volume. In 1928, on November 11, the Edgar Cayce Hospital was opened. Patients came from all over the country and were diagnosed and prescribed for by Cayce. They were then treated by the staff of doctors, nurses, and therapists.

The Depression later forced the hospital to close, in 1931 when financial backing was lost, but later that same year the Association for Research and Enlightenment was formed as a research body for all the information in the readings.

Cayce himself continued to develop psychically, picking up information in the waking state as well as when in trance, seeing auras around people and even diagnosing from these. With the onset of World War II Cayce was inundated with requests for readings and, despite warnings about his own health (given from his own readings), he began to grow weak from overwork. His readings continuously told him to rest, but he felt obliged to keep going. Finally, in 1944, he collapsed. His last reading was for himself, in September of that year, when he was told that he must rest until either he got better or he died. Shortly after, he had a stroke and became partially paralyzed. He died on January 3, 1945. Within three months, Gertrude also died.

Copies of over 14,000 case histories of Cayce's readings, including all follow-up reports received from the individuals concerned, are available for reference at the Association for Research and Enlightenment, Inc. (A.R.E.), in Virginia Beach. This material represents the most massive collection of psychic information ever obtained from a single source. The A.R.E. organization has grown from a few hundred supporters in 1945 to one that is supported worldwide today.

Countless individuals have been touched by the life work of this man who was raised a simple farm boy and yet became one of the most versatile and credible psychics the world has ever known. He has been called "the father of holistic medicine." In history, the Cayce readings gave insights into Judaism that were verified a decade after his death; in world affairs, he saw the collapse of communism nearly fifty years before it happened. Even in the field of physics, a professor and fellow of the American Physical Society theorized a connection between the elementary-particle theory and the way in which Edgar Cayce received his information. Repeatedly, science and history have validated concepts and ideas explored in Edgar Cayce's psychic information.

LESSON THIRTEEN

Table Tipping and Levitation

Table tipping is another method of spirit communication that was very popular in the early days of Spiritualism. It has fallen out of favor in modern times, mainly because it came to be treated by many as no more than a parlor game. Table tipping is simplicity itself. If anything, it's too easy. Consequently many people tried it and, finding that it came easily, misused it. Like all psychic phenomena, and spirit communication in particular, you need to approach it with a certain amount of respect. There is room for humor, yes, but not ridicule.

Serious table tippers can cause large, heavy tables to move. Tables that could not easily be moved under normal circumstances by the total number of persons present can almost dance around the room, under psychic influences.

Choice of Table

To start, choose a small, light table. A card table is ideal. Or you can make your own, specifically for table tipping. Lumber stores and DIY stores sell table tops (rectangular or circular) and table legs. Use wooden parts rather than metal or plastic. A round top about thirty inches in diameter can work well, though the actual size will depend upon how many people are to regularly use it. Attach three or four legs equidistant around it. The legs should be of a comfortable height; again thirty inches is good. If you are planning on working with a regular circle of friends and need to take your table to different homes, it can be useful to have a table where the legs can be unscrewed for traveling. With four legs I would suggest they be perpendicular to the table top, but with a three-legged table, set them in from the edge and have them sloping out (you can buy the necessary fittings, either flat or angled).

Circle of Hands

You don't need to sit in a darkened room for table tipping. Many people do prefer the light to be slightly dimmed, but even that is not mandatory; you can work in full daylight. Try different degrees of light to see which works best for you. You will find, incidentally, that there are many parallels between table tipping and the use of the talking board.

However many persons are participating should sit evenly spaced around the table. Start this, as any psychic exercise, as I described in earlier chapters: everyone should have their feet flat on the floor, hands loosely in their laps (you will put your hands on the table after this preliminary exercise). Breathe deeply and calm yourself. Then, as you breathe, imagine you are breathing in the soft, positive, white or blue light of protection. Feel it filling your body, driving out any negativity as you breathe out. As you continue to breathe it in, see it expanding to fill the circle of friends about the table. Continue to breathe deeply until the light expands to fill the whole room in which you all sit.

If you feel so inclined, you may all say a prayer. Many Spiritualists sing a song together to help create a pleasant, happy atmosphere. This should certainly be a light, happy song. As I said in lesson seven, it doesn't have to be a hymn or anything religious—the purpose of the singing is simply to help attune the sitters to one another and to create a pleasant atmosphere into which you may invite the spirit.

Now all should lay their hands on the table, palms down, along the edge. Initially it's a good idea to make an unbroken circle of the hands. Touch your two thumbs together, spread your fingers and have your little fingers touching the little fingers of the people on either side. If there are not enough people to go all around the table this way, then separate your own hands but do touch little fingers to those of your neighbors.

As the medium, you will be the spokesperson. (As with the talking board, it can get very confusing if everyone just tries to shout out questions.) Let the others relay their questions through you. Better yet, start with a list of predetermined questions though, as you progress, you will need to be more spontaneous—interacting with the spirit you contact.

Start by asking aloud, "Is there anybody there?" Repeat this a few times. You can add, "If there's anybody there, would you please communicate by moving the table?" You should shortly feel the table start to move. Perhaps it will give a creak or two to start, or it may immediately start to rock back and forth. Don't be alarmed; after all, this is what you've been waiting for! Continue to say, "Please communicate by moving the table."

Thumps of Intelligence

The table will start to rock up onto two legs and thump back down onto the floor. When it has done this a few times say, "Please tip twice for yes and three times for no. Are you of the spirit world?" The table will respond by thumping twice.

Why two thumps for yes and three for no? These are used—rather than simply one for yes and two for no—so that there's no doubt about a response. Sometimes there's only a slight movement of the table and you won't be quite certain whether it really was a thump or not. If you have asked for two as a minimum, then there's never any doubt that you are getting a reply.

Once contact has been established you may proceed with questions. Initially stick to those questions that can be answered yes or no. You will get information faster that way and it will give everyone time to get used to the feelings of communicating.

The actual force that initially moves the table is the force of the combined muscle power of the sitters. By that I don't mean that the sitters are consciously making the table rock. It's the spirit who makes use of that muscle power to do the physical

> The table literally slid around the entire room. We had to run to keep up with it at times, and some of the people had to bow out because it became difficult to continue the fast pace. But that did not affect the intensity of the energy flow.
>
> **Elizabeth Owens**

> The hostess, much to his surprise, made the guests play table-rapping. Sitting and placing his hands on a heavy round table, (Leon) Rivail was astonished when the table began to rap out messages. It not only told where Mme. X had misplaced her jewels but that Mlle. Y would soon marry and with whom.
>
> **Zolar**

---

moving but then directs it to provide the intelligence—to provide the answers to the questions asked. You move it, yes, but the spirit provides the answers that come through it. (You'll find that it's possible for things to be moved without the direct help of sitters, but at this stage don't worry about it.)

Question and Answer

When you've got the hang of getting yes or no answers, go on to having actual messages spelled out. Say: "To elaborate on answers, please bang the table once for the letter *A*, twice for *B*, three times for *C*, and so on." You can then ask if there are any messages for anyone in particular (rather than spelling out complete names, go by initials). Thumping down on the floor so many times for the letters of the alphabet can seem long and tedious at first but it's surprising how quickly it can go. Many times, also, you can cut down by guessing what is being spelled, halfway through the word, and saying something like: "Do you mean 'mediumship' (or whatever the word)?"

The information obtained from the table may surprise you. Keep a careful record of all questions asked and all answers received. Appoint someone not sitting at the table as secretary, to keep the record. Afterward, check out as much information as you are able. You'll be surprised at how much is relevant. There will, however, be some that is pure nonsense or even gibberish. It seems that many spirits are desperate to make contact with the physical world . . . with anyone on this plane. They will joyfully come through the table and talk for the pure joy of being in contact. If you are looking for contact with a particular individual—perhaps a dead relative—they may not be averse to pretending to be that relative, just so that they can stay in contact. So don't take anything at its face value. Check and recheck.

When you've already established contact with your guide, as we discussed in lesson five, you can usually get him or her to take charge of "the other side" of the table. Then you have someone to keep the pretenders and foolers at bay! You can ask for specific spirits to come to you through the table, and if they are available you will be put in contact.

Levitation

The table will sometimes go up on just one leg. There have been many séances in which I've participated, where the table has gone up on one leg and spun around quite rapidly. People had to leave their seats and rush around after it, trying to keep their hands on the table surface! The next step from there would seem to be for all the legs of the table to come off the ground, levitating the table. Although this is a most uncommon occurrence, it has happened many times

Photograph of the table resting on the floor

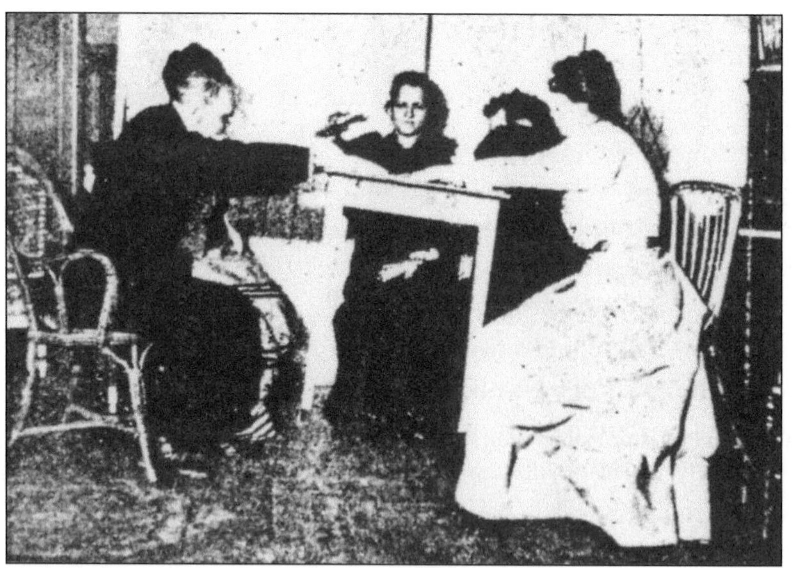

Photograph of the same table raised to a height of twenty-five centimeters

Under some circumstances the table rises and stands, sometimes on one foot, sometimes on another, then gently resumes its natural position. At other times it is balanced, imitating the movement of pitching and rolling. At other times, again—though this requires considerable medianimic power—it is entirely detached from the floor, and maintained in equilibrium in space, without support.

Allan Kardec

I do not think I have ever observed the table absolutely immovable . . . there have always been minute movements and tremors in it; but for practical purposes it can be suspended, as it were, so as to be at rest. Then while levitated it can be moved up and down in a vertical line, and it can be moved to and fro practically horizontally.

W. J. Crawford, DSc

Complete levitation of a table in Professor Flammarion's salon through mediumship of Eusapio Paladino

throughout the history of Spiritualism. It seems totally unbelievable, perhaps, and yet photographs have been taken validating the levitations. Some of these photographs were taken with infrared film, when the phenomenon was taking place in a darkened séance room.

Levitation, and table-tipping itself, comes under the heading of "physical" phenomena. In *Mysterious Psychic Forces* (London, 1907), Camille Flammarion includes some very clear photographs of a table fully levitated at a séance with the famous medium Eusapia Paladino. This took place during an investigation of the medium by various leading men of the time, including Professors Lombroso, Richet, Buffern, Gerosa, and Schiaparelli. Flammarion described it as follows:

> *This levitation, one of the most frequent phenomena that occur in the experiments with Eusapia, stood a most satisfactory examination.*
>
> *The phenomenon always materialized under the following conditions: the persons seated about the table place their hands on it, and form the chain; each hand of the medium is held by the adjacent hand of her two neighbors; each of her feet remains under the feet of her neighbor, who also press her knees with theirs. She is seated, as usual, at one of the small ends of the (rectangular) table, a position least favorable for a mechanical levitation. At the end of several minutes the table makes a slight movement, rises first to the right then to the left, and finally mounts off of its four feet straight into the air, and lies there horizontally (as if it were floating on a liquid), ordinarily at a height of from 4 to 8 inches (in exceptional cases from 24*

Colin Evans levitating

to 27 inches); then falls back and rests on its four feet. It frequently remains in the air for several seconds, and while there also makes undulatory motions, during which the position of the feet under the table can be thoroughly examined. During the levitation the right hand of the medium often leaves the table, as well as that of her neighbor, and is held in the air above.

In order to better observe this thing, we removed one by one the persons placed at the table, recognizing the truth that the chain formed by several persons was neither necessary for this phenomenon nor for others. Finally, we left only a single person with the medium, seated at her left. This person placed her foot upon Eusapia's two feet and one hand upon her knees, and held with her other hand the left hand of the medium. Eusapia's right hand was on the table, in full view—though sometimes she held it in the air during the levitation.

As the table remained in the air for several seconds, it was possible to obtain several photographs of the performance. Three pieces of photographic apparatus were working together in different parts of the room . . . twenty photographs were obtained, some of which were excellent.

This gives some idea of the care that was taken to ensure there was no trickery or fraud, conscious or unconscious. One interesting point is that the fact of the circle being broken—people dropping out and moving away from the table—had no effect on the medium or her phenomenon. Usually mediums are insistent that the chain not be broken.

Nandor Fodor (*Encyclopedia of Psychic Science*, London, 1934) tells of an occurrence, in London in the late 1800s, in the house of Mrs. Guppy-Volckman when the American medium Mary Hardy was visiting. Apparently Mrs. Volckman didn't wish to take part in that evening's séance and so she retired to the far end of the long room. Mrs. Hardy prepared herself with a circle of participants up the other end. As Fodor says:

Suddenly Mrs. Volckman was levitated and carried in sight of us all into the middle of the ring. As she felt herself rising in the air she called out, "Don't let go hands, for Heaven's sake!" We were just standing in a ring and I had hold of the hand of Prince Albert of Solme. As Mrs. Volckman came sailing over our heads, her feet caught his neck and mine, and in our anxiety to do as she told us we gripped tight hold of each other and were thrown forward on our knees by the force with which she was carried past us into the centre of the ring. The influence that levitated her, moreover, placed her on a chair with such a bump that it broke the two front legs off.

Levitation of the table tipping table is one thing; levitation of an actual person is quite another. Yet, again, there are several instances of just that, the above being but one example. Another example is the various levitations of Daniel Dunglas Home, which are legendary (see lesson four) and by far the best known.

Amedee Zuccanni of Bologne frequently levitated. He was the subject of intense investigation by Dr. L. Patrizi, professor of physiology at the University of Modena, and Professor Creste Murani of the Milan Polytechnic. Many flashlight photographs were taken that showed Zuccarini suspended in midair with no visible signs of support. In 1938 excellent photographs were also taken of British medium Colin Evans levitating about three feet off the ground, in London's Conway Hall, during a public séance.

Under or Over?

A question often asked is, does the power that lifts the table come from underneath the table or from above it? It might be assumed that it comes from underneath, giving added credulity to charges that the medium somehow lifts the table with his or her foot, or otherwise. But Colin Brookes-Smith developed and set up electronic apparatus to determine the source of the "lift." So far his research indicates that in fact the lift comes from above the table! There may, perhaps, be some correlation between this and the venturi effect in aircraft whereby the airplane is lifted by the air passing over the top of the wing, not that flowing underneath it.

Flammarion's earlier experiments with Eusapia Paladino included measurement of pressure on the table. Eusapia was made to sit alone at the table, in full light. She had her sleeves rolled up to the elbows and stuck her legs straight out in front of her (under the table) but repeatedly struck her feet together loudly, so that it was obvious she could not be using her legs in any way on the table. The investigators were constantly about her, observing everything.

The table itself was first lifted along one side to a height of about six inches and suspended to a dynamometer that was coupled to a cord, in turn tied to a small beam supported across two wardrobes. With the medium's hands on either side of the dynamometer connection, on top of the table, the meter read seventy-seven pounds. One would normally expect the reading to increase, with everyone's hands on the top surface, if pressure was applied. Instead the reading fell off until it reached only seven pounds, then four, then two, and finally zero! When conditions were reversed, with all hands under the table and Eusapia even turning her hands, so that the backs only were in contact, again instead of the expected decrease, the meter showed an increase to seven and a half and then on up to thirteen pounds!

Many such experiments have been done over the years. About the only conclusion that has been reached is that the medium is in no way responsible for the movement of the table; its lifting or dropping. If anything, the table seems to move directly contrary to the forces that may be applied.

Whether or not you get your table to completely levitate is not important. The main thing is to be able to use it to communicate with the spirits of the dead. Through table tipping you can talk with your loved ones and they with you. Keep a record of all that you do and carefully check out all the information you receive. Only in this way will you be able to verify, to your own satisfaction, whether or not you are truly in touch with level two.

Early French Methods

It was the Comte d'Ourches who introduced table tipping and automatic writing to France. Baron Guldenstubbé gives a description of the methods favored for table tipping (*Practical Experimental Pneumatology,* 1860):

> *The circles consist of twelve persons, representing in equal proportions the positive and negative or sensitive elements. This distinction does not follow the sex of the members, though generally women are negative and sensitive, while men are positive and magnetic. The mental and physical constitution of each individual must be studied before forming the circles, for some delicate women have masculine qualities, while some strong men are, morally speaking, women. A table is placed in a clear and ventilated spot; the medium is seated at one end and entirely isolated; by his calm and contemplative quietude he serves as a conductor for the electricity, and it may be noted that a good somnambulist is usually an excellent medium. The six electrical or negative dispositions, that are generally recognized by their emotional qualities and their sensibility, are placed to the right of the medium, the most sensitive of all being next to him. The same rule is followed with the positive personalities, who are to the left of the medium, with the most positive next to him. In order to form a chain, the twelve persons each place their right hand on the table. Observe that the medium or mediums, if there be more than one, are entirely isolated from those who form the chain.*
>
> *After a number of séances, certain remarkable phenomena have been obtained, such as simultaneous shocks, felt by all present at the moment of mental evocation on the part of the most intelligent persons. It is the same with mysterious knockings and other strange sounds; many people, including those least sensitive, have had simultaneous visions, though remaining in the ordinary waking state. Sensitive persons have obtained that most wonderful gift of mediumship, namely automatic writing, as the result of an invisible attraction that uses the nonintelligent instrument of a human arm to express its ideas. For the rest, non-sensitive persons experience the mysterious influence of an external wind, but the effect is not strong enough to put their limbs in motion. All these phenomena, obtained according to the mode of American Spiritualism, have the defect of being more or less indirect, because it is impossible in these experiments to dispense with the mediation of a human being or medium. It is the same with the table-turning that invaded Europe in the middle of the year 1853.*

Speaking of his experiences with the Comte d'Ourches, Baron Guldenstubbé goes on to describe some of the table tipping experiences:

> *We attained by degrees the point when tables moved, apart from any contact whatever, while the Comte d'Ourches has caused them to rise, also without contact. The author has made tables rush across a room with great rapidity, and not only without contact but without the magnetic aid of a circle of sitters.*

Examination Questions

1. What sort of table is used in table tipping; heavy or light? Which is best to start the practice? Should it be rectangular or round?

2. Where should the sitters' hands be, on the top surface of the table or underneath?

3. What force is moving the table?

4. How is information obtained from a table?

5. Do the sitters have to remain seated around the table? Should their hands be in contact with one another?

Profile

Sir William Crookes

William Crookes was born in London on June 17, 1832. His father was a tailor. As one of sixteen children, Crookes was largely self-taught. At the age of sixteen he enrolled in the Royal College of Chemistry, graduating in 1854. From there he went to Radcliffe Observatory, Oxford, in the position of superintendent of the Meteorological Department. In 1855 he moved on to become professor of chemistry at Chester Training College.

Crookes married Ellen Humphrey in 1856. They had eight children. Five years after marrying, Crookes discovered the element thallium and the correct measurement of atomic weight. He was then elected Fellow of the Royal Society, at the age of thirty-one. As a scientist, he made many important discoveries, in addition to thalium. He also invented the radiometer and edited the prestigious *Quarterly Journal of Science.* At different times he was president of the Royal Society, the Chemical Society, the Institute of Electrical Engineers, and the British Association. Crookes was knighted in 1897 and was the recipient of any number of medals of distinction. He is considered one of the greatest physicists of the nineteenth century.

Keenly interested in spiritualism and mediums, Crookes was president of the Society for Psychical Research from 1896 to 1899. Crookes first came into contact with psychic phenomena in July, 1869, at a séance with Mrs. Marshal. He attended this after the death of his youngest brother, Philip. From there he took an interest in J. J. Morse, Henry Slade, and others, and announced his intention of starting a thorough investigation of psychic phenomena. The newspapers and journals of the time were delighted to hear this, presuming that Crookes would do an exposé of spiritualism. They were extremely disappointed, for Crookes did intensive investigations of many mediums and psychics only to endorse them and to endorse most psychic phenomena. After intensive examination of Daniel Dunglas Home (1833–1886), the sensational British physical medium, Crooke stated, "Of all the persons endowed with a powerful development of this Psychic Force, Mr. Daniel Dunglas Home is the most remarkable and it is mainly owing to the many opportunities I have had of carrying on my investigation in his presence that I am enabled to affirm so conclusively the existence of this force." His examination of the fifteen-year-old medium Florence Cook, and her fully materialized spirit Katie King, was no less exhaustive and equally compelling.

Sir William Crookes

Many years later, in 1917, Crookes told *The International Psychic Gazette,* "I have never had any occasion to change my mind on the subject. I am perfectly satisfied with what I have said in earlier days. It is quite true that a connection has been set up between this world and the next." He worked diligently using scientific methods and often constructing elaborate apparatus to measure and/or monitor the actions of mediums. Under the title "Notes of an

Enquiry into the Phenomena called Spiritualism," he published a lengthy article in the *Quarterly Journal of Science* giving, under thirteen different headings, a detailed account of all the phenomena he had had the opportunity to test and control. The report dumbfounded the men of science of that day.

Although Crookes tempered his activity in the field of Spiritualist phenomena in later years, due to a sensed danger to his scientific position, he never retracted a single statement supporting his findings. In front of the British Association at Bristol in 1898, he said, "No incident in my scientific career is more widely known than the part I took many years ago in certain psychic researches. Thirty years have passed since I published an account of experiments tending to show that outside our scientific knowledge there exists a Force exercised by intelligence common to mortals. I have nothing to retract. I adhere to my already published statements. Indeed, I might add much thereto."

Crookes died in London on April 4, 1919.

LESSON FOURTEEN

Healing

Spiritual Healing

Healing both the physically and the mentally sick can be done using the energies of the spirit world operating through a medium. It is not the same thing as a faith cure in that many people have been spiritually cured even when they had no belief that it could be done. Rather than depend upon the power of the individual's mind, operating consciously or unconsciously, spiritual healing utilizes the power and knowledge of the second level channeled through to this level by the medium.

Spiritual healing can be done in the following ways:

1. By the spiritual influences working directly through the body of the medium.
2. By the spiritual influences illuminating the brain of the medium, and thereby intensifying perception so that the seat of the disease becomes known, along with the remedy (as was done by Edgar Cayce—see below).
3. Through the application of absent treatments, whereby spiritual beings combine their own healing forces with that of the medium and convey them to the (distant) patient, causing them to be absorbed by the system of that patient.

Obviously these definitions cover not only the facts of spiritual healing but also absent treatments and diagnosis.

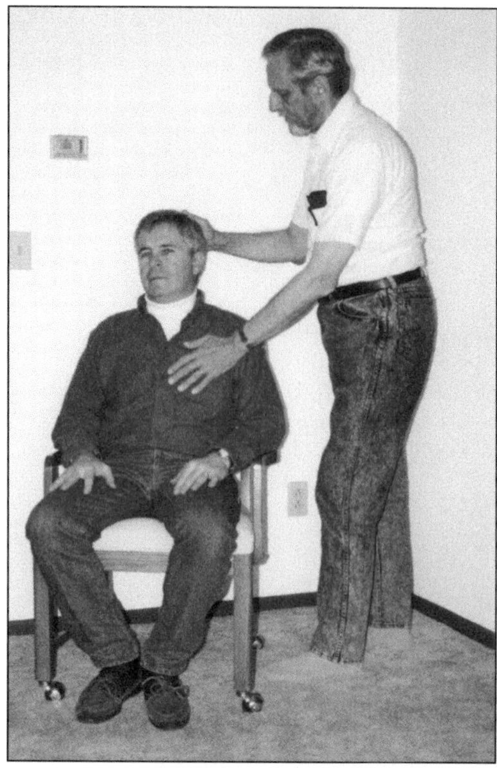

Spiritual healing

Edgar Cayce

Edgar Cayce (1877–1945) practiced healing for forty-three years. He had never studied medicine; in fact, his education didn't extend beyond grammar school. Yet he was able to diagnose illnesses—either with a patient present or thousands of miles away—and to prescribe medicines and treatments that cured. Cayce had exhibited psychic powers from a very young age, but his ability to channel curative energy didn't show up until he was twenty-one. At that time he suffered from very bad laryngitis. Unable to find a doctor who could help, he went to a hypnotist. In trance, Cayce himself came up with his own diagnosis and cure. The hypnotist, Al Layne, then suggested they try to do the same thing for other people with medical problems. Although Cayce was dubious, he agreed to try. He was amazingly successful. Over the period of the next forty-three years he went on to diagnose and prescribe for approximately thirty thousand people. All he needed in order to focus in on them was their name and address. Happily, records were kept of all the readings he did so that even today we are able to treat people according to Cayce's channeled prescriptions. Cayce also did some prophetic readings and came to be known as "the Sleeping Prophet."

From working with Layne, Cayce went on to self-hypnotize—to put himself into trance—so that he was able to work alone. Through the material he channeled, he came to believe strongly in reincarnation; something in which he did not believe initially.

One doctor, who worked with Cayce for some years, said of him:

> *His psychological terms and descriptions of the nervous anatomy would do credit to any professor of nervous anatomy. There is no faltering in his speech and all his statements are clear and concise. He handles the most complex "jawbreakers" with as much ease as any Boston physician, which to me is quite wonderful in view of the fact that while in his normal state he is an illiterate man, especially along the line of medicine, surgery or pharmacy, of which he knows nothing.*

But typically the medical community dismissed Cayce's work, turning a blind eye to the volume and the incredibly high success rate of his cures. Although today the majority of the medical profession still insists on wearing blinders, a few doctors in recent times have come to appreciate what he did and even work along similar lines.

When Cayce went into trance and considered a patient, the first words he would say were always, "Yes, we can see the body"; a clue, I think, to the fact that it was spirit working through him. In his prescriptions he would sometimes include ingredients that had been long out of use. For example, one time he called for the use of balsam of sulfur. The pharmacist trying to fill the prescription had never heard of such a thing. It was only in looking back in a fifty-year-old pharmaceutical catalog that, by chance, he

> Different healers induce entirely different sensations in their patients. The effect of passes on patients should be noted . . . some experience cool breezes passing over or apparently through the entire body during the passes, and blindfolded can tell exactly where your hand is. Others sense warmth, chills or ill-defined electric shocks during treatment. Noting these details, operators will discover the specific sensations their personal magnetism arouses.
>
> **Harry Boddington**

> Her first memory . . . was that during the surgery a group of old Indian men had been standing around the operating table. She had had an odd sense that they were helping her pull through the operation. Later she learned that a Native American healer, whom she had gone to several months previously for a healing ceremony, had called on the spirits of sixty-four medicine men to watch over her.
>
> **Tom Cowan**

---

eventually found mention of balsam of sulfur. This is again, perhaps, indicative of the fact that working through him were spirits from the past.

Some British Spiritual Healers

Probably the best known spiritual healer in England was Harry Edwards (1893–1976). During World War I Edwards was working with some Arabs in the Middle East, building a railroad. In the course of the work many of the Arabs injured themselves and always went to Edwards to heal them. They referred to him as *hakim*—"healer." Edwards himself didn't think he was doing anything unusual, attributing their fast recovery to them rather than to himself. On returning to England, after the war, he didn't trouble to pursue this. It was not until 1935 that he finally looked into Spiritualism, and then he gradually "eased into" the healing side of Spiritualism.

Edwards finally did come to recognize the fact that he was a good medium for healing. He never did think of himself as the healer, but simply as a channel for the energy. He had a great respect for the Native Americans, and their knowledge of herbs and healing, and for other similar cultures. He believed that it was Amerindians who worked through him. In later years he also came to recognize the channeled energies of Louis Pasteur and of Lord Lister. Many Spiritualist healers do claim to have deceased doctors working through them.

My uncle, George Buckland—who was the person responsible for introducing me to the whole wonderful world of metaphysics when I was about twelve—was a Spiritualist, and witnessed Harry Edwards' healings on many occasions. He would tell me of them and give his characteristic shrug and chuckle, saying it was impossible to believe what he had seen . . . and yet it was impossible to deny that it had happened!

Like Cayce, Edwards found that he was able to heal just as successfully absently—when the patient was hundreds or even thousands of miles away. He had many spectacular successes, including several healing cancer. In the final years of his life, Edwards was receiving as many as two thousand letters a day from people seeking help. If he were still alive, I think he might well have done much today to help those suffering from AIDS.

Another British healer of considerable note is George Chapman, of Liverpool, who first became interested in Spiritualism through the death of a baby daughter, in 1945. Having an interest in the healing aspects of Spiritualism, and then developing some success as a medium, Chapman worked initially with the spirit of a Cree Indian healer. He then became associated with the late eminent eye specialist and surgeon Dr. William Lang.

Lang died in 1937, aged eighty-four. A number of people who knew Lang when he was alive have witnessed Chapman working whilst channeling Lang. They say the resemblance is uncanny. As Lang takes over, Chapman's face is transfigured. It seems to become wrinkled and many years older. Chapman assumes Lang's characteristically stooped attitude, speaks in Lang's high-pitched, slightly quavery voice, and snaps his fingers imperatively when he needs surgical instruments passed to him, as Lang did.

No true surgical instruments are used, for the surgery is of a spiritual nature. The patient is fully clothed and the medium/doctor works with his hands just above the surface of the physical body, working on the ethereal body. Yet patients speak of having felt (nonpainful) sensations of, for example, incisions being sewn up. Throughout the operation, and the whole time he is in trance, Chapman's eyes are tightly closed. He says that afterward he remembers nothing of what took place, only of Dr. Lang's initial arrival.

Robert Cull, the husband of another greatly respected British medium, Jean Cull, found himself introduced to spiritual healing in a very forceful manner. Robert Cull was a tremendous skeptic. On the one hand he watched his wife developing as a medium and totally believed in her and trusted her. Yet on the other he could not accept that it was the spirits of the dead who worked through her. In his case even seeing was not believing. Then one day the spirits turned the tables on him!

At the house of some friends, Jean and Robert had been discussing healing with their hosts and another couple who were present. Robert watched some healing done to help a skin complaint one of the men was suffering from, when the subject of his own allergic rhinitis came up. Reluctantly Robert agreed to let one of the male mediums work on him, and sat down in a wooden chair. When he woke up, some time later, everyone was looking at him in a strange way.

It turned out that he had gone into involuntary trance and, while in that state, had spoken as a Chinese gentleman calling himself Chi. Chi said that he would be Robert's constant companion from then onward and would work with him, doing spiritual healings! It took a very long time before Robert could even believe that it was himself speaking on the tape recording they played for him, let alone that he had a spirit guide and was to be a healing channel.

Becoming a Healer

The first requirement for you, as a spiritual healer, is good health for yourself. You cannot hope to heal others if you are the one in need of health. To this end you need to follow a good diet, cutting out junk food and things like sugar (the "white death") and bleached flour. Eat plenty of fruit and vegetables. Acidic fruits, such as the pear, peach, plum, orange and lemon, are especially good for you, since they act upon the liver and tend to cleanse the blood.

I don't for one moment suggest you become a vegetarian (I personally believe that can actually be unhealthy for all but a few people). Don't overindulge in red meats, however. Try to keep a balanced diet—though what is balanced for one may not be for another. Avoid becoming grossly overweight or underweight. Drink only decaffeinated tea and coffee—and make sure they are naturally decaffeinated,

Seated on a hard-backed chair, I was invited to relax. I remember feeling Graham's hands touching my head and then I remember nothing. When I came to, everyone was sitting down looking very pleased and smiling, including Graham. I wondered what had happened. Jean . . . said she would like me to listen to a tape-recording . . . A gentleman introduced himself as Chi. He said he would be my constant companion from the spirit world. Together we would bring comfort and hope to many people . . . (I) asked when the recording had been made and who had been talking. Everyone began to laugh. I was told that the recording had been made only moments before, and that I was the medium through whom spirit had spoken.

Robert Cull

I have no idea what reaction I expected. I had never thought of myself as having healing powers. In touching the child (who had very bad asthma), I did so more in response to the mother's faith in me than any faith I had in myself. Yet what happened was nothing short of miraculous. One moment the child was struggling for breath, and the next he was breathing easily and normally. It was as quick and simple as that and, of all those present, I am sure I was the most dumbfounded . . . The child went on breathing normally, and continued to do so for the next twenty years, when I lost touch with him.

Estelle Roberts

---

not chemically. The teas I drink are actually caffeine free, rather than decaffeinated. One is Celestial Seasonings' "Caffeine-Free Tea," which is fairly easy to find. Another is called "Kaffree" tea (distributed by Worthington Foods, Inc.) and is made from the leaves of the rooibus shrub *(Aspalathus linearis)*; an African herb. There are also the "Rooibos Leaf Caffeine Free Tea Bags" put out by Alvita and available in health food stores. All of these taste very much like a pekoe tea, yet are caffeine free.

Try to develop a mind that is sympathetic and receptive, in an attitude of kind helpfulness. If you feel at all selfish it sets up an immediate barrier to helping others. Work on your mediumship development as I have outlined it throughout this book. It is especially important to get into contact with your spirit guide, since through him or her you will be drawing on the spirits who will help you with healing.

Chakras

In the first chapter of this book I spoke about chakras. I think it bears repeating here, since this is quite important for healing.

The physical body is connected to the etheric or spiritual body at centers known as chakras. Part of the development of any psychic and healing ability is to stimulate those chakras by raising what is known as the kundalini power; power that travels through the body and generates energy.

The chakras are linked with actual physical glands, and there are seven of them. The first, lumbar (or base) chakra is at the gonads; the second, spine chakra is at the adrenals; the solar plexus chakra is at the lyden; the heart chakra is at the thymus; the throat chakra is at the thyroid; the third eye chakra is at the pineal, and the crown chakra is at the pituitary.

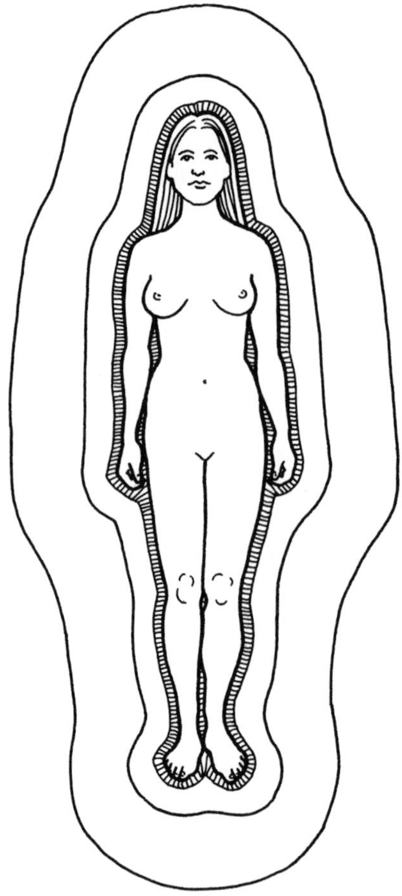

The aura

Here is what I say about this in my book *Buckland's Complete Book of Witchcraft* (Llewellyn, 1986 and 2002):

> *In meditation the mysterious psychic energy can be sent up through these centers. This very potent force is called the kundalini, or "Serpent Power." As this mighty force begins to flow within you, these vital psychic centers—the chakras—begin to open in successive order.*
>
> *As the vital forces begin to flow through the nervous system, the individual achieves a sense of well-being and peace. The subconscious begins to clear itself of the negative and undesired patterns of feelings and images that have been programmed into it through a lifetime. The cosmic force of the kundalini very naturally operates in a calm, relaxed, contemplative atmosphere. As the succession of opening chakras continues, your awareness and perception of life flows continually from within. A new vibrancy permeates your being.*

Yes, getting the kundalini power to flow through the chakras very definitely sets up a new vibrancy. But how to get that power to flow? The first step is the preparation for meditation, as I have outlined in previous chapters. Do your head rolls, deep breathing and relaxation, then awaken the chakras as follows.

Each of these seven centers is associated with a color, going through the spectrum. The base chakra is red, the spine chakra is orange, the solar plexus chakra is yellow, the heart chakra is green, the throat chakra is blue, the pineal chakra is indigo and the crown chakra is violet.

As part of your meditation, imagine each of these centers, one at a time, and see it enveloped in its specific color. Concentrate your energies first on the base chakra, and see it enveloped in a swirling ball of red light. Imagine this light ball spinning around, clockwise, getting faster and faster. After a few moments of this, see the ball of light start to move up to the position of the second chakra, at the adrenals. As it moves up, see it gradually changing color to orange, so that by the time it gets to that second chakra position it is pure orange. Again have it swirl around and around. Then move it on up to the third chakra, at the solar plexus, changing to pure yellow as it moves. Go on up through all the chakras until all have been vitalized in this fashion. Finish off by changing the color to white and seeing the ball of light grow larger and larger until it envelops your whole body.

It is important that the chakras be awakened in the right order, from base to crown. You will find you feel a sensation of warmth with, perhaps, a faint pricking at each center, as you "awaken the fiery serpent." Always do this before you attempt any spiritual healing.

The Human Aura

Baron von Reichenbach, an industrial chemist, in the mid-nineteenth century, discovered what he termed odyle, or the odic force. He showed that it emanated from all objects, but especially from the human body, and could be seen by sensitives. The thoroughness and soundness of his scientific experiments—controlled by Dr. William Gregory, professor of chemistry at Edinburgh University—made a great impression on the mind of the public at that time.

In 1911 Dr. Walter J. Kilner, of St. Thomas' Hospital, London, published a book called *The Human Atmosphere,* dealing with these same emanations but referring to them as the human aura. Kilner was able to prove their existence by developing a screen that could be used by anyone. This screen made the aura visible and was a solution of dicyanin (a product of coal tar) sealed between two pieces of glass. Today it is possible to buy what are known as "aura goggles" that, when worn, allow anyone to see auras.

Three Layers of Light

The human aura consists of a number of layers of light, as it were, expanding outward from the physical body. The first of these, which is very dark in color and is generally known as the etheric double, extends no more than a half-inch or so beyond the body's extremities. Beyond that is the inner aura, which extends outward for two or three inches. Then, beyond that, is the outer aura, which has been observed extending out six inches or more before becoming invisible. The inner aura is the one most commonly seen. Its color(s) can vary depending upon the physical and mental health of the person. The outer aura colors also vary, but are usually of a darker hue and therefore harder to discern.

What is meant by the colors of the aura? There doesn't seem to be a consistent interpretation of the colors seen, for they vary with the individual. In very general terms it can be said that dark colors, especially browns and reds, indicate anger. A grayish-brown shade might mean selfishness; a greenish-brown, jealousy. Red can indicate sensuality and physical love, whereas pink is connected with love on the mental and spiritual planes. Orange is frequently a sign of pride and ambition; yellow shows intellectuality; deep blue-green is sympathy. Light blue is indicative of devotion while dark blue is spirituality and religious feeling. These colors are as suggested by Charles W. Leadbeater, an Anglican clergyman who became a leading figure in the Theosophical movement.

Many psychics claim that when they see gaps in an aura it indicates a physical problem. Others speak of seeing black clouds in areas where there is disease. You need to be very cautious in diagnosing with the aura, however, because, as I've said, the colors seen can vary with the individual. Where brown means one thing for one person it can mean something totally different for another. And where a gap in the aura may mean cancer for one person it could just as easily be indigestion for another! Just because one sensitive sees a person surrounded in a pink cloud, and assumes they are madly in love, don't be surprised if you see that same person in blue, and think of them as being highly spiritual. It all has to do with vibrations and wavelengths. Like a radio, the one psychic might tune into one wavelength of the person while you are tuning into another—she may be on AM while you are on FM! (For a full discussion of color vibrations, see my book *Color Magick,* [Llewellyn, 2002.])

Train Yourself to be Sensitive

While persevering in psychometry (see lesson eleven), also cultivate these aura-seeing abilities, for the one complements the other. Try to see and feel the vibrations coming from people you meet, in all walks of life. Look at them against a light background, with the light behind them, and also with dark shadow behind them. You will find that either one or the other is better for you to be able to see their aura. Try to focus on

> The vital currents which these psychic channels carry to nourish our bodies, are fed to the physical organism through focal centers called chakras. In Sanskrit, the word chakra means wheel or disc. Since the subtle centers appear to psychic sight to be round, vibrating vortices, it is easy to see why the word "wheel" was used to describe them.
>
> **Omar Garrison**

---

any emanations issuing from their body. If you are standing or sitting near them, try to sense everything they are giving off unconsciously. Try to pick up on their emotions and on their state of health.

When walking down the street, get into the habit of picking up on people as they pass. Just a brief sense of them will do. What colors do you see? Are they happy or sad? Intense or carefree? Busy or relaxed? You will soon find you are able to pick up certain vibrations from just a casual meeting.

Then go on to "probing" them. How are they, physically? Do they have any health problems? If so, what are they? Practice anywhere and everywhere.

You, the Healer

Now you are ready to try some psychic healing, or at least some diagnosis. You will (hopefully) get to the point where the spirits will be coming through you and they will be doing all the diagnosis and prescribing. But to start with, get an idea yourself of the feel of a patient; an idea of what is probably wrong with her or him.

Your "patient" can be sitting up in a chair or lying down, it doesn't matter which. Tell her (or him) to close her eyes and relax. To start, join hands with her and ask her to match breathing with you. Take some good deep breaths together then allow her to settle into a regular, normal breathing pattern. This will help both of you attune to the same wavelength.

Start by drawing off any negativity in the patient's body. One suggested way to do this (which I have practiced for years) is to slowly draw your hands down the sides of the patient; one hand on either side, palms in toward the body. Draw down the sides of the head, outsides of the arms, hips, legs, and so on to the ground in one fluid motion. There give your hands a shake, just as though you were shaking water off them only you are here shaking off the negativity you've drawn from the patient. Repeat this drawing off. Do it seven times in all. (Some feel seven times to be excessive but I don't. Go by your own feelings.)

Now, with your hands about an inch or so off the body, pass them slowly over the patient, in all directions, and see if you sense any physical marks or problems. You will be surprised how easily you pick up on cuts and bruises; even moles and pimples! Be aware of any anomalies in her aura. Don't yet try to interpret their meaning but move your hands to any such area and concentrate.

Now close your eyes and mentally call upon your spirit guide to come. Ask for assistance in diagnosing the patient. Relax and let your hands move wherever you feel they should. Let your mind remain open so that whatever comes into it can come in unopposed. It's often better to have the patient sitting in a chair or on a backless stool so that you can pass one hand over the front of the body and the other hand over the back. The palms of the hands should be in line with one another. Imagine power flowing back and forth between the two. Gypsies (who work with their hands in actual contact with the body) think in terms of the right hand representing the sun and the left hand the moon. They then see the light pass from the sun to the moon and being reflected back. See my book *Gypsy Witchcraft & Magic*, Llewellyn, 1998.

Say whatever comes into your head. You may well find yourself using words and terms you are unfamiliar with. Have a tape recorder going, or someone taking notes. Afterward, check out all that you are able. If you know anyone familiar with medical terms—a nurse, doctor, medical assistant, or whomever—ask them to go through the notes or listen to the tape, and explain or confirm what is said (confirm in the sense of acknowledging the correctness of the terms or phraseology).

Do this diagnosis with as many people as you can. It's good if you can work on someone who has already had a medical examination and can therefore, afterward, confirm what you have said. The more you do it; the more the spirits will grow accustomed to working through you.

Distant Healing

Whether or not you are successful at spiritual healing by working on a patient who is physically present, you may well be very successful at absent, or distant, healing. Many successful healers have actually found they have far better results with patients who are far away than they do with those immediately present.

Work as you do for normal spiritual contact, as medium in a séance. Sit and prepare yourself. Move on to contact with your guide. Now have someone read out the name and address of the person seeking healing. Ask for contact with that person, and for a diagnosis to be made. Relax and let come what may, making note of what you say, hear, see, or sense. Having made your diagnosis, now ask what would be the best treatment, and again make note of what you receive. Ask your guide for healing energies to go to that person.

At this stage in your progress, don't attempt to pass on your received prescriptions for cure. Have the patient go through normal medical channels, so that you can verify all that you have learned through spirit. You will be amazed how accurate you will find the second level medical experts to be. And you will know when the time is right to pass on all that you receive.

If you have no success—no matter how long and how hard you try—don't feel rejected. Not everyone is meant to be a spiritual healer. It may mean that your talents as a medium between this level and the next lie in another direction. Or it may simply mean that the time is not yet right for you to enter into the field of healing. As with so much in mediumship, perseverance is the keyword. Keep practicing; especially keep working on communicating with your guide.

Examination Questions

1. Who or what brings about the healing? Is this the same thing as faith healing?

2. Does the person/patient have to be present to be healed?

3. Who was known as "the Sleeping Prophet" and what did he always say when he first started work on a patient? What may we infer from this?

4. Who was probably the best-known British healer? Where was he working when he first discovered and displayed his healing talents?

5. Whose healing energies did British healer George Chapman channel? Why do witnesses feel this to be so?

6. Are actual surgical instruments used in Spiritualist surgery?

7. What is the first requirement of a spiritual healer?

8. What is the name for the etheric centers that are connected throughout the human body? What is the name of the power that passes through these centers?

9. What is the etheric double? Can this be seen with the naked eye? How can the aura be of use in doing healings?

10. When working on a person who has come to you for a healing, you receive from the spirits the diagnosis and the cure for what ails them. Do you share this knowledge with the person?

Profile

Gerard Croiset

Gérard Croiset was born at Laren, in the Netherlands, on March 10, 1909. He had an unhappy childhood, being neglected by his parents who were in show business. His father, Hyman, was a prominent actor and his mother was a wardrobe mistress. The parents separated (never having been officially married) when Croiset was eight, leaving him to move through a series of orphanages and foster homes.

From the age of six, Croiset had visions and over his early years was frequently punished by his elders when he spoke of them. He dropped out of school when he was thirteen and took a variety of unskilled jobs, none of which he held for very long. He finally got a job as a grocery helper at one of the stores in the Albert Heyn chain. This he managed to keep for several years.

At age twenty-five Croiset married Gerda ter Morsche, an Enschede carpenter's daughter, and the following year he opened a grocery store with money loaned by his inlaws. Unfortunately it didn't last long, Croiset going bankrupt very quickly. But about that time he came into contact with some local Spiritualists and was finally able to work on developing his clairvoyant talents. These developed quickly and his reputation blossomed, as both a psychometrist and psychic. He was instrumental in locating lost children and animals. He found that he also had an inherent healing ability. He predicted World War II at least four years before it began, and with its start he was able to do healing on injured soldiers. There were a number of scenes from the war that he saw before the actual outbreak of hostilities. During the war, Croiset spent time in a concentration camp but was released in 1943. He was able to aid the Dutch resistance with his clairvoyant powers but was arrested again, by the Gestapo, in October of 1943.

After the war, in December 1945, Croiset attended a lecture on parapsychology, given by Professor Tenhaeff. The two men spoke together after the lecture and Tenhaeff went on to run tests on Croiset. Croiset accompanied the professor to the University of Utrecht, where he was subjected to such tests as the Rorschach personality (ink blots), the Murray Thematic Apperception (story-telling), the Pfister-Heisz (color pyramid), the Lüscher color selection and the Szondi. Professor Tenhaeff reported, "In early 1946 I made many psychoscopic tests with him. I realized fairly soon that he was very gifted. The more I tested him, the more I became persuaded that Croiset was a remarkable subject for parapsychological research." Tenhaeff went on to introduce Croiset to the Dutch Society for Psychical Research. They came to admire his abilities and to look upon him as a talented artist with rare paranormal gifts. Soon nearly all of Holland began to accept this view of Gérard Croiset.

One of the most amazing tests, in terms of startling results, was known as the chair test. This was devised by Professor Tenhaeff. The number of a chair in a lecture hall was chosen at random, days or even weeks ahead of time. The seats could not be reserved and sometimes even the actual venue was not determined till close to the date of the lecture. Anywhere from a few hours to several days before the lecture, Croiset would describe, and give a number of personal details of, the person who would occupy the chair on the date in question. These descriptions were never vague or in any way general, but could include hair and eye color, height, physique, age, dress, even marks on the body. Croiset's predictions would be recorded; the recording being placed in a sealed bag and locked away in a safe. At the lecture, the recording would be played back and the occupant of the chair asked to stand up and comment on Croiset's observations. Croiset showed incredible accuracy with this test, and with many others. Occasionally Croiset would seem unable to get any information. On those occasions it turned out that the seat remained empty for the lecture. Sometimes he got very confusing images, which were later explained by the fact that more than one person used the chair.

The Croiset cases have been meticulously documented over the years. He worked with the police, with private individuals, and with institutions, tracing lost people and objects, tracking down thieves and murderers, and solving numerous puzzles and problems both in his own country and in many other countries. He was tested by parapsychologists all over the world and all reached the same conclusions.

Croiset specialized in cases dealing with young children, especially when they were missing. Many of the cases he dealt with over the telephone. He accepted no payment for any of the things he did, though he did accept donations to his healing clinic. At the clinic, it was not unusual for him to deal with over one hundred cases a day. Much like Edgar Cayce, Gérard Croiset could sense the condition of a patient, what was wrong, and how to correct it, but unlike Cayce he did not have to go into trance to do so. Gérard Croiset died on July 20, 1980. His son took over the running of the clinic.

Gérard Croiset Jr., second oldest of five children, seemed to have inherited his father's talents. From Holland he directed South Carolina police in a search for two missing girls. He drew a detailed map of the area where he saw them to be, at a place called Folly Beach, near Charleston. The bodies of the girls were found in shallow graves in the sand.

LESSON FIFTEEN

Channeling

Channeling vs. Mediumship

A COMMON QUESTION seems to be, "What is the difference between channeling and spiritual mediumship?" In some ways they are very much alike, insofar as the channeler is acting as a medium for nonphysical entities to come through to this plane. But nonetheless, there are some distinct differences.

First of all, the majority of channelers are acting as direct voice conduits for the personalities they access. Very, very few engage in clairvoyance, clairaudience, or similar activities, but seem to be strictly direct voice (though some work, or start, with automatic writing). Secondly, the personalities they transmit are not always the spirits of those who have previously lived on this physical plane. This is not the case with all channels, admittedly, but certainly with a large number. Thirdly, there is usually only one personality who is channeled on a regular basis by any one channeler. And, as an extension of this, the personality comes through and, in effect, lectures or preaches to the audience; some having very definite directives they wish to impart. There is not the introduction of a variety of spirits, as in spiritual mediumship.

In spiritual mediumship, as we have seen, the medium is acting as a channel for the spirits of recently deceased loved ones to return to this level and reconnect with those left behind. Primarily there are exchanges of a personal nature, with references to family matters.

In channeling, it is as though the audience is attending a lecture by a visiting dignitary who has a general message to deliver. There may well be a chance for questions at the end of the lecture but these are usually limited to one or two questions only—not necessarily of a personal nature—by whomever manages to get recognized.

People who channel come from all walks of life, from every profession. The qualities most highly valued by the guides are dedication, enthusiasm, and the willingness to be a channel. Those of you who are intelligent, or intuitive, who like to think for yourselves, who value truth, and who can recognize higher wisdom will become very good at channeling.

Orin and DaBen

Just because the entity claims to be five thousand years old, from the lost continent of Atlantis, or from the galaxy Spurious XXI, doesn't make it so!

Raymond Buckland

Origins

It is not always easy to establish the origin of a channeled entity. Some entities claim to have last been alive on this planet at the time of Atlantis, or of ancient Egypt. Others say they have never lived in this physical plane at all. Some say they are from a far distant planet in another galaxy.

Jane Roberts' "Seth" said he was "individual portions of energy, materialized within physical existence." Elizabeth Clare Prophet channeled what she described as "ascended masters"—spiritually advanced beings who no longer live on the physical plane. Judy "Zebra" Knight (born Judith Darlene Hampton) claims that her "Ramtha" once lived thirty-five thousand years ago on the now-lost continent of Lemuria, or Mu. Jessica Lansing's "Michael" says he is "of the mid-causal plane"—made up of a thousand fragments of an entity like itself. Jach Pursel's "Lazaris" says that he has never been in human form; he is a "group form" living in another dimension. Darryl Anka's "Bashar" says that he is from the planet Essassani, five hundred light years away. Elwood Babbitt has had Jesus speak through him, or so he and the entity claim.

These are perhaps typical of channeled entities and are some of the better known ones. One thing they have in common is that they all are, or claim to be, more highly evolved than we poor mortals and are here to help us advance. Another point I personally find interesting—and one that I don't think has ever been addressed—is the fact that, regardless of the sex of the channel, virtually all the entities manifest as males.

Channeled Material

Most of the material that is channeled boils down to the same general teachings. We are taught that the universe is a multidimensional, living being; that we create our own reality, and that love conquers all.

As Jon Klimo says, in *Channeling* (1987):

> *Virtually all of the sources above the lower astral levels tell us that from their vantage points they know the entire universe to be a living spiritual being of which each is a living part. According to Universal Law, we are evolving through a series of embodied and disembodied lives toward an eventual reunion with the one God, which is the underlying identity of All That Is. In the meantime, we maintain an ongoing condition of identity with this God, though we are unaware of it. It is by virtue of*

First, are the teachings limited? Are the teachings giving you the sense that you are less than you are? Second, can I apply this? Can I use this? What's it going to do for me? Third, as I apply what's being said, am I happier? Am I more myself and is my life working better? Fourth, when I come away from the experience, am I feeling and am I thinking more positively?

Lazaris

I do not believe that I could get the equivalent of Seth's book on my own. This book is Seth's way of demonstrating that human personality is multidimensional, that we exist in many realities at once, that the soul or inner self is not something apart from us, but the very medium in which we exist.

Jane Roberts

---

the higher Self that we are connected to this deeper truth.

Some few channeled entities have been "doom and gloom" prophets; notably the egotistical and strangely materialistic "Ramtha" of J. Z. Knight. They have warned of impending disaster, urging that we get our act together and hurry up and save the world. Still others have urged their followers to give away all their worldly goods, stockpile food and water, and wait for armageddon!

What should you believe? Whom can you trust? The answer, as with any Spiritualist medium, is to study and judge the quality of what is being received and then to make up your own mind. Don't be told what to do. Listen to the advice and decide if it is right for you.

Most of the lectures that come through channelers are good and positive. If you find that the channel you are listening to on a regular basis is other than positive, you might want to question a little more. An entity from another galaxy (for example) might well be more advanced in many ways, but that doesn't necessarily mean that he is in the best position to tell you what to do with your life savings, your home, or your family. Don't sell your real estate; don't give up your job; don't leave your spouse and family, just because a channeled entity says you should. Think it through. Question the source. And research the background of the channeler.

Again to quote Jon Klimo:

We must guard against the charisma of authority . . . just because we may believe that information comes from some glamorous paranormal source, we should not fail to scrutinize its content and weigh our response to it as carefully as if it came from a more pedestrian source . . .

How to Channel

Many of the established channels started spontaneously. My wife, Tara, and I were once talking with Jach Pursel, who channels "Lazaris." Jach said that he had been in the insurance business, living in Florida. He had no great interest in matters metaphysical and certainly knew nothing of channeling. His wife, of that time, Peny, did introduce him to meditation, since he was working long hours and finding himself in need of a good relaxation technique. One day he did his meditation and, so far as he knew, fell asleep during it. Jach said that when he woke up,

> The guides and teachers who speak through me are primarily energy, and I act not unlike a human telephone or radio receiver . . . The spirits who speak through me are human personalities who lived in another historical period. They are no different from you or me. They are merely in discarnate state.
>
> **Kevin Ryerson**

> I greet you in love and peace. My identity is Ashtar, commandant quadra sector, patrol station Schare, all projections, all waves. Greetings. Through the Council of the Seven Lights you have been brought here, inspired with the inner light to help your fellow man.
>
> **Ashtar, through George Van Tassel**

Peny was sitting looking at him in amazement. Apparently, Lazaris had come through and started talking. The voice was completely different from Jach's—a most distinctive voice; at that time heavily accented. The voice also had different speech patterns from Jach's. Peny had the presence of mind to write down what was said. When they found that this same thing was happening every time Jach tried to meditate, they started using a tape recorder. Jach just couldn't believe it when he heard the voice!

Many other channels have had similar initiations. So it is possible that you can start channeling at just about any time, if the entity to come through decides that the time is right! But if you don't want to just sit and wait and hope, then there are steps you can take.

Exercise

Start out as with all your Spiritualist and psychic development exercises. Do your deep breathing, relaxation, and go into your meditation. Don't forget to set up that barrier of blue or white (or whatever color you prefer) light about you. Set a tape recorder to record; then give out to the universe that you are ready and open to channel; you are willing to accept and direct any intelligence that should wish to come to you. You can make this statement silently within, if you so wish, but I feel it probably has more impact (on your own conscious and subconscious, apart from anywhere else) if you make it aloud. Just say, in effect, "I hereby give permission for any positive force to speak through me. I am ready and willing to channel information for the education and for the good of all concerned." Then sit quietly and wait.

Several channels speak of mentally "falling away" from themselves as they give themselves over to the channeled force. To achieve this kind of sensation, after making your statement mentally, take yourself on the start of the meditation journey you did in lesson five. Take yourself to where you start moving down the steep path, descending to the lower level. But keep going down. Imagine a cave, a tunnel, or an opening of some sort into the earth. Go into it and find more steps, a ladder, or something similar, whereby you can descend further and further.

You may well find that when you go down you never reach the bottom, for the channeling takes over before you do. Some established channels say that they are climbing down a ladder and then, before they know it, they are falling off the ladder, backward, into a deep sleep. The next thing you may know is that you are waking up again. But if you do reach the bottom, see yourself in a large cavern, or small earth home, or something of that nature, and simply sit down quietly to wait. If, after sufficient time (about twenty minutes, I'd suggest), nothing has happened, then start the return journey. Try again another day.

Don't forget that not everyone is a channel. Not everyone will get results. Try no more than about twenty minutes at a time. Try once, twice, or three times a week over several weeks. Be prepared for a long wait. You may be lucky and receive contact in a short time, but it may take long weeks of perseverance.

Real or Imagined? Channeled or Inspirational?

A lot of what is presented as channeled material is probably no more than the vocalized unconscious mind of the channeler. The person is not consciously pretending to be a foreign entity but is unconsciously presenting material from his or her own mind "packaged," as it were, as if coming from a separate source.

This has been described as inspirational speaking. The channel might never be able to speak so well—to be so eloquent—in everyday life. But he or she, speaking as a "channeled entity," is able to bring out material that he didn't even know he had access to.

How do you, the listener, judge this material? The same way you judge all other channeled material—ask yourself "Does it make sense?" "Does it apply to me?" "Will it work, in a positive way, to advance my life?" If the answers to all of these are "Yes," then it really doesn't matter what is the true source of the material you are hearing.

Examination Questions

1. There is a difference between channeling and mediumship that relates to the material produced. What is/are the main difference(s)?

2. Is a channeled entity the spirit of someone who once lived on this plane?

3. Has anyone "accidentally" become a channel, without setting out to do so?

4. How seriously should you take any warnings given by channeled entities?

5. How certain can you be that the material that comes through a channel actually comes from the entity claimed?

Profile

Lily Dale Assembly

Lily Dale Assembly, beside beautiful Lake Cassadaga in upstate New York, is the world's oldest and largest Spiritualist community. It presently covers in excess of one hundred and sixty acres, and has its own fire department and post office.

The community was founded in 1879 though it had its beginnings earlier than that, in 1855, with the formation of the First Spiritualist Society of Laona (a few miles from where Lily Dale is now located). This society had previously (from 1844) been known as the Religious Society of Free Thinkers.

In 1871 Spiritualists started holding regular picnic meetings on the land of William Alden, beside Lake Cassadaga. These began as simply excursions for fun and recreation, but quickly led to the dedication of Alden's Grove to the special care of the Spiritualists, with a series of one-day meetings featuring discussions and prominent lecturers. In 1877 Jeremiah Carter, one of the foremost members of the group, heard a voice telling him to "Go to Alden's and arrange for a camp meeting." The following morning he walked the six miles to the Alden Farm and sat down with William Alden to arrange the meeting. Extended camp seasons followed, the first such occurring on Tuesday September 11, 1877, and running till Sunday September 16, 1877. The following year the camp season was extended by ten days, the grounds were fenced in, and a cottage was built. Despite terrible rain storms, the crowd was bigger than before and an even longer meeting was planned for the next year.

Following William Alden's death, problems developed in that his son, Theodore Alden, demanded rent for use of the grounds. This led to the board deciding to purchase their own property, which they did in 1879. Twenty acres was purchased on what is the present Lily Dale Assembly site. Mrs. Amelia Colby named the camp the Cassadaga Lake Free Association.

Lily Dale Assembly entrance sign

In 1903 the name was changed to the City of Light, and three years later to the Lily Dale Assembly (because of the large number of water lilies on the lake). Albert Cobb was elected the first president of the association. Whole families —men, women, and children—toiled to clear trees and brush for camp sites, to build a horse stable, and to erect what became known as the Bough House. This was a building made of entwined boughs, and with rough hewn logs for seats, that would be used for services. The first speaker was suffragette Elizabeth Lowe Watson.

The grounds were laid out for lots, which could be rented (the land was not to be sold), for future cottages. The rental fees for these lots were kept low, with regard to the fact that the assembly was for everyone, regardless of wealth or social standing. On August 7, 1880, a hotel was opened. It was originally the barn. It's known as a "hung suspension building." When additional floors were needed each floor was raised and the new additions placed underneath. It was originally known as the Grand Hotel but today is the Maplewood Hotel. The first cottage

Forest Temple

was built (by a Mr. Sage) on what is today the site of the Marion Skidmore Library building. By 1893 there were 215 cottages with approximately forty families living there year round. The Lyceum (Spiritualist's Sunday School) was started in 1881, in a tent. By 1928 this had grown into today's beautiful building. By August 1883 a large and impressive auditorium had been built. The floor was fifty feet by fifty feet with eleven rows of raised chairs. A tent housed the library, though this was later moved into the Assembly Hall. In 1924 the present impressive library building was built.

In 1887 an additional eighteen acres of land was purchased and the following year the United States Postal Service installed a post office, officially recognizing the community. In 1888 the Assembly Hall was built and became famous for its "Thought Exchange." In 1892 construction started on the Octagon Building, which today houses the Medium's League. It is one of only seven such buildings in the state of New York. There was a dance school in Lily Dale and, for a short while, there was even a ferris wheel there. This finally had to be removed, however, because the excessive noise of its steam engine "disturbed the various programs."

Many celebrities visited Lily Dale. Susan B. Anthony was a regular. Among other notables to visit were Mahatma Gandhi, Sir Arthur Conan Doyle, Mae West, Franklin & Eleanor Roosevelt, and Leo Tolstoy's daughter Russian countess Alexandra Tolstoy.

In 1895 the Alden House was purchased by Mrs. Abby Pettengill and renamed the Leolyn, after her granddaughter. The Leolyn then was purchased from Mrs. Pettengill by the Assembly. The auditorium was remodeled in 1916 and seating increased to twelve hundred, yet many times during the history of Lily Dale people stood three deep outside the auditorium

Early Lily Dale Assembly signs

in order to hear the lecture. A beautiful Healing Temple was added by Louis Vosburg in 1955, under the direction of T. J. Kelly's spirit guide.

The original Fox family cottage was moved from Hydesville to the Lily Dale site in 1916, a gift from Benjamin Bartlett of Cambridge Springs, Pennsylvania. Tragically it was destroyed by fire in 1955. Arson was suspected. Some relics were saved, including the original peddler's tin box and the Fox family Bible. Both are now on display in the excellent little museum at Lily Dale, run by an enthusiastic Ron Nagy and Joyce LaJudice.

As many as thirty thousand people flock to Lily Dale each year. It is certainly a community that should be visited by every Spiritualist and everyone seeking comfort and proof of survival after death on this earthly plane.

LESSON SIXTEEN

Development and Development Circles

Lack of Good Mediums

Looking back over the relatively short history of Spiritualism, it seems there was a vast number of mediums from the late 1800s well into the twentieth century, but the years since World War II have seen a very definite decline. Today it seems difficult, if not impossible, to find a medium; good, bad, or indifferent. Why is this? There are several reasons. The most cogent, I feel, is due to the advancement of home entertainment and leisure pursuits.

Spiritualism was born in the mid-nineteenth century. It's not surprising that there then came a sudden blossoming of mediums, as more and more people became aware of the possibility of spiritual contact and of the latent talents they themselves possessed. As I said in earlier lessons, we all have these "powers" within us. It's simply a matter of realizing we have them and then drawing them out. Many were able to develop them, in the past, and many became very accomplished as intermediaries between this world and the next. We must also admit that many more were not so accomplished or were too lazy to develop themselves—but found the various phenomena of Spiritualism easy to duplicate in a fraudulent manner.

With the doorway to the next world cracked open, whole groups of people joined together to communicate with those they had known and loved and who had passed on to the next level of existence. Groups would get together—"Home Circles"—meeting on a regular basis to help each other develop and to bring out the abilities of mediumship in one another. These Circles of enthusiasts were the core of the Spiritualist movement.

As long as we feel any emotion about them, whether of love, grief, resentment, or fear, we are actively in touch with them; we are affecting them, and they are affecting us. We should therefore strive by all means in our power to achieve right relations with those who have passed over, and the most effectual way of achieving right relations is to possess accurate knowledge of inter-life conditions.

Dion Fortune

The mediumistic faculty in all its forms can be cultivated by sitting in the spirit circle, which tends to perfect and spiritualize the magnetism of the sitters by their mutual action on each other and by the influence of the spirits.

Emma Hardinge Britten

But then came the invention of radio and, later, of television. By then the novelty of communication with the world of spirit had worn off. It experienced an upsurge—quite a sizable one—throughout the periods of the two world wars since, at those times, people felt the need to contact loved ones killed in the conflicts. But afterward the necessity wasn't there, or wasn't so immediate, for most people.

With vast numbers of the population wooed away from Spiritualism by the magic of radio and television (plus the advent of movies, women in the work force, time and money for a wide variety of readily available recreation), the number of Home Circles—and thereby the number of developing mediums—declined until mediumship became almost nonexistent. The number of Spiritualist devotees shrank to minute proportions, and it's no wonder. Yet Spiritualism did not die out.

New Wave of Psychics

At first glance it might seem that the modern education received by the younger generation would sound the death knell on such a practice, and religion, as Spiritualism. Yet the reverse is true. Previously children have slavishly followed the religion and beliefs of their parents, and their grandparents before them, without question. But today children are taught to think for themselves. No longer do they automatically become Roman Catholics, Jews, Episcopalians, or whatever. No longer do they mouth, parrot-fashion, the beliefs and arguments of their elders. Today young people are far more capable of making up their own minds, and don't hesitate to do so. And in doing so there is a tendency to reject many of the traditional values.

I think it's a bad thing to reject anything out of hand. But I think it's a good thing to give serious thought to what you have been told and to reach your own decision on whether or not it is believable. Perhaps, not surprisingly, this has led to a swing back to interest in spirit communication, among other things.

Many people are becoming jaded with television. They are bored with the endless repetition of inane situation comedies and police dramas. People are now looking for alternatives to being couch potatoes. Astrologers will say that it's the dawning of the Age of Aquarius that is responsible, and so it may be. But whatever the reason, there is today a far greater awareness of other realities, of psychic senses and sensibilities, of alternate paths of religious belief and expression. Rather than mediums, specifically, we are finding a veritable plethora of "psychics" who read tarot cards, palms, runes, crystal balls; who chart horoscopes, do healing using a variety of methods, and even use talking boards and tip tables. The psychic has replaced the medium in many ways and psychic fairs and New Age centers flourish.

Full Circle

Life goes in circles, or cycles. Nowhere is this more noticeable, perhaps, than in the field of fashion. What was "in" ten years ago suddenly makes a comeback. Short skirts for women, wide ties for men, double-breasted suits, flared pants, hairstyles. But it's not only fashions. Interests, fads, whole lifestyles, all seem to come and go in huge circles. And interest in Spiritualism is but one example.

As part of the "New Age"—a misnomer, since the vast majority of the practices that are put under this unsatisfactory heading are ancient ones—we have seen the advent of channeling on a grand scale. This is a phenomenon we looked at in the last lesson, that is akin to mediumship and, indeed, has been a stepping stone in the journey back to Home Circles.

Channeling has been quite a fad, with well known personalities becoming involved with it, just as in earlier days well known personalities become involved in Spiritualism (Sir Arthur Conan Doyle, author of the Sherlock Homes stories, is an example of this). One of the positive things about channeling was that it did remind many people of the phenomenon of mediumship. Consequently, Spiritualist churches have seen an increase in membership. Home Circles have started up again.

In England, the Home Circles never did die out as completely as they seemed to here in the United States. Today there are still development groups meeting, throughout Britain, who have been doing so for years. But even so there was a noticeable decline in membership and now there, also, the Circles are once again on the increase.

Development Circles

It would seem, then, that today is an ideal time to establish more Home Development Circles for mediumship. Actually this is already happening. Small institutes and metaphysical bookstores have never stopped giving classes, lectures and workshops on various aspects of Spiritualism, clairvoyance, psychometry, table tipping, healing, etc. But now these classes and workshops are also being held in people's homes. Groups of friends are getting together, just as they did in "the old days," to investigate and experiment with these forever fascinating subjects. Books are being published: James Van Praagh's *Talking to Heaven,* Sylvia Browne's *Adventures of a Psychic,* John Edward's *One Last Time* and *Crossing Over.* The last mentioned is tied-in to John Edward's very popular television show of the same name, which has really brought mediumship front and center.

If you have a strong interest, whether as a potential medium or just from curiosity, why not form a development circle of your own?

Exercises

Your Own Development Circle

A Home Circle should be made up of six to ten people; twelve at the most. All should be dedicated to the point of committing themselves to attending every meeting, unless there are truly exceptional circumstances. Meetings should be held once a week—the actual day is not important but it should be on the same day every week, at the same time and in the same place. It is possible to meet at a different house each time, on a rotating basis, but far better if you can keep to one house and even one particular room, for you will find there will be quite a build-up of vibrations over the months.

New people should not be introduced haphazardly. The idea is for the members to grow completely comfortable with one another, to develop together, and also for the spirits to be able to attune and develop with them. Any new person coming into the established Circle tends to throw everyone "out of sync," as it were. This is not to say that you may never bring in others, just that it should not be done on a whim. No more should "visitors" be invited, for they, too, will interfere with the harmonious atmosphere that has been generated.

So you need a group of people who, from the start, know that they must be responsible and dedicated. You can expect to work together for a very long time. Most established Circles have been going for years. Appoint a leader. He or she should be the most experienced and/or most well read. The leader is responsible for everyone and responsible for recognizing where talent is showing itself, so that it can be especially encouraged. All should be supported in their development, with no one ignored.

Everyone should be encouraged to read as much as they possibly can, on all aspects of spiritual contact and psychic development (see bibliography). Time should be taken at the start of every meeting to discuss what has been read and learned and for people to ask questions of one another.

There's no need to work in darkness; however, a low light setting does seem to help development in its earlier stages. Later on you can come back to full light if you wish. As I mentioned in lesson nine, it's a good idea to have fresh flowers in the room. Make sure the telephone is disconnected and that there are going to be no interruptions. The group may want to decide whether or not the burning of a light incense will contribute positive vibes (I find it does, but not all feel that way).

Start by everyone going through the relaxation and breathing exercises, then join in together with a little singing. Again as mentioned in lesson nine, the song should be light and happy. Now take a moment to relax and make yourself comfortable—feet flat on the floor, legs uncrossed. Take hands in a circle and, if you wish (this is not mandatory), join together in a short prayer. Then let the leader make a statement of purpose. This will initially be to the effect that you are all there to make contact with the spirit world and to develop yourselves as mediums. The leader will ask for help and guidance from the spirit guides in all that you undertake, and will emphasize your dedication to the work before you.

The very first exercise might be focused on the meditation that leads to everyone encountering their spirit guide (see lesson five). Probably not everyone *will* make contact the first time. Spend time discussing each person's experience in the meditation. At the next meeting, repeat the meditation, with those who connected reestablishing contact and those who didn't connect perhaps this time making contact. Certainly, those who don't immediately meet up with their guides can keep trying at home, between Circles. It should be emphasized, however, that not everyone may have a guide, at least initially. Also, some may well have more than one. As mentioned earlier, there's no relevance to how many guides a person has. It's not a case of "I have more guides than you do! (Ergo, I'm more important!)" Six guides, one guide, no guides—it's all the same.

In the first weeks of meeting you might concentrate on psychometry, going on to clairvoyance and clairaudience, and developing much as I have indicated in this book. Do readings for one another; get the feel of letting things come through. As I've said before, no matter how strange something sounds to you, it may have great significance to another. Don't try to interpret, just relay what you receive. In these early weeks everyone should be encouraged to participate.

Into Mediumship

When the leader feels that all are comfortable with one another, that the initial shyness of speaking out has passed, then you should start concentrating on one person at a time. Here is one good reason for not having too many people in your Circle. With a

By a home circle we simply mean a group of persons who meet on a regular basis with the express purpose of making spirit contact . . . it is important that this circle meet at the same time and in the same place each week. In fact, to as great an extent as is possible, the group assembled should be limited to the same persons as well, and include only those persons who are sincerely committed to making spirit contact.

Zolar

The psychic demonstrator . . . (was) highly respected for her gifts and her integrity. She singled me out at once, saying in unequivocal terms: "You are a medium and have much work to do. Chosen by the spirit world, you must not ignore the call."

Estelle Roberts

---

smaller number, you'll be able to work with everyone having some development time each week. With a large number, you wouldn't have the time to fit everybody in. Later on, certainly—some months down the path—you'll get to the point where you will only concentrate on one person each meeting, but in the early days it's nice if everyone has an opportunity to try their hand.

So, take the first person for concentrated development and let the leader stand behind that person while they and everyone else joins hands to form a circle. The leader should hold out his or her hands over the head of this designated medium, concentrating energies into her, or him. Everyone should try to send positive energies to the medium, around the chain of hands, as the leader asks the medium's guide to come through.

At this point it may be that the medium gets some direct connection with her guide, or with a spirit. She should speak out with whatever comes through. It is unlikely, at this stage, that any physical phenomena will be experienced, though it certainly has been known to happen. More likely, the medium will see or hear her guide, or the spirit, and will relay what is seen or heard. If such contact is made, you may progress much as I described in the chapter on the talking board, with the leader acting as spokesperson and asking questions.

If nothing comes through, don't be discouraged. Don't let the medium feel ineffective. All the energies there are important. Not everyone will develop as a good medium; this should be understood from the start. Also, some will be more attuned to working at, say, psychometry while others excel at clairaudience, for example. But everybody's energy is useful in the Circle. Like the cells of a huge battery, you are all contributing to the energy of whoever is working on their progress at the moment.

After a Circle all should feel refreshed and energized. You shouldn't feel depleted in any way. If you find yourself exhausted on a regular basis, then you might need to leave that particular development group. Energy should flow freely from you, and flow freely to you from spirit. If your energy is being sapped, leaving you the worse for it, then you need to make a break. This is not to say that there is anything "evil" happening in such a group. It is just that some individuals do strongly draw other people's energy to themselves. They do this quite unconsciously, but they can adversely affect others. If you happen to be one of those who is being sapped by such a person (you won't necessarily be able to tell

We have never found it necessary or helpful actually to sit in a circle formation. We sit on the settee and in armchairs, with other chairs brought in if required, in the most convenient positions in the room. We do not sit round a table touching hands . . . We all sit as comfortably as we can, because this helps everyone to relax. We sit in total darkness, though some circles we have conducted have been held in subdued light.

Robert Cull

Only faith in a life after death, in a brighter world, where dear ones will meet again—only that and the measured tramp of time can give consolation.

Winston Churchill

---

who it is), then it is better to leave rather than spend all your time feeding them.

Record Keeping Is Important

It is most important that you keep accurate notes of all that takes place in the Circle. Only in this way can you see the progress you are making. Run a tape recorder and also, if possible, have someone taking notes. These days some groups even have a video camera going, just in case there are any physical manifestations. This is a good idea. You can probably keep just one videotape for this, since it can be used over and over when there's nothing of any importance in the session. Keep only what is worthwhile on video. But do review what was taped; this is the whole point. You probably won't be aware of any phenomena at the moment of it happening; until you watch the videotape and see it! But it's good to keep the audiotapes in their entirety and to build up a library of them, showing how the Development Circle has progressed over the months and years. Also, incidentally, it's not unknown for spirit voices (that were not heard during the Circle) to be heard when tapes are played back! (See lesson seventeen.)

If you keep at it, you will get to the stage where you have two or three really good mediums in your Circle and where you can enjoy regular communication with the second level.

Rescue Circles

Once established, some Circles like to spend time on what they term "rescue work." It seems there are a large number of spirits who do not realize that they have died. They wander about, literally haunting their old neighborhoods, wondering what has happened to them.

Should you, or your Circle, come into contact with such a spirit, take time to explain to him (or her) where he is. (Such spirits are often contacted by way of the Ouija board.) Tell him that he is preventing his own progress by attaching himself to an area to which he can never return. Tell him to go forward into the light.

Those people who are accomplished at astral projection, and can decide where they want to travel, frequently go out searching for these "lost spirits" in order to help them cross over to the second level.

Let your Circle always be on the lookout for those spirits who seem confused and uncertain as to where they are or what has happened. Ask your guide(s) to direct any such lost ones to you and to your Circle.

Examination Questions

1. What is a "Home Circle?"

2. A Home Development Circle meets when, and as often, as it can. Members come and go and visitors are welcome. Is this a good thing or not? If so, why? If not, why not?

3. How many people should there be in a Home Circle?

4. What's the best way to start the proceedings?

5. How many mediums can be developed at a Home Circle?

6. Does everyone get a turn at mediumship every week?

7. How can such things as tape recorders and video cameras aid the development of a Circle?

8. Should you expect to feel exhausted or refreshed after spiritual development work?

9. Why is good record-keeping important?

10. What is a Rescue Circle?

Profile

Dion Fortune

Dion Fortune was the pseudonym of Violet Mary Firth. Born in Wales, in 1891, she grew up in a Christian Science family. Firth demonstrated mediumistic talents when in her teen years and claimed to have memories of a past life as a priestess in Atlantis. She studied Freud and Jung (preferring Jung) and worked for the Medico-Psychological Clinic in London. She had plans to build up a practice as a lay analyst and took classes at the University of London to that end. She even undertook clinical work under the auspices of the London (Royal Free Hospital) School of Medicine for Women. After some years, however, Firth came to the conclusion that neither Freud nor Jung had all the answers and that the truth lay in the occult.

Although fascinated by the works of Helena Blavatsky, Firth was not enthused about occultism presented in an Eastern setting and therefore was not drawn to the Theosophical Society, though she was a member of it for a brief period. At the age of twenty-eight, Firth joined the Alpha and Omega Lodge of the Stella Matutina, an outer division of the Hermetic Order of the Golden Dawn led by J. W. Brodie-Innes. On initiation, she took the magical name Deo Non Fortuna ("By God, not chance"). This Firth later shortened to Dion Fortune and used as her pen name. Five years later Firth/Fortune left the Order after a disagreement with Moina Mathers (widow of MacGregor Mathers) who then led the group. She went on to found the Community and Fraternity of the Inner Light, based on contacts she claimed to have made with "Inner Planes" of wisdom. Today this is known as the Society of the Inner Light.

Fortune had learned Ceremonial Magic from Brodie-Innes and quickly became an adept. In 1927 she married a Dr. Thomas Penry Evans. In 1936 she wrote one of her best-known books, *The Mystical Qabbalah,* dealing with the use of the Qabbalah by modern occultists. She had previously written *Sane Occultism* (1929) and *Psychic Self-Defense* (1930), the latter as the result of a psychic attack she received from an employer back in 1911, when she was twenty-nine. She had, at that time, been working in a school where the principal took a dislike to her. It was, in fact, this attack that had led to her study of Jung and Freud.

Fortune went on to write a number of books, fiction and nonfiction, teaching the Western esoteric tradition. The two novels *The Sea Priestess* (1938) and *Moon Magic* (published posthumously in 1956), contain much practical occult knowledge, telling the story of a priestess of Isis who comes to restore paganism to a world that has lost touch with nature. *The Goat-Foot God* (1936) is another novel enjoyed by modern-day pagans, dealing as it does with the powers of Pan.

In *Spiritualism in the Light of Occult Science* (1931), Fortune says:

> *What have Spiritualists to do with the ancient wisdom? More than most of them realize, for occultism is traditional Spiritualism. Whether we study the Delphic Oracles or the Witch trials of the Middle Ages, we encounter authentic psychic phenomena. Spiritualists would find themselves on familiar ground if they penetrated to the caves of Tibet or the temples of Ancient Egypt, for the Secret Tradition has been built up by generations of psychics and spirit-controlled mediums.*

It's a little-known fact that Dion Fortune was herself an accomplished medium. She had been taught by Margaret Lumley Brown, who took over many of Fortune's functions at the Society of Inner Light after the latter's death, from leukemia, in 1946. (Margaret Lumley Brown has been called by some the finest medium and psychic of the twentieth century.) Gareth Knight—a student of Fortune's and literary executor of Margaret Lumley Brown—stated that, "The mediumship of Dion Fortune has been a well-kept secret within the Inner Group of the Fraternity, but it has recently been decided to make a secret of it no longer in order that certain of the teachings thus received may be made available for all who follow the Path."

In the early 1920s, Fortune had acted as a medium when working with Frederick Bligh Bond, at Glastonbury. Bond was absorbed in psychic archaeology at the site of Glastonbury Cathedral. The July 1922 issue of the journal *Psychic Science*—published by the College of Psychic Science—carried an article by Fortune, using her name Violet M. Firth, titled "Psychology and Occultism." In the article, she says, "In entering the trance condition one sees the medium become abstracted, and then, closing down the avenues of the five physical senses, enter a subjective state. In some mediums one can observe this condition very well, (and) especially when it is the intention to get trance speech, the contact is maintained with the vocal organs."

LESSON SEVENTEEN

Electronic Spirit Contact

Modern Tools of Communication

Spiritualism's modern form started in 1848, as was shown in lesson three. But it has been around, in various forms, for thousands of years. It would seem logical, therefore, that it would keep up with the times; would change and adapt as humankind changes. And so it seems it does. According to Harold Sherman, writing in 1974 *(You Can Communicate With the Unseen World)*, "By use of an ordinary tape recorder and/or a radio set attuned to unused frequencies, spirit voices of purported entities are being received." This is known as Electronic Voice Phenomenon (EVP).

In the 1920s, Thomas Alva Edison is reported to have said: "If our personality survives, then it is strictly logical or scientific to assume that it retains memory, intellect, other faculties, and knowledge that we acquire on this Earth. Therefore … if we can evolve an instrument so delicate as to be affected by our personality as it survives in the next life, such an instrument, when made available, ought to record something." In the June 1922 issue of *Popular Radio* there was a major article titled "Can the Dead Reach Us by Radio?" Other periodicals of the period also touched on the subject. But today, spirit communication goes even further than tape recorders and radios; it includes television and computers, cell phones, and satellite dishes.

People have been experiencing amplified and recorded spirit contact since the birth of electronic receiving and recording devices. From the earliest days of the telephone, spirit voices have been heard on that instrument. From the days of the first radios, spirit voices have come through the radio speakers. But the phenomena first became really noticeable at the end of World War II, with the gradual spread of the use of the first wire

Millions of spiritual creatures walk the Earth
Unseen, both when we wake, and when we sleep.
What if earth and heaven be to each other like
More than on earth is thought?

John Milton

I hope you have seen some bit of evidence of the continuity of life, and the faculty of mind and soul that each and every one of you have. It's there. Develop it, unfold it, use it unselfishly for the benefit of your fellow man.

Rev. B. Anne Gehman

---

recorders, which then gave way to tape recorders. Wire recorders had been used by the services during the war and had worked well. But it soon became apparent that tape was a better medium than wire for recording; first coated-paper tape and later magnetized plastic tape.

Two of the first serious investigators of electronic spirit communication were Friedrich Juergenson and Dr. Konstantin Raudive. Over a number of years, Raudive collected dozens of tapes of recorded spirit messages, totaling seventy-two thousand voices. According to Worlditc.org:

> *In 1959, the man who was to become a great pioneer in the recording of voice phenomena, Swedish film producer Friedrich Juergenson, captured voices on audiotape while taping bird songs. He was startled when he played the tape back and heard a male voice say something about "bird voices in the night." Listening more intently to his tapes, he heard his (deceased) mother's voice say in German, "Friedrich, you are being watched. Friedel, my little Friedel, can you hear me?" Juergenson said that when he heard his mother's voice, he was convinced he had made "an important discovery." During the next four years, Juergenson continued to tape hundreds of paranormal voices. He played the tapes at an international press conference and in 1964 published a book in Swedish:* Voices from the Universe *and then another entitled* Radio Contact with the Dead. *In 1967, Franz Seidel, Vienna, developed the "psychophone" and Theodore Rudolph developed a goniometer for Raudive's experiments. Thomas Edison spoke through West German clairvoyant Sigrun Seuterman, in trance, about his earlier efforts in 1928 to develop equipment for recording voices from the beyond. Edison also made suggestions as to how to modify TV sets and tune them to 740 megahertz to get paranormal effects. . . .*

In 1967, Juergenson's *Radio Contact with the Dead* was translated into German, and Latvian psychologist Dr Konstantin Raudive read it skeptically. He visited Juergenson to learn his methodology, decided to experiment on his own, and soon began developing his own experimental techniques. Like Juergenson, Raudive, too, heard the voice of his own deceased mother, who called him by his boyhood name, "Kostulit, this is your mother." Eventually he catalogued tens of thousands of voices, many under strict laboratory conditions.

At the eleventh annual conference of the Parapsychological Association, held at the University of Frieburg, Germany, in September 1968, Dr. Raudive played some of these tapes to Dr. Jules Eisenbud (who worked with Ted Serios on thought photography—see lesson eight), Mrs. K. M. Goldney from

Spiritualists cannot accept the ideas forged by theology which teaches the necessity for a personal savior to save mankind from the consequences of Adam's sin. Genesis is now regarded by Christians themselves as allegorical. It follows that Adam and Eve are allegories too, and therefore never existed in the flesh. The educated Christian also accepts the teachings of evolution, which prove that man rose from lower forms and never 'fell' from perfection. Added to these extraordinary contradictions, many of them repudiate the theory that Jesus was God, but still refer to the Christ within, which does not really mean Jesus at all but implies God in manifestation. Christians have thus borrowed from the Quakers' idea of divinity expressing itself through man after terribly persecuting them for teaching it.

Harry Boddington

---

the British Society for Psychical Research, Dr. Walter Uphoff of the University of Colorado, and others. As Dr. Uphoff described it:

> *All we could do was listen and try to figure out what might explain what we were hearing. Some voices were clearer and more distinct than others; the level of static or background noise was high because the volume had to be turned to maximum level in order to reproduce the otherwise faint voices; and the cadence certainly suggested that these were not likely to be bits of stray radio signals.*

Most of the received voices had been inaudible at the time of recording. The strategy was for the moderator—in this case Dr. Raudive—to announce the date and time and then to invite any spirits to communicate. Later playback called for increasing the volume and, in most instances, changing the speed. In 1971 Raudive had performed a controlled experiment with technicians at Pye Records. In the sound lab, special equipment was installed that would cut out any possible intrusion of outside radio or television signals. Raudive used one tape recorder, monitored by a control deck. He wasn't allowed to touch the equipment himself but could only speak into the microphone. This he did for eighteen minutes. The engineers were sure that no other sounds had been picked up yet, on playback, they found over two hundred voices recorded.

George W. Meek's book *After We Die, What Then?* (1987) deals with the 1980s breakthroughs of electronic spirit communication. In the book Meek made the prediction "A workable, dependable, repeatable two-way communication with the mental-causal levels of consciousness should be demonstrated in Europe, the United States, or South America well before the end of the century." In 1982 Meek traversed the globe distributing recordings of communications between his associate William O'Neil and a scientist who had been dead for fourteen years. Meek also provided wiring diagrams, guidelines, photographs, and technical data for research in a 100-page technical report he had prepared.

Experiments were conducted using such things as low frequency oscillators, ultraviolet and infrared lights, and variable speed tape decks. In the mid-1980s, Ken Webster received messages on his computer that supposedly came from a Thomas Harden of sixteenth-century England. Harden seemed to be of the opinion that Webster was living in his house (an ancient building dating back to that time). The many messages have been examined through research at Oxford Library and confirm the language, dialect, spelling, etc., of the period. Webster

Death is just a change in lifestyles.

Stephen Levine

Death is not the end; it is simply walking out of the physical form and into the spirit realm, which is our true home. It's going back home.

Stephen Christopher

---

later produced a book, *The Vertical Plane,* which details the events.

In the mid 1980s Klaus Schreiber received, on his television, pictures of the faces of various deceased people—including Romy Schneider and Albert Einstein. He got the pictures by focusing a video camera on to the screen of the television and feeding the camera's output back into the television, forming a feedback loop. About this time a couple in Luxembourg started getting amazing voice contacts through their radio. The then-deceased Konstantin Raudive spoke through the apparatus to them in 1994, saying that, "It can only work when the vibrations of those present are in complete harmony and when their aims and intentions are pure."

The list goes on; innumerable people have received contact from deceased persons—relatives, friends, and others they had never known. Sarah Estep started the American Association of Electronic Voice Phenomena in 1982. In the 1990s, the International Network for Instrumental Transcommunication (INIT) was started by Mark Macy, though this was later fragmented due to the skepticism and pressure of the scientific community. The world wide web features www.worlditc.org as a purveyor of useful information on the whole subject.

Exercises—Your Own EVPs and ITC

EVP is Electronic Voice Phenomenon. ITC is Instrumental Transcommunication. These are the two levels of the electronic work. The former is capturing voices—however faint—on tape, or hearing them on the telephone or radio (where, of course, they won't be recorded). The first contacts were made using a tape recorder and microphone. ITC includes two-way communication between this first level and the second level; by telephone, radio, computer, fax, or any special devices. This latter communication may be stored by use of technical means and can include images and text as well as voices.

Tape Recorder

It would probably be best to start your experiments with a simple tape recorder and microphone. Start by relaxing. Play some soothing music, or perhaps read something satisfying, or even go for a pleasant walk. All of these can help put you in the right mood for attuning to the transcommunication contact.

1. Be in a positive state of mind. In other words, know that you are going to make contact.

2. Set up your equipment—be it tape recorder, computer, telephone, or whatever—in a room that is comfortable, quiet, and where you feel relaxed.

3. If it helps you, burn incense and/or light candles; lower the lights.

4. Do your white light protection barrier. Say a brief prayer; do a short meditation.

State your name, the date, and the time. Speak softly, so that you can turn up the volume to full when you play back. You can ask for a specific spirit (no guarantee that he or she will come, of course)

> There is no death of the spiritual being you truly are; only a change, a transformation, as you release your physical body.
>
> **Bill & Judy Guggenheim**

> Your world and our world are the same world; the same universe. It is something like two pictures of the same place, one in black and white and the other in color. There is only the curtain or veil or frequency between us. Our frequency is simply too high for people to sense.
>
> **The spirit Benjamin, speaking through medium Wilbur Hull to Anne Gehman**

---

or just for "any spirit." You can leave the tape running, without words from you, just to see what message(s) might come through. Or you can have a list of questions and ask them, leaving sufficient pauses for answers. You almost certainly won't hear any response as you go along. When you have finished, thank the spirit(s) and close with a short prayer.

The spirit world of the second level operates at a different frequency from ours. In order to communicate, mediums have to speed up their vibrations, in effect, while the spirits slow down theirs. It's a delicate operation that takes practice for both sides to arrive at the same vibration suitable for communication. With your tape recording, since the spirit messages will be at a higher frequency, it would help if you have more than one speed on the machine, or are able to vary the speed. Let it record at a fast speed and then play back at a slow speed. Crank up the volume as high as you can. If you have access to an amplifier, to bring it up even more, that will help.

It may take a number of times playing back before you recognize what is there— if there is anything there, of course. It may be that you get nothing the first time—or the first several times—you try the experiment. Just persevere. As you listen, it may sound like nothing but background "hiss." It's only by repeatedly playing that you start to make out words.

Television

Try the method mentioned above, for getting a television picture. With the dial set on a blank channel number, you can simply sit and stare at the screen—but that will probably induce eye strain! Train a video camera on the screen. You can set it on a tripod and leave it for a while, if you like. Have the output of the camera plugged into the input of the television set. Alternatively, just have the camera recording the blank screen. When playing back, if it's possible to play back at a different speed, then do so. One way to do this is if you have access to a European VCR (PAL system). By playing back the recorded tape in the PAL system, you will be playing it at a different speed from that recorded, which may (or may not) bring out spirit pictures. You may have to experiment to see whether it's best to record on the U.S. system and play back on the PAL or vice versa.

Computers

Messages purporting to be from the spirit world have arrived by way of computers but it's very difficult to prove this, since computers are so open to "hacking" by others. One suggestion for experimentation is given below, in "From Slates to Laptops."

From Slates to Laptops

Almost from the beginning of Spiritualism one of the tools of the séance room has been the slate. This is the old-fashioned, schoolroom, writing slate—a piece of actual slate set in a wooden frame, which can be written on with chalk. Slates are used to demonstrate a form of physical phenomena known, appropriately, as "slate writing." Two slates are placed face to face with a piece of chalk between them. They are tied together and left on a small table, or on the floor, in the middle of a circle for the duration of the sitting. It's common practice to place slates and a trumpet together. With most circles the slates are simply placed there and left, with the hopes that when examined at the end of the sitting writing will be found on the slates. This has certainly happened, and was quite common in the past. The Lily Dale Museum contains a number of slates with intricate messages written on them, obtained under séance room conditions.

Computer screen ghost writing

A modern form of slate writing might be experienced using a laptop computer. This could be set to a word-processing program, with a new, blank, file opened. Closing up the computer (which will actually turn it off), it can then be left in the center of the circle. At the end of the sitting, turn on the computer and examine the empty file that had been created. It's possible that it will be found to contain a message. Sometimes the slate process can be hurried by having the medium—or just one, or more, of the sitters—hold the bound slates and concentrate on them, asking spirit to make contact. So with the computer. It can be held, by medium or sitters, and concentrated upon.

As with slate writing, great patience is needed. These days it seems that it's very seldom that slate writing materializes, but slates are always put out "just in case." It will probably be the same way with the laptop. It may be a long while before you actually get a message materialized in the file, but keep trying anyway.

Examination Questions

1. For how long have electronic voice phenomena been in existence? What pioneer of electronic communication believed in the possibility of spirit contact through mechanical/ electronic means?

2. What method of recording was used during World War II and what did its development lead to?

3. Friedrich Juergenson, the Swedish movie producer, found he had recorded his deceased mother's voice while recording bird songs. What other pioneer also recorded his dead mother's voice, and went on to amass over seventy-two thousand spirit voice recordings? What was his strategy when setting out to make spirit voice recordings?

4. What two things are necessary to hear recorded spirit voices from a tape recording?

5. Describe how a laptop computer might be used in a Spiritualist Circle. Of what would it be the modern equivalent?

AFTERWORD

THROUGHOUT THIS BOOK I've spoken of developing your abilities in the various aspects of mediumship. In everything I've talked about, practice is the keyword. One thing to remember, however: don't overdo things. Don't try to do something—be it scrying, clairvoyance, psychometry, or whatever—and keep trying till you're blue in the face! Apart from getting discouraged, you'll rapidly terminate your interest in the activity you are focusing upon, and perhaps lose interest in the whole field, and you'll drag down your psychic defenses to the point where you could suffer both physically and emotionally. But by taking small bites on a regular basis you will progress, gain in strength, and much sooner reach success in your endeavors.

I encourage you to take courses and workshops—most of the Spiritualist communities and many of the churches offer them. Do talk with those who have already taken the course to get some feedback. As in so many things, all are not equal. For those who are really serious about their mediumship, then I cannot speak too highly of the courses offered by the Morris Pratt Institute and by the NSAC's College of Spiritual Science.

There has been a lot of fraudulence in Spiritualism. There still is some, though nowhere near as much as in the past. But I repeat what I've said before: that doesn't mean that it is all fraudulent. There have been and still are many good, sincere mediums. In the early days D. D. Home was outstanding, as was Leonora Piper. In more recent times Gladys Leonard, Winifred Coombe Tennant, Geraldine Cummins, Eileen Garrett, Ena Twigg, and Estelle Roberts were excellent. George Anderson is an outstanding present-day medium, as is James Van Praagh and my personal favorites John

Edward and Anne Gehman. Others include Elizabeth Owen, Shirley Calkins Smith, Jean Cull, Pamela White, Cheryl Williams, Douglas Johnson, and many more. There are many good, dedicated Spiritualists out there, if you just take the time to track them down. And remember to judge each of them on an individual basis. Examine what they say. Make up your own mind whether or not you believe them.

Know that mediumship is not necessarily a special gift. I strongly believe that we all have the capability within us to make contact; to bridge the gap between this level and the next. I hope that this book will help bring out that specialness in each of you, so that there will be less need for the frauds and so that all can see that death is not the end. There is a life beyond, and we will see our loved ones again.

Raymond Buckland

> I believe that whether we receive one word of validation or enough to fill a book, it is important to acknowledge the enormous energy spirits are expending in order to come through. They are coming through for us—because they love us, and because they know the ultimate message is a vital one: In these modern, often cynical times it is important to remember that we are all spiritual beings, and as such, we cannot die. We can only live and learn forever.
>
> **John Edward**

APPENDIX A

Fraudulent Practices

The Fraudulent Mediums Act

In Great Britain prior to 1951, if anyone was caught swindling using Spiritualism, fortunetelling, or the like, the only way they could be prosecuted was under the old Witchcraft Act. This seemed rather silly in the middle of the twentieth century, so the Witchcraft Act was repealed and it was replaced by the Fraudulent Mediums Act.

The Fraudulent Mediums Act, 22nd June, 1951

An Act to repeal the Witchcraft Act, 1735, and to make, in substitution for certain provisions of section four of the Vagrancy Act, 1824, express provision for the punishment of persons who fraudulently purport to act as spiritualistic mediums or to exercise powers of telepathy, clairvoyance or similar powers.

Be it enacted by the King's most Excellent Majesty, by and with the advice and consent of the Lords Spiritual and Temporal, and Commons, in this present Parliament assembled, and by the authority of the same, as follows:

I. (1) Subject to the provisions of this section, any person who:

(a) with intent to deceive purports to act as a spiritualistic medium or to exercise any powers of telepathy, clairvoyance or other similar powers, or,

(b) in purporting to act as spiritualistic medium or to exercise such powers as aforesaid, uses any fraudulent device, shall be guilty of an offence.

(2) A person shall not be convicted of an offence under the foregoing subsection unless it is proved that he acted for reward; and for the purpose of this section a person shall be deemed to act for reward if any money is paid, or other valuable item given, in respect of what he does, whether to him or to any other person.

(3) A person guilty of an offence under this section shall be liable on summary conviction to a fine not exceeding fifty pounds or to imprisonment for a term not exceeding four months or to both such fine and such imprisonment, or on conviction on indictment to a fine not exceeding five hundred pounds or to imprisonment for a term not exceeding two years or to both such fine and such imprisonment.

(4) No proceedings for an offence under this section shall be brought in England or Wales except by or with the consent of the Director of Public Prosecutions.

(5) Nothing in subsection (1) of this section shall apply to anything done solely for the purpose of entertainment.

II. The following enactments are hereby repealed, that is to say:

(a) the Witchcraft Act, 1735, so far as still in force, and

(b) section four of the Vagrancy Act, 1824, so far as it extends to persons purporting to act as spiritualistic mediums or to exercise any powers of telepathy, clairvoyance or other similar powers, or to persons who, purporting so to act or to exercise such powers, use fraudulent devices.

III. (1) This Act may be cited as the Fraudulent Mediums Act, 1951.

(2) This Act shall not extend to Northern Ireland.

The Constitution of the United States of America doesn't contain anything similar to the British Fraudulent Mediums Act. There are various state and local laws, however, which do cover the legality of so-called fortunetelling and mediumship. The present-day legal position of mediums varies from state to state, and many mediums go under the protective shell of ordination; adopting the religious title of "Reverend," since there is no equivalent to the British Fraudulent Mediums Act in the United States. The National Spiritualist Association of Churches is one legal protective organization, offering legal ordination of mediums.

Spiritualist Fraud

Spiritualist mediumship is easy to fake. But just because it is easy to fake doesn't mean that all mediums are fraudulent. Far from it! Yet this is a conclusion to which many seem all too ready to jump. Professional conjurers especially seem to make this elementary mistake. They see, or hear of, a medium levitating a table (for example) and just because stage magicians know how they could fake such a thing, they immediately assume that that must be the only way to do it, and therefore that the medium also must be faking it!

It would be possible to place a home-movie projector in a cabinet and rear-project film onto a screen so that the whole thing outwardly looked like a working television set. Yet what you actually would have is far from being a television set; it would be working in a totally different way. This is a good analogy for the workings of a conjurer, or a fake medium, compared to a true medium. The end product may seem the same but it really isn't at all alike; the mechanics are completely different. Yet, as I have said, the conjurer invariably assumes that his way of doing things must be the only way.

But having said that, I would be the first to admit that there are fraudulent mediums . . . just as there are fraudulent cops, fraudulent bank managers, fraudulent salespeople, and frauds in all walks of life. Yes, there is a very high percentage of fraud in psychism and Spiritualism. Why is this? It's because mediumship is a very easy thing to fake. And it's also because there are many, many people who are grieving over the death of a loved one and are therefore in an extremely vulnerable position when it comes to the possibility of communicating with that lost spirit. Fake mediums who take advantage of such bereaved people are probably the most contemptible swindlers of all.

In his book *The Psychic Mafia*, Lamar Keene, a repentant, formerly fraudulent medium/minister, describes how he rose to fame and, especially, fortune. He was operating a Spiritualist church where all the mediumship was of the fraudulent variety. Keene and a fellow conspirator kept a complete filing system on all the regular members of their congregation, plus others who came sporadically. All the details concerning these people, their lives, and the lives of those near and dear to them, who had died, were carefully filed and cross-indexed. The purpose, of course, was so that these facts could be presented by the "medium" minister at opportune moments to impress the recipient.

Tricks Of the Trade: Billets

One of the most popular forms of spiritual reading done in the church setting is using billets. The premise is that by the sitter writing the name(s) of the deceased on the paper and/or asking a question, it is easier for the medium to make contact with the spirit on the second level. In a manner similar to psychometry, the billet makes the connecting link. In reality, of course, it can also provide a fake "medium" with a certain amount of information to start off with—if he or she can somehow get to read it.

The sitter writes on the billet, signs it, and it is then either folded up a couple of times or it is placed, unfolded, into an envelope and sealed. A basket is passed through the congregation and the billets are dropped in. This basket is then taken up to the front of the church and placed beside the medium. There are now several ways for him or her to handle the billets. It might simply be by holding the folded paper in the hand, or between both hands, concentrating on it, and then starting to speak. Or the operator may lay the paper on an open Bible. One effective way I have seen is for the "medium" to take up the billet, hold it for a moment, and then to light it from a burning candle nearby and drop the burning paper into a receptacle. While it's burning, the medium identifies the writer and goes into making contact with the spirit(s). This is, as I say, very effective, from the sitter's point of view, for how could the billet possibly be read when it has just been destroyed? The answer is that it was not actually destroyed—or not the whole thing!

Sometimes—and especially if this type of cheating is to be done—the pads of paper given out for billets are made up of sheets with nice little decorations, or Biblical quotations, printed around all four edges. Consequently the sitter is forced to write his or her name or question in the center section of the sheet. The instructions given are that the sheet should then be folded in half and in half again. Ostensibly this makes it impossible for anyone to be able to read what is written on it. When the "medium" picks the folded paper out of the basket, however, he holds it by the corner that is the center of the folds and surreptitiously tears off that section. The rest of the billet is quite visible in his fingers and looks as though it is still whole. It is this that is lit and dropped into the receptacle. Meanwhile the minister, with his hand below the level of the pulpit, has only to tuck his thumb into the palmed center piece, and it opens up so that he can read what is written there!

A billet switch and the one-ahead method is another way of doing things. The medium has a blank billet (let's call it A) palmed in his hand. He takes up a folded billet (B) from the pile and unobtrusively switches the two. He can then holds up the visible, and blank, billet (A) to his forehead, or wherever he likes, as though concentrating on it. Meanwhile he is looking down at his other hand, out of sight, which is flipping open the written billet (B) so that he can read it. At the end of the reading he openly drops the (blank) billet (A) into the receptacle and takes up the next one (C) from the basket. He can now use B in the same way he used the blank, switch them and read the new one (C) while holding up B, and so on. Outwardly he is picking up a billet from the basket, holding it up in plain sight while he "reads" it, then putting it down and doing the same with the next. This can be very effective.

Another method is used when the billet is placed, unfolded, in a sealed envelope. The envelope is simply laid down for a few moments on top of the Bible. But the Bible is a fake, being hollowed out with a light inside it. Unseen by the congregation—since the top of the pulpit or rostrum slopes backward—the light is switched on and the minister can read what is written, through the envelope.

Another variation on this, not requiring a fake Bible, is for the minister to wipe some lighter fluid over the face of the envelope. This will momentarily make it transparent, so that the billet can be read through it. The fluid will quickly evaporate so that even if the writer wants the billet envelope back, it will show no signs of tampering.

Tricks of the Trade: Materializations and Trumpets

In darkness many things are possible. Even with the usual low-wattage red bulb alight, it is not possible for sitters to detect accomplices who are dressed all in black. If the medium works from inside a cabinet, he or she may also be dressed in black and come out to help make things happen. It has been said that ectoplasm looks a little like gauze or chiffon. In many cases it *is* gauze or chiffon! In a totally dark séance—and most physical mediums call for total darkness, to facilitate materialization—it is easy for someone dressed all in black to slip on a simple covering of chiffon, or something similar, and be dimly seen by the sitters as a materialized spirit. The main problem, for the medium, is how to get the material into the séance room. Lamar Keene spoke of stuffing material into his undershorts! One female medium he talks about did it even more effectively. She was not in the least perturbed if investigators wanted to search her beforehand. In fact she welcomed it, for she had carefully folded a sheet of chiffon and packed it into a condom, which she then inserted in her vagina!

Some permanent séance rooms are set up with hidden doors, so that accomplices can slip into the room under cover of darkness and move objects, appear as materializations, whisper in people's ears, or whatever else is called for. Martha Lomax, a "medium," was a very large woman. At her séances three diminutive "spirits" would materialize and flit about the room, sometimes even climbing into the laps of the sitters. They were, in fact, Lomax's three small children, who entered through a trapdoor, under cover of the darkness, or even hid beneath her skirts.

Movement of the trumpet can similarly be accomplished by black-clad mediums and/or assistants. The trumpet usually has a band of luminous paint around its bell and mouthpiece, so that its movement can be seen by the sitters in the dim red light. Sometimes a trumpet will actually have secret extra length that can be pulled out of it to extend it beyond the luminous bands—without the sitters' knowledge, of course. This means that the medium can manipulate the trumpet from a distance and make it fly about the room and rise up to the ceiling. The trumpet is usually very light in weight. Another way to move it is for the medium to slip what normally looks like a pen out of his pocket. It is actually a telescoping rod, much like the pointers that can be purchased for lecturers to point at maps, etc. Extending the rod, the medium can then cause the lightweight trumpet to move, even while sitting some distance away from it.

To have voices come from the trumpet is simply to have the "medium," or accomplice in black, speak through it as it "hovers" close to the sitter.

Tricks of the Trade: Levitating Tables and Banging Tambourines

With the above it obviously behooves the sitter to be very wary at séances held in complete darkness (or with no more than a low-wattage red bulb alight). Happily, few of these types of séances are held these days. Most reputable mediums will operate in full light, or at most with only slightly dimmed lighting. Even in better lit rooms, however, it is possible for fraudulent mediums to operate. Take the levitating of a table, for example. After some tipping, and rotating up onto two or even one leg, it may well happen that the table finally lifts all four legs off the floor.

One way a fake medium can accomplish this is by having a short length of wood or metal attached to the forearm (one or both arms) and to slip this under the edge of the table at the same time that their hands are placed on the top surface of the table. In an emergency they can slip an ordinary dinner knife, or even a fork, into their sleeve to do the job; putting the handle under the watch strap is one way of holding it firmly. With this projection under the table—if it is a light one, such as a card table—it is easy to lift the table into the air. Everyone present would swear that there was no way it could be faked. Another way is to have a nail driven into the table top, with just the smallest amount of its head still projecting. By the "medium" slipping the ring she is wearing (such as a wedding band) under the head of the nail, as she places her hands on the table top, a purchase can be gained enough to give a lift to a lightweight table.

Sometimes a medium will sit inside the cabinet with tambourines, bells, and/or musical instruments on a small table beside her. She is tied into the chair, so that there is, apparently, no way she could even touch the things on the table. Yet when the curtain is drawn across, and she has gone into trance, the sitters hear the tambourine being banged, the bell rung and all the other sounds. At the end of the séance the medium is found still securely tied in the chair.

Fraudulent Table Tipping

Some of the fakers are simply good at getting out of, and back into, knotted rope. But others are sneakier. They will use a chair with an arm, or arms that can be detached. The sitters may tie the medium into the chair, and tie the knots as tightly as possible. But when the curtain is drawn across, all the medium has to do is press a button, or twist the arm, or in some way cause the upper arm of the chair to come free so that he or she can use the still-bound hand quite freely. At the end she simply slips the chair arm back to click into place, and the rope and knots remain untouched.

Gathering Information

If you should go to a séance, church meeting, or Spiritualist demonstration where you are asked to write out a question, and given a clipboard on which to write . . . beware! There are a variety of fake clipboards available through professional conjurers' supply houses that look absolutely like the genuine article. You can write on a piece of paper resting on the clipboard, then tear off the paper and keep it, yet the damage has been done; the clipboard itself now has a copy of what you wrote. The clipboard can then be taken backstage before the start of the sitting or demonstration and the accumulated information transferred to the medium. The fact that you have kept the piece of paper on which you wrote has no bearing on it. Usually the clipboard has a cleverly hidden sheet of carbon paper and second sheet of paper, to pick up all that is written. No matter how slim and normal the clipboard may look, it can be such a fake. Today you might encounter sophisticated electronic listening and video devices. Best, then, to guard against discussing your background and/or loss while standing around, or in line, before going into the service or demonstration!

But let me finish by emphasizing that today the vast majority of mediums are totally honest. And still the best way to judge is by the evidence they produce. Did anyone—anyone—know of the information forthcoming, ahead of time?

Such top-class mediums as John Edward, James Van Praagh, George Anderson, and others consistently produce material that is not even known to the sitter, but has to be checked out later to confirm it. Yes, there are frauds in all walks of life, but that doesn't mean that everyone is fraudulent.

In contrast to the deviousness exhibited by fake mediums, as detailed above, here is the Declaration of Principles under which true Spiritualists and mediums operate. It is included here thanks to the kind permission of the National Spiritualist Association of Churches at Lily Dale, New York.

Declaration of Principles

Adopted by the National Spiritualist Association.

1. **We believe in Infinite Intelligence.**

   By this we express our belief in a Supreme Impersonal Power everywhere present, manifesting as life through all forms of organized matter called by some God, by others Spirit, and by Spiritualists, Infinite Intelligence. Though this power is impersonal, our understanding can only be gained by our personal perception of this creative force.

2. **We believe that the phenomena of Nature, both physical and spiritual, are the expression of Infinite Intelligence.**

   In this matter we express our belief in the immanence of Spirit and that all forms of life are manifestations of Spirit or Infinite Intelligence, and thus, all of humanity are children of God.

3. **We affirm that a correct understanding of such expression and living in accordance therewith constitute true religion.**

   A correct understanding of the Laws of Nature, on the physical, mental and spiritual planes of life, and living in accordance therewith, will unfold the highest aspirations and attributes of the Soul, which is the correct function of true Religion.

4. **We affirm that the existence and personal identity of the individual continue after the change called death.**

   "Life here and hereafter is all one life whose continuity of consciousness is unbroken by the mere change in form whose process we call death." *(Lilian Whiting)*

5. **We affirm that communication with the so-called dead is a fact, scientifically proven by the phenomena of Spiritualism.**

   Spirit communication has been in evidence in all ages of the world and is amply recorded in both sacred and profane literature of all ages. Orthodoxy has accepted these manifestations and has interpreted them in dogma and creed in terms of the supernatural. Spiritualism accepts and recognizes them in the understanding and light of Natural Law.

6. **We believe that the highest morality is contained in the Golden Rule: "Whatsoever ye would that others should do unto you, do ye also unto them."**

   This precept we believe to be true. It points the way to harmony, peace and happiness. Wherever tried, it has proven successful, and when fully understood and practiced, will bring peace and happiness to all of humanity.

7. **We affirm the moral responsibility of individuals, and that we make our own happiness or unhappiness as we obey or disobey Nature's physical and spiritual laws.**

   Individuals are responsible for the welfare of the world in which we live, for its welfare or its misery, for its happiness or unhappiness. If we are to obtain Heaven on Earth, we must learn to make that Heaven for ourselves and for others. Individuals are responsible for their own spiritual growth and welfare. Errors and wrong-doing must be outgrown and overcome. Virtue and love of good must take their place. Spiritual growth and advancement must be attained by aspiration and personal striving. Vicarious atonement has no place in the philosophy of Spiritualism. Each one must carry their own load in the overcoming of wrong-doing and replacing it with the right.

8. **We affirm that the doorway to reformation is never closed against any soul, here or hereafter.**

   We discard entirely the terribly wrong and illogical teachings of eternal damnation, and in place thereof we accept and present for consideration of thinking people the thought of the continuity of life beyond the change called death.

   It is a natural life. The opportunities for growth and progress toward more spiritual conditions are open to all, as they are here on the Earth Plane. We accept no such teaching as a damnation. We do teach that wrong-doing will necessarily bring remorse and suffering that will be difficult to describe in words and that can only be relieved by the individual's own efforts, if not here then in the hereafter. If we make our lives better while here, and that of our neighbors happier, we shall unfold that happiness, or Heaven on Earth, which we shall carry with us into the Spirit World.

9. **We affirm that the precepts of Prophecy and Healing are Divine attributes proven through Mediumship.**

   We thus affirm our belief in and acceptance of the truths of prophecy and healing. Being associated with the spiritual aspects of humanity, we assert that the practice or the two are not unique nor of recent occurrence alone, but that they are universal and everlasting, and have been witnessed and observed in all ages of the world.

Definitions

1. Spiritualism is the Science, Philosophy and Religion of a continuous life, based upon the demonstrated fact of communication, by means of Mediumship, with those who live in the Spirit World.

2. A Spiritualist is one who believes, as the basis of his or her religion, in the communication between this and the Spirit World by means of Mediumship and who endeavors to mould his or her character and conduct in accordance with the highest teaching derived from such communication.

3. A Medium is one whose organism is sensitive to vibrations from the Spirit World and through whose instrumentality intelligence in that world are able to convey messages and produce the phenomena of Spiritualism.

4. A Spiritualist Healer is one who, either through one's own inherent powers or through Mediumship, is able to impart vital, curative force to pathologic conditions.

5. The Phenomena of Spiritualism consists of Prophecy, Clairvoyance, Clairaudience, Gift of Tongues, Laying on of Hands, Healing, Visions, Trance, Apports, Levitation, Raps, Automatic and Independent Writings and Paintings, Voice, Materialization, Photography, Psychometry, and any other manifestation proving the continuity of life as demonstrated through the Physical and Spiritual senses and faculties of man.

Social Policy Statements of the National Spiritualist Association of Churches

(Included here thanks to the kind permission of The N.S.A.C. at Lily Dale, New York.)

The following Social Policy Statements are published to the world, not to bind the conscience of any individual, but to address the social conditions of society and the world to express the majority consensus of the delegation as adopted at the National Spiritualist Association of Churches one hundredth Annual Convention in St. Louis, Missouri, October 1992. As far back as 1900, many of these statements were adopted as resolutions at previous delegate convention of the NSAC.

Therefore, the NSAC:

Religion

Demands freedom of religious thought and expression as the cornerstone of all lasting good in the world.

Discrimination

Promotes and provides an environment free of all discrimination based on race, color, sex, national origin, disability, age, or sexual orientation. (Adopted October 2001)

Ministry

Affirms that our Ministry has the right, honor, and privilege to perform all life celebrations. (Adopted October 2000)

Equal Rights

Recognizes the purifying and uplifting power of woman in both public and private life. We demand for her all the privileges political, social and industrial that are accorded her brother man.

War

Abhors war in any form and supports every effort by any nation or group to maintain peace in the world. We do support our nation's young men and women who serve in the armed forces but do not support war itself as a method of resolving disputes and differences. Wars at any stage of human progress are brutal and morally injurious to the welfare of society, and all international disputes should be settled by board of arbitration, thus ushering in the era of universal peace on earth, good will to all.

Justice
Stands shoulder to shoulder with those who are opposing grafters, high and low, and works to secure justice for the oppressed of the earth; we condemn child labor, the sweat shop and industrial oppression and the practical and political disenfranchisement of all. We will work ceaselessly to make this nation in reality a government of the people, by the people and for the people.

Capital Punishment
Considers it a disservice to humanity to support capital punishment. Crime is but the result of ignorance and a diseased mentality and capital punishment is a relic of a partially civilized age. Knowing of the continuation of life after so-called death and that the individual carries with them the same type of mentality that was expressed before leaving the physical world, we know that minds of different thought exist on the Earth Plane and can be influenced by this mentality, thus the crime can be compounded. We support reform measure in the penal system and humane treatment of inmates. Through treatment and education, the criminal is given the opportunity to reform. We heartily commend those states and nations that have abolished the practice.

Life and Death with Dignity
Affirms the right of each individual to determine for self, or through a guardian, the extent through which the medical community or family may interfere with the treatment or a terminal, or irreversible condition, by the use of Living Wills, Advanced Directives, and Durable Powers of Attorney, available in all states in various form. We, as Spiritualists, are bound to follow the law. If we, as individuals, would have the current laws changed or extended beyond their present scope, it is our individual right to work for this through the proper channels.

Medicine and Spiritual Healing
Recommends that all medical cases pronounced incurable or terminal by medical doctors to be submitted to one or more spiritual healers.

Parenthood
Advocates planned parenthood and the widest dissemination of sex and hygiene knowledge to the end that poverty and social diseases may be eliminated.

Abortion: Informed Choice
Stands on the premise that the individual is responsible for her own happiness regarding abortion. It is not the prerogative of organized religion to mandate what constitutes happiness to an individual. It is the individual's right to make an informed choice in the matter as she alone would be responsible for her actions. This statement does not say we are pro-choice; it states we are in favor of informed choice.

Legitimacy of Birth
Denounces the cruel and heartless custom of designating any of God's children as illegitimate because of the circumstances of their birth.

World Peace
Recommends the interchange of students between colleges and schools of the nations of the world to the end that foolish, local prejudices be broken down by simple expedient of young people living and learning together as citizens of the world.

APPENDIX B

Answers to Examination Questions

Lesson One

1. Examples of mediumship and channeling can be found as far back as human history stretches. The Paleolithic cave paintings that show hunting and fertility rituals indicate that a human played the part of the God of Hunting, or the Goddess of Fertility, for those magical rituals. In so doing, the individual almost certainly (consciously or unconsciously) channeled the words and directions of the deities.

2. Mozart heard music in his head and then wrote it down exactly as he heard it. He did not consciously "compose." By doing this, he was channeling the material; acting as a medium to bring it to this consciousness.

3. Throughout the Bible there are references to the use of mediumistic gifts. For example, in 1 Corinthians 12:8-10 it says: "For to one is given, by the Spirit, the word of wisdom; to another the word of knowledge by the same Spirit; to another faith by the same spirit; to another the gifts of healing by the same Spirit; to another the working of miracles; to another prophecy; to another discerning of spirits; to another divers kinds of tongues; to another the interpretation of tongues." Also 1 Corinthians 14:31: "For ye may all prophesy one by one, that all may learn, and all may be comforted." There are numerous other examples, throughout the Bible, showing the use of mediumship through dreams, augury, and the like.

4. Possession takes place without the permission of the person involved. Usually the entire body is taken over by the possessing entity, which usually represents negative energy. But in certain types of mediumship, the individual allows the positive energy of a departed spirit to make use of his or her hand, arm, vocal cords, or similar, without giving up complete control.

5. No. As mentioned in the previous question, the medium allows the visiting spirit to use certain faculties without surrendering complete control.

Lesson Two

1. No. They believe that there is just one place to which everyone goes. It is sometimes referred to as the "Summerland."

2. From the reports of people who have had near death experiences and from the spirits of the dead who speak through mediums, at séances.

3. It seems highly unlikely that there is any immediate confrontation with any infinite intelligence.

4. No. On death we are able to assume the guise we most favor. This may be as we remember ourselves when young or at any other time. For purposes of recognition, at a séance, however, the deceased assumes the guise best remembered by the sitter(s).

5. In dreaming we are on the astral plane, which may be linked to the afterlife in that we are there able to meet, and speak, with those who have died. It is possible that our astral body is, in fact, our spirit or soul.

6. Not at all. In fact death may bring release from pain experienced up until that time.

7. Generally speaking, the dead have no more knowledge of future events than have the living, though there are individual instances when some spirits seem to have knowledge of some future possibilities. But on the whole, there is no "all-knowing" that comes with death.

8. They both believe themselves to be right, if these were the deeply held beliefs they had in life. It will take time, in the afterlife, to learn the truth so that there is no sudden shock on learning that your life-long beliefs were incorrect.

9. Yes, there are all things, for all things—animal, vegetable, and mineral—possess spirits.

10. Although the silver cord is infinitely elastic for astral travel in life, at death the cord will separate from the body so that there is no return of the spirit to the deceased physical form.

Lesson Three

1. Spiritualism was founded in Hydesville, Wayne County, New York, in 1848, at the home of the Fox family: John and Margaret and two of their daughters, Catharine (Kate) and Margaretta.

2. By making knocking or "rapping" sounds on the walls. Initially it made two raps for "Yes" and one rap for "No." Raps were also used to indicate numbers, such as dates and ages. Later, long messages were rapped out by one of the girls calling out the letters of the alphabet and waiting for a rap at the indicated letter. This, of course, necessitated the girl having to go through the alphabet repeatedly, which could prove very tiring.

3. On the same day that the initial contact was made in Hydesville, the "Poughkeepsie Seer," Andrew Jackson Davis, then in New York City, heard a voice he described as "tender and strong" that told him "Brother, the good work has begun—behold a living demonstration is born."

4. Horace Greeley, editor of the *New York Tribune.* He worked with Fenimore Cooper, George Bancroft, and two poets, then wrote an article attesting to the validity of the Fox sisters' phenomena.

5. Catherine, or Kate, worked with Charles F. Livermore, bringing him a long series of messages from his deceased wife Estelle. Estelle even managed to materialize on occasions and to send notes in her own handwriting, which was recognized by Livermore. Kate worked with the banker exclusively for five years.

6. Leah tried to have Kate separated from her children because of the mother's drinking problems. Margaretta also had a problem with alcoholism and swore to avenge herself and her sister Kate on Leah. She did so by going before a panel, in front of a very large audience in New York City, in October 1888, and stating that all the Spiritualist phenomena had been produced fraudulently by the sisters. Kate, although not active in the denunciation, appeared to back Margaretta. Approximately a year later, Margaretta made a retraction, indicating that she had been having financial problems and that persons and groups with vested interests had paid her to make the accusations.

7. He did so under hypnosis, first with a man named Levingston and then with a Dr. Lyon. By the time he was twenty-one, however, Davis was able to work without a hypnotist, putting himself into a light trance. Later still he progressed to doing inspirational writing, without going into any sort of trance.

8. Jackson had very little schooling and in his normal, waking state had no knowledge of anything other than his native language. In the course of dictating his books under hypnosis, however, he displayed an amazing facility for the Hebrew language and for historical and Biblical archaeology.

9. There were knockings that came from the wall, heard distinctly by the attending physician, Dr. Mellen.

10. M. Cahagnet, who did mesmerism.

Lesson Four

1. There were many other mediums but, before the Fox sisters, none had displayed the courage to stand up and speak publicly about their gift. The Fox sisters showed that such gifts were not unnatural nor anything to be ashamed of. Those who were still apprehensive about reactions, practiced quietly at home, for family and close friends.

2. The craze was for table tipping, which occurs at a séance, with sitters around a table and with their hands resting lightly on the top, causing the table to tip up on two legs then drop down again, to give answers to questions. When the craze reached England, it was taken seriously enough that prominent scientists examined the phenomenon and tried to explain it in their own terms.

3. Daniel Dunglas Home exhibited levitation at Ashley House, Victoria Street, London,

when he floated out of one window and into another, seventy feet above the ground. He was able to produce a large number of phenomena, including causing apparitions to appear and demonstrating telekinetic (TK or PK) abilities.

4. Lees was a thirteen-year-old boy living in Leicester, England, who began to receive messages from Prince Albert shortly after the prince's death (in December 1861). After being tested, he was taken to Queen Victoria, who was greatly impressed by the fact that he was able to tell her things known only to herself and the prince.

5. The Society for Psychical Research. It's first president (Professor Henry Sidgwick) stated, in his first presidential address, that in the enlightened age of the times it was scandalous that the phenomena of Spiritualism—with its many competent witnesses—was in dispute as to its reality and acceptance. He described it as being of scientific importance and urged full and proper investigation and research, which the society planned to undertake.

6. In the early days of Spiritualism, in England, mediums could be charged with fraud, which was done under the Witchcraft Act of 1735. In 1951 this Act was repealed and replaced with the Fraudulent Mediums Act, which stated that mediumship was legal so long as it was not done "with intent to deceive" or using "any fraudulent device."

7. Mrs. Leonore E. Piper (1859–1950) was the medium and she was subjected to stringent testing for decades. She was never once found to be fraudulent.

8. Abraham Lincoln attended séances in both Washington D.C. and New York. He was very interested in Spiritualism. Nettie Colburn (later Mrs. Maynard) was in her late teens when, in trance, she lectured the president on the need for emancipation of the slaves. She did so on more than one occasion, emerging from trance with no recollection of what she had said.

9. By the end of the nineteenth century many Spiritualist groups had formed themselves into churches, connecting the mediumistic activities with Christianity. The Roman Catholic Church labeled such phenomena as the work of their devil. The Anglicans were somewhat more tolerant, though stopped short of promoting the activity.

10. Rivail changed his name to Allan Kardec. He became the father of what he termed "spiritism," which flourished (and still flourishes) in both his native France and in South America.

Lesson Five

1. There is no set number. Most people have at least one, though not all; some do not have any and others have several of them. It is not connected with the Fox sisters' contact with a spirit but is a belief that is found throughout the ages. The ancient Greeks, Romans, Egyptians, Chinese, and many others held this belief, in one way or another.

2. This is the guardian who works most closely with the medium, acting as a filter for those spirits trying to gain access to the medium.

3. This is because the guide or guardian does not "control" the medium. The guide will suggest what is in the medium's best interests, but will not force the issue in any way.

4. No, not all. Many—probably the vast majority—do have their own individual doorkeepers, but there are mediums who seem to operate without one.

5. His or her purpose is to "filter" the spirits trying to come through to the medium. He or she will ensure that no more than one at a time tries to come through, that they are all positive, nonthreatening spirits, and that they have good reason for wanting to make contact.

Lesson Six

1. Ask yourself such questions as "Do I really want to be a medium and, if so, why?" Are you really serious about it? There needs to be more than just a feeling that "This would be cool!" or "Let's just see if it really works." You should have a very real empathy with those trying to make contact with deceased love ones, and there should be a strong motivation to explore the world beyond death. Do you want to become a medium just to work with family and friends, who are close to you? Or do you want to become well enough practiced at it to use your gifts to help large numbers of people, most of whom will be strangers to you? Either one of those is sufficient reason, but it may help to see an ultimate goal.

2. It certainly is not "wrong." Many mediums of the past have achieved both fame and fortune; though many of them without seeking it. If that is your main reason for becoming a medium, however, you may well find that it influences (negatively) the success you have at mediumship, in that you may lose spiritual focus. (At the same time, it must be conceded that through becoming famous as a medium you would be in a better position to help more people. It can be a two-edged sword.) British medium Ivy Northage said, "The less of me, the more of spirit, the better medium I become."

3. There are too many distractions today. In the past there were large numbers of development circles—families and friends working together to develop in this field. Today, with television and computers, movies, plus huge numbers of sports activities, ready transportation for travel, and similar things, people just don't spend the time they used to on activities such as psychic development.

4. With practice it becomes easier but initially it can be very difficult. It requires a "sender" and a "receiver" together with a "bridge" (the medium) between the two. Both sides need to be trying to make contact at the same time. From the other side there are many problems of attunement to the medium, then there are problems of reception (due to what might be termed "atmospherics"), and also the interpretation of what is being sent.

5. The reason is frequently that the medium tries to interpret what comes through to him or her, rather than simply relaying it and leaving the interpretation up to the receiver. It is very easy for a medium to put a wrong interpretation on some word or action received from the spirit world and, in doing so, to seem not to have made contact with the spirit who actually is there.

6. The reason is that the medium must surrender use of some part or parts of his or her body, be it vocal cords, arm and hand muscles (for automatic writing), or whatever. For the spirit to assume these and operate them deftly can take time. There is usually a period of familiarization before good strong messages start to come through.

7. It is the very triviality that provides the proof that the message comes from who it is claimed to be. Seemingly minor, trivial pieces of information are generally the best ones in that they are known only to the sender and receiver, and could not be discovered or guessed at by a third party. Therefore, a spirit referring to the general terrors of World War II (for example) would not carry the same weight as reference to having once owned a small black dog known as Midnight. The latter may seem trivial to an observer but is definite proof of survival to the recipient of the message.

8. (a) the key to success. (b) a celebration; frequently a wedding. (c) a birth, whether of a child, an idea, or a movement. These and other symbols are often used in spirit communication to get an idea across in the simplest terms. These and others are known as universal symbols and are recognized by most mediums. Many mediums also develop their own personal symbols that work as a sort of shorthand for them in communication. There is a parallel with the universal symbolism and personal symbolism found in dream interpretation.

9. Probably by supplying an image of a blacksmith working at a forge. It is difficult to get names across so, when the name is one that can be shown in some way, that is often what the spirit resorts to.

10. Although most people have the potential to become mediums, there are no guarantees. The key is practice—the more you try; the better chance you have of developing. As to becoming a direct voice medium, specifically, again there is no guarantee. Some people seem more suited to one form of mediumship than another, as in so many things. Some are especially talented at direct voice, some at clairvoyance, some at physical mediumship. Try them all and practice assiduously.

Lesson Seven

1. The talking board known as the Ouija was first commercially produced in 1892, by William Fuld's company, in Boston. The idea behind the board, however,—and a wide number of variations of design—has been around for centuries. It was known in ancient Greece, Rome, and in China as early as 600 B.C.E.

2. No. Although the majority of sales are for the purposes of fun and light entertainment, the board is a serious tool for spirit communication, when used properly. In a court case in 1920 the then-makers of the board, the Baltimore Talking Board Company, tried to get out of paying sales tax by claiming that it was "a form of amateur mediumship and not a game or sport." Although one judge agreed with them, the majority ruled that most boards were sold for "social amusement" and so the company lost the case. The reviewing board , however, did say that, "The court knows in a general way that the Ouija board is seriously used by some persons in the belief that it affords mysterious spirit communication."

3. As many as can comfortably fit around it. The instructions issued with the commercial board suggest just two people, with the board balanced between them, on their knees. In fact the board can be placed on a table and many people can sit around it, each with a fingertip resting on the planchette. Probably the best, most manageable number, however, is six.

4. No more so than, for example, the telephone. It is purely an instrument of communication. What comes through the board is dependent upon the sender and, to an extent, the receiver(s). In itself, the board is not evil.

5. Because of having a central window in addition to being shaped like a pointer, there is a tendency for the spirits to get confused and indicate the letters with either one of these. It often becomes necessary, therefore, to keep a record of two sets of letters. To overcome this defect, the "window" should be covered over so that all indications of letters depend upon the pointed end of the planchette alone.

6. It is the unconscious use of the muscle-power of the sitters that moves the planchette. The messages then come from the spirit intelligence that then *directs* the planchette to the specific letters.

7. That would defeat the whole object. It is the spirit communicating that directs the planchette to point to the individual letters. To attempt to push the planchette to a consciously chosen letter would not relay the spirit's true intentions.

8. It is receipt of a message by two (or more) separate teams working with talking boards, in different places and at different times. The intended message would be delivered/received in two (or more) parts; one part given to each team. A separate monitor would review the results of both teams' séances and try to recognize the complete message, putting the pieces together. Such cross-correspondences underscore the fact that the people using the boards are not in any way controlling the messages that come through. So long as no one—including the monitor—knows what is to come, the message cannot be credited to the use of ESP.

9. A pencil planchette has a pencil, or pen, pushed through a hole in the surface so that the pencil point acts as one of the legs. If used on a large sheet of paper, as the plachette moves around, the pencil will leave a mark, which invariably develops into writing. This is known as automatic writing. The message is therefore written out, rather than being conveyed by pointing to a series of letters. The handwriting can vary with different spirits communicating.

10. No, not always. Listen to the advice but take it only if it seems right for you. Just because the advice is coming from a spirit does not make it infallible. Be very cautious of any tendencies by a sprit to control your thoughts and actions. If you get too many negative messages, stop using the board.

Lesson Eight

1. You should do both. One of the necessities of automatic writing—at least when you first start doing it—is to separate your mind from what your hand might be writing. An excellent way to do this is to read a book while the spirit is making use of your hand and arm.

2. This is so that you will not influence what is being recorded. Even if you are trying not to "compose" the missive, unconsciously you might be directing what is written. It is therefore best to completely disassociate yourself from what is taking place.

3. (a) Moses (1839–1892) was one of the most famous physical mediums, who produced a great deal of automatic writing from 1872 through until 1883. These scripts were published under the title *Spirit Teachings* (London, 1883). A former skeptic of Spiritualism,

Moses later demonstrated levitation and produced apports. (b) Stead (1849–1912) was a British journalist who also produced a quantity of automatic writing. He was unusual in that he started receiving messages from living friends, as well as from dead ones. He had repeated dreams that seemed to be precognitive ones of the later sinking of the *Titanic.* Stead himself died in the *Titanic* disaster, twenty-six years after having received the dreams. (c) Patience Worth was the name of the spirit channeled by Pearl Curran, from 1913 until the late 1920s. Altogether two thousand five hundred poems were produced along with short stories, plays, allegories, and six full-length novels.

4. Automatic writing is produced without the writer's knowledge of what is being written; the writer usually being engaged in some other activity at the same time that he or she is writing. Inspirational writing is done with the writer having full knowledge of the process but receiving the material in his or her head and putting it down on paper as it is received.

5. To directly type the material received, as inspirational writing, can be a big time-saver in that it does not then have to be transcribed. But the material can never be regarded as totally "pure" in that it may well be influenced by the unconscious—or the conscious—mind of the medium.

6. William Mumler, an engraver who lived in Boston, was the first to produce spirit photographs. In 1862 he was trying to take photographs of himself with a delayed exposure, moving into the picture after opening the lens. He found that a spirit had been captured in the pictures. He had not set out to get spirit photographs.

7. Ted Serios was a medium able to produce images on Polaroid film that were prints of anything he focused his mind on. He would concentrate, point the lens at his head, and click the shutter. Serios was thoroughly investigated and yet produced several hundred images that covered more than a hundred different themes.

8. Since we all have latent psychic and mediumistic powers, it is quite possible for anyone to produce spirit photographs. During a séance would probably be the best time. High speed film is recommended, such as 400 ASA or higher; the higher the better. To experiment photographing in darkness or near darkness, infrared film should be used.

9. Using strips or squares of photographic paper, enclosed in light-tight material, these can be held on or near the person, concentrated upon, held between the palms of the hands, held against the heart or the forehead, or in any other way brought within the aura of the experimenter. Sheets can be scattered around a darkened room during a séance, or passed among the sitters. A number of people can concentrate on one piece of photographic paper. Later processing of the paper should show some results.

10. There is no reason why a digital camera should not capture such an image. It has been done with security cameras, for example.

Lesson Nine

1. There are four levels, known as beta, alpha, theta, and delta. Beta is the normal, wide-awake level, with delta the deepest.

2. A medium is not always aware of being in trance since some trances are extremely light. For example, when doing such activities as psychometry, the medium may be in a light trance without being aware of it. Although some early mediums described trance as a painful experience, today's mediums do not do so. It's not necessary to go into trance for all forms of Spiritualist mediumship. Many mediums never go into trance. Trance seems to be more necessary in cases of physical phenomena.

3. Going into trance is a feeling of freedom; of leaving the earthly restrictions on the physical body. Many mediums have found it useful to have someone hypnotize them for their first experiences of trance (Andrew Jackson Davis started this way).

4. Hypnotism can be used to initially bring about a trance state that can be used for Spiritualistic purposes. The advantage is that the hypnotist can verify the medium's progress as he or she is taken down into the deeper trance levels. Suggestions can then be given that will allow the medium to use self-hypnosis in the future. Hypnotic trance differs from pure mediumistic trance in that there has to be the third party present (medium, spirit, and hypnotist), while in the usual mediumistic trance the connection is purely between the medium and the spirit.

5. The first rule is that the medium's health should be good. This is generally dependent upon a good diet, breathing, and exercise. Secondly, when entering trance the medium should keep the conscious mind alert, keeping his or her awareness of identity and of the ability to return to consciousness whenever desired. Lastly, the medium should repeatedly assure him or herself of the presence of the guide (or guardian angel) and the spirits on level two who are there to help and assist in all possible ways.

Lesson Ten

1. Clairvoyance means "clear seeing." Clairaudience is "clear hearing." Clairsentience is "clear sensing."

2. Not necessarily. Mediums adept at clairvoyance are not necessarily good at clairaudience, hence may only see and not hear. In this case they have to rely on signs, symbols, and gestures made by the spirits.

3. By researching to find the truth, the actuality, of what is presented. Many times this means digging far back into the past to find verification.

4. Probably the medium—or, more correctly, the spirit. Although the sitter may have no knowledge of such a figure in the family tree, not everyone and everything is generally known without researching the family background. Just such a figure, on horseback and in military uniform, may well turn up in an old family photograph album. Sitters should not be too quick to disclaim what is presented.

5. Concentration is probably the most important element of clairvoyant development—the ability to concentrate on one thing for a period of time, to the exclusion of all else, in order to get all the details of the object or person.

6. A cardboard mailing tube (real or imaginary), a telephone, and a seashell, are all tools that can be used for development exercises.

7. No real significance in itself, but the sound can become the voice(s) of spirit(s). It is an excellent tool for developing clairaudience.

8. Hopefully not (a)! It is almost certainly an example of clairalience (or clairgustance), where a particular scent or odor associated with a spirit be-comes known to the medium and/or sitters at a séance.

9. Look for a ball with no bubbles, scratches, or other imperfections, so that there will be nothing to distract when gazing into it. The size of the ball is unimportant. Larger balls are generally more expensive but also more likely to have imperfections.

10. Give it a rest! If you gaze for too long—with or without results—your eyes will become tired and strained. Stop the scrying and try again another day.

Lesson Eleven

1. She is practicing psychometry; the art of attuning to the vibrations of the object held and, through them, being able to see the past as it relates to that object.

2. It is more commonly found in women. As many as one in four women have the ability while only one in ten men have it.

3. No. It is said that "spirit speaks first." In other words, the very first impression you get is invariably the correct one. Later impressions are more likely to be influenced by conscious or unconscious logic on the part of the medium.

4. By shaking hands with them or making personal contact in some way.

5. They may all be correct. Objects absorb information from many, if not all, stages of the owner's life. One medium may pick up from one period and another medium from a completely different period.

6. Yes, it can be a useful tool in spiritual mediumship. By aligning with the vibrations of an object, the medium can be helped to align with the vibrations of the object's owner, even if deceased. By virtue of the medium holding that object, he or she can invariably tune-in more easily to the spirit on the second level.

Lesson Twelve

1. Physical mediums produce direct voice, levitations, apports, rappings, the playing of musical instruments (without physical contact), movement of objects (again without contact), transfiguration, production of ectoplasm, and similar experiences. There was so much fraud associated with physical mediumship in the past that few such mediums were taken seriously and the class generally had a poor reputation. This led to a decline in any who might otherwise have proven adept at such phenomena.

2. Eusapia Paladino frequently resorted to fraud, if she thought she could get away with it due to the poor quality of investigation. But when studied by serious, well-qualified investigators, she produced a great deal of seemingly genuine phenomena and is rated as one of the best physical mediums ever.

3. They both had a background in stage magic and conjuring, which made them aware of how some of the fraudulent mediums operated.

4. It is a small area of a room usually formed by hanging a curtain diagonally across a corner. Often a small table is placed inside the cabinet, on which are musical instruments and other items that might be useful in a séance. Sometimes the medium will sit inside the cabinet but mostly he or she will sit outside, facing away from it.

5. A trumpet is a cone-shaped object, much like a megaphone, used for projecting the voice. It is generally of tin or aluminum but can be of any material. It is often painted with luminous paint; either entirely or in rings around the mouthpiece and the bell end. It will frequently seem to float about the room during a séance, amplifying the voice of a spirit so that the sitters can hear it. It is a good idea to always have one in the séance room, just in case it should be used.

6. Some physical mediums do seem to change their facial appearance when a spirit is speaking through them. This might be a very slight change or a substantial one. Some sitters can actually recognize the face of a deceased loved one when this happens.

7. This is known as ectoplasm. It is a white substance that exudes from various orifices of the medium, such as the mouth and nose. Although it seems insubstantial, it can be strong enough to lift trumpets and other objects, some of them quite heavy. It can also form into the shape of faces and even full figures. At the end of a séance the ectoplasm seems to return into the body of the medium.

8. It looks almost like flimsy cloth. It has been described as feeling like "chiffon cloth" and being icy cold. Fraudulent mediums have used such substances as cheesecloth and fine gauze to simulate it. Sometimes it is so fine that it appears almost like a fine mist. It is sensitive to light but can be photographed using infrared film.

9. This is an apport. It is usually something small, like a stone, flower, or piece of jewelry, but not necessarily so. A full human being—a very large lady—has been apported. So has a large sunflower, complete with soil-covered roots. Both animate and inanimate objects have been apported to séance rooms.

10. Some mediums claim to feel a "cobwebby" sensation, like very fine threads, when physical phenomena are about to manifest. This is nothing of which to be afraid. There is no harm that will come to the medium.

Lesson Thirteen

1. The weight of the table doesn't matter. Light tables are used a lot but very large, heavy tables have also been moved around as though there was no weight to them. It is, however, best to start with a light table such as a card table, to get used to table tipping. The table can be square, rectangular, octagonal, round, or any shape.

2. The sitters' hands should rest on the top surface of the table.

3. It is the combined muscular forces of the sitters that are utilized, in some way, to do the actual moving of the table. It is, however, the spirit communicating who directs the answers to the questions.

4. By a spokesperson asking questions. Those that can be answered "Yes" or "No" are easiest but whole messages can be spelled out by the table "counting out" the letters of the alphabet or by a spokesperson calling out the letters and the table thumping at the appropriate ones.

5. Many times a table will move about and even spin around so that it's impossible for the sitters to remain seated. Even though it seems to be best for the sitters to have fingers touching initially, it seems that as the séance progresses, the immediate contact can be broken.

Lesson Fourteen

1. It is the energies of the spirit world, operating through the medium, that bring about the healing, both physically and mentally. It is not the same thing as faith healing, since the person does not even have to believe in spiritual healing for it to work.

2. No. Healing can be done at a distance; even a very great distance—like, halfway around the world.

3. This was Edgar Cayce (1877–1945), who worked under self-hypnosis. Whenever he was about to consider a patient he would say, "Yes, we can see the body." From this it might be inferred that there was a spirit or spirits working through him.

4. Harry Edwards (1893–1976). During World War I, he was working in the Middle East, building a railroad, and healed many of the Arab workers when they injured themselves. It was not until the mid-1930s, however, that he became involved with Spiritualism and with Spiritualist healing per se.

5. Chapman channeled the healing energies and expertise of deceased surgeon and eminent eye specialist Dr. William Lang, though he did work for a while, initially, with a Cree Indian healer. Many witnesses who knew Dr. Lang recognized the mannerisms, stance, and even the face of the surgeon when Chapman became entranced and transfigured.

6. No, they are not. The instruments may be used by the spirit surgeon on the second level, but such tools are never handled and used by the medium channeling the healing.

7. Good health for him- or herself. To this end a good diet is one of the essentials, as are exercise and psychic development.

8. These are the chakras. There are seven of them. The power that passes through them is the kundalini power.

9. The etheric double is the first of the "layers of light" that expand outward from the physical body. It extends no more than a half inch and then becomes the inner aura, which is followed by the outer aura. From there, any further layers are invisible to the human eye. The etheric double can be seen with the naked eye by most people (with training and practice; though some see it immediately), and some can even see the next two layers. These auras can be useful in determining a person's health, mood, and general mental and physical condition, though care must be exercised in interpreting the colors observed.

10. Not immediately. It is better (and more prudent) to allow them time to consult with competent medical practitioners first. There can then be confirmation of what you have learned.

Lesson Fifteen

1. Spiritual mediumship relates to contact and messages between deceased persons and those family, friends, and loved ones they have left behind. The material is usually of a personal nature. A number of different spirits may come through. With channeling there is usually only one entity, who may or may not have previously lived on earth and

who is primarily concerned with delivering a message or a series of lectures aimed at a large audience. There is seldom, if ever, any personal give and take. While mediumship may involve a large number of different means to transmit messages, channeled material is more likely (though not exclusively) to be solely by direct voice or automatic writing.

2. A channeled entity may be from any one of a number of possible origins. Some few do claim to have once lived on this plane but as many—if not more—claim to be from other universes, other dimensions, to be group entities, or to be from such possible sources as long lost continents.

3. Most channelers seem to have become so accidentally. Several have started speaking as an entity during a meditation session.

4. Such warnings should be borne in mind but not instantly acted upon. Consider the source and its probable veracity. Just because an entity claims certain things doesn't necessarily make them so. Examine the full teachings received. Keep in mind the admonitions of Lazaris. Are the teachings giving you a sense that you are less than you are? Can you apply the advice? What is it going to do for you (and to you)? Is your life better thanks to the advice so far received? Does it all leave you thinking and feeling positive?

5. You probably can't be 100 percent positive. Although the majority of channelers do not consciously present material from their own unconscious minds, it's always possible that that is the true source and that it's "dressed up" as coming from a romantic-sounding entity. You have to judge by the material given to you and decide whether or not it will make a positive difference to your life. If it will, then it doesn't really matter what the true source might be.

Lesson Sixteen

1. A Home Circle is a group of people interested in bringing out their mediumistic talents, meeting together on a regular basis to support one another in developing those powers.

2. This is not the best way to run a Home Circle. Such a Circle should meet on a regular basis—the same day of the week (once a week), the same time of day, in the same house—and should keep to having the same people with no visitors allowed. In this way the members of the Circle grow to feel completely comfortable with one another, and it also allows the spirits to attune to them better.

3. The best size for a Circle is six to ten people, with twelve being the absolute maximum.

4. Start by going through the relaxation and breathing techniques, then do a little singing of something light and uplifting. If desired, a short prayer can be said, though this is optional. Then the members should take hands, in a circle, and ask for guidance of the spirits.

5. As many as show the ability. This will usually be only a small percentage of really good ones—perhaps two or three—though there's no reason why there shouldn't be more. But certainly most of the people will come to display a number of different psychic skills.

6. Not necessarily. They take it in turns. In the early stages of working more will be able to have some development time each week, but as the group progresses the concentration will come to be upon only one or two each session.

7. It is extremely important to record the sittings so that progress can be the better judged. Written records can and should be supplemented by tape recordings and video. But these last two can sometimes reveal things that weren't noticed during the actual sessions. Occasionally spirit voices may be heard when the tape is played back. It's even possible that spirit lights, or even actual figures, may show up on a video when it's later viewed.

8. You should never feel exhausted due to psychic work. You should feel refreshed. If you constantly feel drained then there's the possibility that someone, or more than one person, is drawing off your energy (almost certainly unconsciously). If this should be the case it would behoove you to join some other Home Circle.

9. So that the progress and development of everyone involved can be judged, as stated in Question 7 above. Sometimes it's hard to see that progress really is being made unless we are able to look back at earlier attempts. Additionally, sometimes what has been suggested in the past is not validated until much later.

10. This is a Home Development Circle that focuses more on the redirection of lost spirits than on the development of their own members. Some spirits do not realize that they have died and need direction to move them on in their journey. All Circles should be on the look-out for such confused spirits.

Lesson Seventeen

1. Phenomena have been in existence since the very beginning of electronic broadcasting and recording. In the late 1920s Thomas Alva Edison stated that " . . . if we can evolve an instrument so delicate as to be affected by our personality as it survives in the next life, such an instrument, when made available, ought to record something."

2. The wire recorder was used and, shortly after the war, developed into the tape recorder. It first used a paper-based magnetic tape but plastic tape was later developed.

3. Dr. Konstantin Raudive also received a recording of his mother speaking to him. He later developed the method of setting up his tape recorder, stating the date and time (for the record), and then simply asking questions or allowing the spirit to speak uninterrupted.

4. It is necessary to play back the recording at a high volume, since the spirit voices are very faint. It is also generally necessary to slow down the speed of the recording, since the messages are made at a higher rate of speed.

5. A laptop could be used by opening a new file in a word processing program, leaving the file blank, then closing the computer and placing it inside the séance circle. At the end of the circle there may be a message in that file. This is a modern equivalent of the spirit slates, where two slates are placed face to face, with a piece of chalk enclosed. They would be tied together and writing would be found on them at the end of the sitting.

Essay/Discussion Projects

For the serious student, it often helps to re-tain information by writing an essay on a particular subject. For a group, discussion is always enlightening. Both can provoke further thought and can also lead to research. Below are some suggested subjects for either essays or for discussion (I'm sure you can think of more). There are no right or wrong "answers" to these, of course, but it's hoped they will add to the usefulness of this book. Don't forget to use the bibliography.

The Beginnings of Spiritualism

Was the Hydesville episode an isolated happening that then grew out of all proportion, or could it be viewed as a necessary step in the gradual development of spirituality along humankind's path of progress? Look at the history of spirit contact and what forces might have led up to that Friday in March, 1848. Where did the Quakers and Shakers fit into the whole picture?

The Afterlife—the Spirit World

How can the varying reports of the life after death, given through mediums, be assimilated with those reports from people who have had near death experiences? Is there any correlation with the reported experiences of shamans?

Reincarnation

Some Spiritualists believe in reincarnation but others do not. Examine arguments for and against. Is there any compelling evidence for either side? What are the differences, if any, between Spiritualism and Spiritism? How did Spiritism evolve?

Healing

Examine some of the many ways of doing spiritual and psychic healing. How effective have these methods been (case studies)? Many medical doctors, and even some hospitals, are coming to understand the positive effects of these healing techniques. Examine this.

The Part of Prophecy in Spiritualism

What, if any, is the part of prophecy in Spiritualism? The Declaration of Principles of the National Spiritualist Association of Churches contains the following: "We affirm that the precepts of Prophecy and Healing are Divine attributes proven through Mediumship. We thus affirm our belief in and acceptance of the truths of prophecy and healing. Being associated with the spiritual aspects of humanity, we assert that the practice of the two are not unique nor of recent occurrence alone, but that they are universal and everlasting, and have been witnessed and observed in all ages of the world." Examine and comment on this.

GLOSSARY

Affirmations: positive statements—usually brief—that are regularly repeated, thereby establishing them in the subconscious mind and reinforcing the conscious mind.

Apport: a gift brought, by spirit, to a sitter at a séance. The word comes from the French *apporter,* "to bring." Weight and size seem not to matter; small items such as precious stones have been apported, as have large objects like blocks of ice and statuary. The objects seem to materialize out of thin air in the presence of physical mediums.

Astral plane: the spiritual dimension beyond the physical world. Nandor Fodor aligns it with the second level, or "the first sphere after bodily death." It is the plane visited during sleep. It is also the plane visited when astrally projecting, or having an out-of-body experience.

Automatic writing; drawing: writing, drawing, or painting produced by spirit, when the conscious mind is otherwise engaged. Spirit makes use of the muscles of the arm and hand of the subject, who may be reading a book, watching television, talking with a friend, or doing any one of a number of tasks and is unaware of the spirit work.

Billet: from the French word for a letter or note. In the Spiritualist sense it is a written note on a small piece of paper that is passed to a medium, for making contact with spirit. Billet reading is a form of psychometry.

Cabinet: a sectioned-off part of a séance room where the medium can consolidate the energy from the sitters. It may be a simple curtain across a corner of a room or it may be a large wooden construction. With physical mediums, many times ectoplasmic figures will emerge and return to the cabinet. The medium may or may not be inside the cabinet.

Chakra: a Sanskrit word meaning "wheel." The chakras are at seven points located in the human body. They are connected to each other and aligned with certain physical glands. The chakras are connected to the etheric or spiritual body. By "awakening" them, the kundalini power is raised, which generates psychic energy.

Channeling: acting as an intermediary to bring information directly from an entity in another dimension. In effect, mediumship is a form of channeling but the term is more generally applied to those who channel information from nonphysical beings, who may or may not have previously lived on this plane, rather than from the deceased spirits of family members.

Circle: the term given to a sitting, or séance, or to a development group, since the usual form is to sit in a circle of chairs. These may or may not be around a table.

Clairalience (also clairgustance)**:** literally "clear smelling." Many times a perfume, or the smell of a cigar, or similar, is recognized in a circle. To smell something of the spirit world is, then, known as clairalience.

Clairaudience: meaning "clear hearing," it is the ability to hear sounds, music, and voices from level two; from the world of spirit. These are not audible to normal ears but are picked up by mediums.

Clairgustance: another term for clairalience.

Clairhambience: to get a taste in the mouth, coming from spirit.

Clairsentience: meaning "clear sensing." Without actually "seeing" or "hearing," a medium can sense information being brought by spirit. It is a psychic perception of information, be it sounds, smells, names, dates, dress, etc.

Clairvoyance: meaning "clear seeing," it is the ability of a medium to see, in his or her mind's eye, spirits and to see scenes and other information being brought to sitters at a séance.

Control: a term sometimes applied to a spirit guide, or gatekeeper, though "control" is something of a misnomer since it does not actually control the medium. It may, however, control the order in which spirits come through to the medium.

Development circle: a group of like-minded people who wish to develop their mediumistic abilities. They usually meet on a regular schedule and work on various psychic development exercises. Also known as a home circle.

Doorkeeper: the main spirit of a medium, who acts as a screen for the medium at a séance, regulating which spirits are allowed to come through. Known variously as a gatekeeper, life guide, control, and similar.

Ectoplasm: from the Greek *ektos* and *plasma,* meaning "exteriorized substance." It is a white substance that may exude from various bodily orifices when a medium is in trance. This usually takes place in low light or darkness. The ectoplasm varies from a fine mist to a solid. It may form into the shape of spirits who are present or it may be used to move and lift objects, such as trumpets and tables. It is sensitive to light but may be photographed using infrared film.

Etherialization: this is an incomplete materialization (which see).

Guide: a spirit who watches over a living person. Each person may have any number of such guides; some being specific to such a specific task as healing. The guide may act as gatekeeper at a séance, arranging who should come through and when.

Infinite Intelligence: sometimes referred to as "Mother/Father God," this is a spiritualist term for the incomprehensible power of the universe.

Inspirational writing: writing from inspirational thoughts received from spirit rather than from conscious composition. While in automatic writing, the writing is actually done by spirit, utilizing a person's arm and hand, in inspirational writing the writing is consciously done by the person but the thoughts and words come from spirit. It might be equated to taking spirit dictation.

Karma: the word means "action" and is the law of return. There are various beliefs concerning it—found especially in Brahmanism, Buddhism, Hinduism, and Theosophy—one being that in each life one is rewarded for or pays for actions done in a previous life. Basically it is saying that as you sow, so do you reap. In Buddhism it is the cycle of cause and effect that may be played out over a series of lives.

Kundalini: the power, or life force, that is raised when the chakras are activated. This may be done consciously—at the start of meditation, for example. Kundalini is often referred to as "the sleeping serpent," since it is a powerful force that may be awakened.

Levitation: to raise up an object contrary to the known laws of gravity. It is a phenomenon of psychokinesis (pk). Examples of levitation are usually seen in the presence of physical mediums. Occasionally, table tipping can lead to the levitating of the table.

Manifestation: the appearance of a spirit, in visible form, usually at a séance. It may be in solid form or it may be transparent, as an apparition. A spontaneous manifestation can occur under various conditions and be regarded as a "ghost."

Materialization: the manifestation of a spirit (see above).

Medium: a person sensitive to the vibrations of level two; the spirit world. By adjusting his or her vibrations —consciously or unconsciously—a bridge is established between the two worlds, enabling spirit to communicate with those of this world. Mediumship is an ancient and universal practice, found throughout history in all parts of the world.

Mental phenomena: this includes clairvoyance, clairaudience, clairsentience, psychometry, scrying, billet reading, and various forms of healing such as auric and color. Mental mediumship is subjective.

Natural law: the principles of nature, which includes humankind along with all forms of life—animal, vegetable, and mineral. Understanding of the natural law determines our actions and reactions. It's possible to create our own realities by the choices we make.

Physical phenomena: these include levitation, ectoplasm, direct voice communication, apports, automatic writing, talking boards and planchettes, table tipping, trumpets, slate writing, manifestations, transfiguration, rappings and knockings. Physical mediumship is objective.

Planchette: a small platform used with a talking board—such as a Ouija board—or, with a pencil in it, used for automatic writing.

Platform: a stage from which mediums may deliver messages.

Possession: possession takes place when a spirit or entity takes over the body of another, without that person's permission. (It's not as common as some movies would have it believed.)

Precognition: to know ahead of time.

Psychic: to know information by sensing it; a person who obtains knowledge without having normal access to it, through extra sensory perception. All mediums are psychic though not all psychics are mediums.

Psychometry: from the Greek *psyche* ("soul") and *metron* ("measure"). This is the handling of an object and, from its vibrations, picking up information about its history: owner(s), origin, value, etc.

Rapping: knocking noises produced by spirit. The origins of Spiritualism date from the rappings made by the spirit of the murdered peddler, Charles B. Rosna, communicating with the Fox sisters in 1848.

Reading: the giving of information by a medium, or a psychic, to a sitter. It implies that the mind/vibrations of the sitter are being "read." A psychic may actually read a palm, tarot cards, runes, or other objects to focus his or her mind. A medium would "read" from the information provided by spirits.

Rescue circle: a group of sensitives sitting for the purpose of aiding and guiding spirits who are unaware that they have died or who, for whatever reason, seem unable to move on to the second level.

Retrocognition: knowledge of things from the past, by other than normal means.

Scrying (also skrying): using a reflective surface as a focal point for seeing the past, present, or future. Crystal balls are common objects for scrying but polished metals, ink blots, water, and any other reflective surfaces have been, and are, used by scryers around the world.

Séance: literally a "sitting." It is a sitting with a medium for the purpose of communicating with the spirits of the dead. Depending upon the type of medium (mental or physical) and the sorts of phenomena expected, the séance would be conducted in bright light, subdued light, or even complete darkness.

Silver cord: the spiritual "umbilical cord" that connects the astral body to the physical body. It is infinitely elastic, enabling an astral projector to travel any distance and yet remain in contact with, and return to, his or her human form. When a spirit materializes at a séance there is usually a "silver cord" (visible or not) of ectoplasm that connects the materialization to the medium.

Skotograph: a name given to some spirit-produced photographs, usually produced on raw photographic paper without the aid of a camera.

Slate: the same as the old school slates used for writing but in Spiritualism used in pairs, fastened together face to face, with a piece of chalk between them. Left out at a séance, spirit may produce writing on one or both of the slates.

Spirit: generally used in the sense of the essence of a person that moves on from the physical body to the ethereal; from level one to level two. It is the post-deceased aspect of a person that communicates with earthly people from the spirit world.

Spiritism; Spiritist: terms introduced and used by Allan Kardec in place of the words "Spiritualism" and "Spiritualist," for his representation of the beliefs and philosophies of the religion. These terms were used in Kardec's native France and are still used extensively in South America (especially Brazil) and the Philippines.

Spirit photography: the capturing of spirit forms in photographs, either accidentally or purposefully.

Spiritualism: the religion, science, and philosophy that teaches a belief in a continuous life, based upon communication with those who have progressed to the spirit world. Contact is made through the agencies of a medium. The main tenet of Spiritualism is what is termed the "Golden Rule."

Spiritualist: one who practices Spiritualism. A Spiritualist may or may not be a medium.

Synchronicity: simultaneously, or near simultaneously, happening events that appear to be coincidental and meaningful.

Talking board: a board, usually marked off with the letters of the alphabet, numbers, and short phrases, that is used for communicating with spirit. The sliding pointer of the board is known as a planchette and its movement is directed by spirit. The best-known commercially produced board is the Ouija board.

Third eye: also known as the "all-seeing eye," it is located in the position of the forehead, between the two eyebrows. This is also the position of the sixth chakra, at the pituitary gland. It is called the third eye because it is associated with psychic senses and spiritual enlightenment.

Trance: an altered state of consciousness where the brainwave activity moves to a certain level. There are basically four such levels: beta, alpha, theta, and delta. Beta is the normal, wide-awake level. Next level down is the alpha level (what might be termed a "light" trance). Below that is the theta, and deepest (equivalent of somnambulism in hypnosis) is delta; a deep trance state. Mediums enter trance, consciously or unconsciously, to various levels.

Trumpet: a light, usually aluminum, cone like a megaphone that is a tool of physical mediumship. Placed inside a circle during a séance, it can become an instrument through which spirits speak, amplifying their voices.

X-ray clairvoyance: a form of clairvoyance where the medium is able to see inside closed areas such as closets, boxes, safes, etc.

BIBLIOGRAPHY

This bibliography includes those books mentioned in the text plus others that I feel may be of help or of interest to you.

Abbott, David P. *Behind the Scenes With the Medium.* Chicago: Open Court, 1907.

Atkinson, William. *Mind-Power.* Chicago: Progress, 1908.

———. *Reincarnation and the Law of Karma.* Chicago: Yogi Publications, 1936.

Bach, Marcus. *Miracles Do Happen.* New York: Waymark Books, 1968.

Badham, Paul and Linda. *Immortality or Extinction?* London: Macmillan, 1982.

Bagnall, O. *The Origin and Properties of the Human Aura.* London: Routledge and Kegan Paul, 1957.

Barbanell, Maurice. *This is Spiritualism.* London: Jenkins, 1959.

Bardens, D. *Ghosts and Hauntings.* New York: Taplinger, 1968.

Barrett, Sir William. *Death-Bed Visions: The Psychical Experiences of the Dying.* London: Psychic Press, 1926.

Bayles, Allison L. *Essence of Religion.* St. Paul: Galde Press, 1993.

Bayley, Harold *The Lost Language Of Symbolism.* London: Citadel, 1988, 1990

Beard, Paul. *Survival of Death: For and Against.* London: Hodder and Stoughton, 1966.

Bentine, Michael. *Doors of the Mind.* London: Granada, 1984.

———. *The Door Marked Summer.* London: Granada, 1981.

Bernstein, M. *The Search For Bridey Murphy* (new edition). New York: Doubleday, 1965.

Berry, Jason. *The Spirit of Black Hawk.* Jackson: University Press of Mississippi, 1995.

Besterman, T. *Crystal-Gazing.* London: Rider, 1924.

Blackmore, Susan J. *Beyond the Body: An Investigation of Out-of-the-Body Experiences.* London: Heinemann, 1982.

Blundson, Norman. *A Popular Dictionary of Spiritualism.* London: Arco, 1961.

Boddington, Harry. *The University of Spiritualism.* London: Spiritualist Press, 1947.

Boros, Ladislaus. *The Mystery of Death.* New York: Herder and Herder, 1965.

Bradley, D. B. and R. A. *Psychic Phenomena.* New York: Parker, 1967.

Bringle, Mary. *Jeane Dixon: Prophet or Fraud?* New York: Tower Books, 1970.

Brinkley, Dannion & Paul Perry. *Saved By the Light.* New York: Villard, 1994.

———. *At Peace In the Light.* New York: HarperCollins, 1995

Britten, Emma Hardinge. *Autobiography* London: Unwin, 1900.

———. *Ghostland, Spiritualism, Occultism.* Chicago: Progessive Thinker, 1909.

Broughton, Richard S. *Parapsychology, the Controversial Science.* New York: Ballantine, 1991.

Brown, Rosemary. *Unfinished Symphonies: Voices from the Beyond.* New York: William Morrow, 1971.

Brown, Slater. *The Heyday of Spiritualism.* New York: Hawthorn, 1970.

Browning, Norma Lee. *The Psychic World of Peter Hurkos.* New York: Doubleday, 1970.

Buckland, Raymond, and Hereward Carrington. *Amazing Secrets of the Psychic World.* New York: Parker, 1975.

Buckland, Raymond. *A Pocket Guide to the Supernatural.* New York: Ace Books, 1969.

———. *Anatomy of the Occult.* New York: Weiser, 1977.

———. *Buckland's Complete Book of Witchcraft.* St. Paul: Llewellyn, 2002.

———. *Color Magick.* St. Paul: Llewellyn, 2002.

———. *Secrets of Gypsy Fortunetelling.* St. Paul: Llewellyn, 1988.

———. *The Truth About Spirit Communication.* St. Paul: Llewellyn, 1995.

———. *The Fortunetelling Book.* Detroit: Visible Ink Press, 2003.

———. *Signs, Symbols & Omens.* St. Paul: Llewellyn, 2003.

Budilovsky, Joan, and Eve Adamson. *The Complete Idiot's Guide to Meditation.* New York: Alpha Books, 1999.

Butler, Willam E. *How to Develop Clairvoyance.* New York: Weiser, 1971.

———. *How to Develop Psychometry.* New York: Weiser, 1971.

———. *How to Read the Aura.* New York: Weiser, 1971.

Carrington, Hereward. *Your Psychic Powers and How to Develop Them.* New York: Dodd Mead, 1920.

———. *The Physical Phenomena of Spiritualism.* New York: American Universities, 1920.

Christopher, Milburne. *ESP, Seers & Psychics.* New York: Thomas Y. Crowell, 1970.

———. *Mediums, Mystics and the Occult.* New York: Crowell, 1975.

Circlot, J. E. *A Dictionary of Symbols.* New York: Philosophical Library, 1962.

Cook, Mrs. Cecil. *How I Discovered My Mediumship.* Chicago: Lormar, 1919.

Covina, Gina. *The Ouija Book.* New York: Simon and Schuster, 1979.

Cowan, Tom. *The Book of Séance.* Chicago: Contemporary Books, 1994.

Crawford, W. J. *The Reality of Psychic Phenomena.* New York: E. P. Dutton, 1918.

Crinita, Joey. *The Medium Touch.* Virginia Beach: Donning, 1982.

Crookall, R. *The Study and Practice of Astral Projection.* London: Aquarian, 1960.

Cull, Robert. *More to Life Than This.* London: Pan, 1987.

Cummins, Geraldine. *The Road to Immortality.* London: Psychic Press, 1967.

Davis, Andrew Jackson. *The Principles of Nature.* New York: 1847.

———. *Death and the After Life.* New York: 1865.

Dingwall, Eric, and John Langdon-Davies. *The Unknown: Is It Nearer?* New York: Signet, 1968.

Dixon, Jeane. *Yesterday, Today and Forever.* New York: Bantam Books, 1977.

Doyle, Sir Arthur Conan. *The Edge of the Unknown.* New York: Putnam's, 1930.

———. *The History of Spiritualism.* New York: Doran, 1926.

Eadie, Betty J., and Curtis Taylor. *Embraced By the Light.* Placerville: Gold Leaf, 1992.

Eaton, William Dunseath. *Spirit Life, or Do We Die?* London: Stanton and Van Vliet, 1920.

Ebon, Martin (ed.). *True Experiences in Communicating With the Dead.* New York: New American Library, 1968.

Eddy, Sherwood. *You Will Survive After Death.* Evanston: Clark Publishing, 1950

Edmonds, John W. *Spiritualism.* New York: 1853.

Edmunds, Simeon. *Spiritualism: A Critical Survey.* Hertfordshire: Aquarian, 1966.

Edward, John. *One Last Time.* New York: Berkley Books, 1998.

———. *Crossing Over.* New York: Princess Books, 2001.

———. *After Life.* New York: Princess Books, 2004.

Edwards, Harry. *The Evidence for Spirit Healing.* London: Harry Edwards Sanctuary, 1952.

———. *The Healing Intelligence.* New York: Taplinger, 1971.

———. *The Mediumship of Jack Webber.* London: Harry Edwards Sanctuary, 1946.

———. *The Science of Spirit Healing.* London: Harry Edwards Sanctuary, 1945.

Enright, D. J. *The Oxford Book of Death.* Oxford University Press, 1983.

Eisenbud, Jule. *The World of Ted Serios.* New York: Morrow, 1967.

Feilding, Everard. *Sittings with Eusapia Palladino.* New York: University Books, 1963.

Fishley, Margaret. *The Supernatural.* London: Aldus, 1976.

Flammarion, C. *Mysterious Psychic Forces.* London: Unwin, 1907.

Flynn, Charles P. *After the Beyond.* New York: Prentice Hall, 1986.

Fodor, Nandor. *Between Two Worlds.* New York: Parker, 1964.

———. *Encyclopedia of Psychic Science (1934).* New York: University Books, 1966.

Ford, Arthur, and Margueritte H. Bro. *Nothing So Strange.* New York: Harper and Row, 1958.

Ford, Arthur. *The Life Beyond Death.* New York: Berkley, 1971.

———. *Unknown But Known.* New York: Harper and Row, 1968.

Fortune, Dion. *Through the Gates of Death.* York Beach: Weiser Books, 2000.

———. *Psychic Self-Defense.* London: Aquarian, 1967.

———. *Spiritualism and Occultism.* Loughborough: Thoth Publications, 1999.

Fournier, D'Albe. *The Life of Sir William Crookes.* London: T. Fisher Unwin, 1923.

Gallup, George Jr., and William Proctor. *Adventures in Immortality: A Look Beyond the Threshold of Death.* London: Souvenir, 1983.

Garfield, Laeh M,. and Jack Grant. *Companions in Spirit.* Berkeley: Celestial Arts, 1984.

Garrett, Eileen J. *Many Voices.* New York: Putnam's, 1968.

———. *The Sense and Nonsense of Prophesy.* New York: Creative Age, 1950.

———. *Behind the Five Senses.* New York: J.B. Lippincott, 1957.

Garrison, Omar. *Tantra the Yoga of Sex.* New York: Julian Press, 1964.

Gauld, Alan. *The Founders of Psychical Research.* New York: Random House, 1968.

———. *Mediumship and Survival: A Century of Investigations.* London: Heinemann, 1982.

Glass, Justine. *They Foresaw the Future.* New York: G. P. Putnam's, 1969.

Godwin, John. *This Baffling World.* New York: Hart, 1968.

Grey, Margot. *Return From Death. An Exploration of the Near-Death Experience.* London: Arkana, 1985.

Gross, Don H. *The Case for Spiritual Healing.* New York: Thomas Nelson, 1958.

Guggenheim, Bill & Judy. *Hello From Heaven!* New York: Bantam, 1997.

Guiley, Rosemary Ellen. *Harper's Encyclopedia of Mystical and Paranormal Experience.* San Francisco: Harper, 1991.

———. *The Encyclopedia of Ghosts and Spirits.* New York: Facts On File, 1992.

Hall, Manley P. *Solving Psychic Problems.* Los Angeles: Philosophical Research, 1956.

Harber, Francis. *The Gospel According to Allan Kardec.* New York: Original Publications, 1980.

Hardinge, Emma. *Modern American Spiritualism.* New York: University Books, 1970.

Harlow, S. Ralph. *A Life After Death.* New York: Doubleday, 1961.

Harris, Barbara and Lionel C. Bascom. *Full Circle.* New York: Pocket Books, 1990.

Hart, Hornell. *The Enigma of Survival.* Springfield: Charles C. Thomas, 1959.

Headon, Deirdre (ed.). *Quest for the Unknown—Charting the Future.* Pleasantville: Reader's Digest, 1992.

Heywood, Rosalind. *The Sixth Sense.* London: Pan Books, 1959.

———. *Beyond the Reach of Sense.* New York: E. P. Dutton, 1961.

Hick, John. *Death and Eternal Life.* New York: Harper & Row, 1976.

Hill, Douglas, and P. Williams. *The Supernatural.* New York: Hawthorn, 1966.

Hogshire, Jim. *Life After Death.* Boca Raton: Globe, 1991.

Hollen, H. *Clairaudient Transmission.* Hollywood: Keats, 1931.

Holzer, Hans. *Born Again.* New York: Doubleday, 1970.

———. *Ghosts I've Met.* New York: Ace Books, 1965.

———. *Psychic Photography.* New York: Schiffer, 1986.

Hunt, Stocker. *Ouija, the Most Dangerous Game.* New York: Harper and Row, 1985.

Hutton, J. Bernard. *Healing Hands.* New York: David McKay Co., 1966.

Hyslop, James. *Life After Death.* New York: (publisher unknown), 1918.

———. *Contact with the Other World (1919).* New York: Lightning Source, 2003.

Iverson, Jeffrey. *More Lives Than One?* London: Souvenir Press, 1976.

Jaegers, Beverly C. *Practical ESP and Clairvoyance.* Richmond Heights: Aries, 1974.

Jaffé, Aniela. *Apparitions and Precognition.* New York: University Books, 1963.

Jones, Lloyd K. *Development of Mediumship.* Chicago: Lormar, 1919.

Kardec, Allan. *The Book of Mediums.* York Beach: Weiser, 1970.

———. *The Spirits' Book.* Mexico: Amapse Society, 1857.

Keene, M. Lamar. *The Psychic Mafia.* New York: St. Martin's, 1976.

Kelsey, Denys, and Joan Grant. *Many Lifetimes.* New York: Doubleday, 1967.

Khei, F. R. C. *A Brief Course in Mediumship.* Mokelumne: Health Research, 1965.

Kilner, Walter J. *The Human Aura* (Original Title: *The Human Atmosphere*). New York: University Books, 1965.

Kirk, Eleanor. *The Bottom Plank of Mental Healing.* New York: Kirk, 1899.

Klimo, Jon. *Channeling.* Los Angeles: Tarcher, 1987.

Knight, Gareth. *Dion Fortune & the Inner Light.* Loughborough: Thoth Publications, 2000.

Knight, Marcus. *Spiritualism, Reincarnation and Immortality.* London: Duckworth, 1950.

Kubler-Ross, Elisabeth. *On Death and Dying.* New York: Macmillan, 1969.

Langley, Noel. *Edgar Cayce on Reincarnation.* New York: Paperback Library, 1967.

Leadbeater, C. W. *Clairvoyance.* Adyar: Theosophical Publishing House, 1903.

Leonard, John C. *The Higher Spiritualism.* Washington, D.C.: Philosophical Book Co., 1927.

Leonard, Sue (ed.). *Quest For the Unknown: Life Beyond Death.* Pleasantville: Reader's Digest, 2002.

Litvag, Irving. *Singer in the Shadows.* New York: Macmillan, 1972.

Lorimer, David. *Survival? Body, Mind and Death in the Light of Psychic Experience.* London: Routledge & Kegan Paul, 1984.

Martin, Joel, and Patricia Romanowski. *We Don't Die.* New York: Putnam's, 1988.

———. *We Are Not Forgotten.* New York: Putnam's, 1988.

———. *Our Children Forever.* New York: Berkley Books, 1994.

———. *Love Beyond Life.* New York: HarperCollins, 1997.

Meek, George W. *After We Die, What Then?* Columbus: Ariel, 1987.

Melville, J. *Crystal Gazing.* New York: Weiser, 1970.

Monroe, Robert A. *Journeys Out of the Body.* New York: Doubleday, 1971.

Montgomery, Ruth. *A Gift of Prophecy.* New York: Morrow, 1965.

———. *A World Beyond.* New York: Coward McCann & Geoghegan, 1971.

Moody, Raymond. *Life After Life.* New York: Bantam, 1976.

———. *Reflections On Life After Life.* New York: Bantam, 1977.

Moody, Raymond, and Paul Perry. *Coming Back.* New York: Bantam Books, 1991.

———. *The Light Beyond.* New York: Bantam Books, 1989.

———. *Reunions.* New York: Villard, 1993.

Mora. *The Psychic.* Canaan: Mora Press, 1983.

Moses, William Stainton. *Direct Spirit Writing.* London:(publisher unknown), 1878.

———. *Higher Aspects of Spiritualism.* London: (publisher unknown), 1880.

———. *Spirit Teachings.* London: (publisher unknown), 1883.

Mühl, Anita M. *Automatic Writing.* Dresden: Steinkopff, 1930.

Myers, F. W. H. *Human Personality and Its Survival of Bodily Death.* London: Longmans Green, 1903.

Neiman, Carol, and Emily Goldman. *After Life: the Complete Guide to Life After Death.* London: Boxtree, 1994.

Nelson, Robert. *Secret Methods of Private Readers!* Columbus: Nelson, 1964.

Northage, Ivy. *Mediumship Made Simple.* London: College of Psychic Studies, 1986.

Overlee, Vernon W. *The Psychic.* Canaan: Mora, 1983.

Owens, Elizabeth. *Discover Your Spiritual Life.* St. Paul: Llewellyn, 2004.

Owens, Elizabeth. *How to Communicate With Spirits.* St. Paul: Llewellyn, 2002.

Panchadasi, Swami. *A Course in Clairvoyance and Occult Powers (1916).* Chicago: Kessinger Publishing, 1997.

Pearsall, Ronald. *The Table-Rappers.* New York: St. Martin's, 1972.

Peebles, J. M. *The General Principles and the Standard Teachings of Spiritualism.* Mokelumne: Health Research, 1969.

Pike, James A. *The Other Side.* New York: Doubleday, 1968.

Podmore, Frank. *Mediums of the Nineteenth Century.* New York: University Books, 1963.

Pollack, J. Croiset. *The Clairvoyant.* New York: Doubleday, 1964.

Price, Harry. *The Most Haunted House in England (1940).* London: New York: Time-Life, 1990.

Prince, W. *The Case of Patience Worth.* New York: University Books, 1964.

Proskauer, Julien J. *Spook Crooks.* New York: Burt, 1932.

Psychic Magazine editors. *Psychics: In-Depth Interviews.* New York: Harper & Row, 1972.

Randles, Jenny & Peter Hough. *The Afterlife. An Investigation into the Mysteries of Life After Death.* London: Piatkus, 1993.

Regardie, Israel. *The Art of True Healing.* London: Helios, 1964.

Reilly, S. W. *Table-Lifting Methods Used by Fake Mediums.* Chicago: Ireland Magic, 1957.

Ridall, Kathryn. *Channeling.* New York: Bantam Books, 1988.

Rita (Mrs. Desmond Humphreys). *The Truth of Spiritualism.* Philadelphia: J. B. Lippincott, 1920.

Roberts, Estelle. *Fifty Years a Medium.* London: Corgi Books, 1969.

Roberts, Jane. *The Seth Material.* Englewood Cliffs: Prentice-Hall, 1970.

———. *Seth Speaks.* Englewood Cliffs: Prentice-Hall, 1972.

Roberts, Kenneth. *The Seventh Sense.* New York: Doubleday, 1953.

Roman, Sanaya, and Duane Packer. *Opening to Channel.* Tiburon: H. J. Kramer, 1987.

Shepard, Leslie A (ed.). *Encyclopedia of Occultism and Parapsychology.* New York: Avon, 1978.

Sherman, Harold. *The Dead Are Alive.* New York: Fawcett, 1981.

———. *You Can Communicate with the Unseen World.* New York: Fawcett, 1974.

———. *You Live After Death.* New York: Fawcett, 1972.

Smith, Alson J. *Immortality, the Scientific Evidence.* New Jersey: Prentice Hall, 1954.

Somerlott, Robert. *"Here, Mr. Splitfoot."* New York: Viking, 1971.

Spence, Lewis. *Encyclopedia of the Occult (1920).* New York: University Books, 1960.

Spraggett, Allen. *The Unexplained.* New York: New American Library, 1967.

Stearn, Jess. *Edgar Cayce, The Sleeping Prophet.* New York: Doubleday, 1967.

———. *The Search for the Girl with the Blue Eyes.* New York: Doubleday, 1968.

Steiger, Brad. *Voices From Beyond.* New York: Award Books, 1968.

———. *You Will Live Again.* New York: Dell, 1978.

Sugrue, Thomas. *There Is a River: The Story of Edgar Cayce.* New York: Dell, 1966.

Theobald, Morell. *Spirit Workers in the Home Circle.* London: Unwin, 1888.

Turner, Gordon. *An Outline of Spiritual Healing.* London: Talmy, Franklin, 1963.

Tuttle, Hudson. *The Arcana of Spiritualism.* Manchester: Two Worlds, 1921.

Twigg, Ena, and Ruth Hagy Brod. *Ena Twigg: Medium.* New York: Hawthorn Books, 1972.

Van Praagh, James. *Talking to Heaven.* New York: Dutton, 1997.

Verner, Alex. *Practical Psychometry.* London: British Psychological Institute, 1935.

———. *Table Rapping and Automatic Writing.* London: Fowler, nd.

Wallis, E. W. and M. H. *A Guide to Mediumship.* Mokelumne: Health Research, 1968.

Wavell, S. *Trance.* London: Dutton, 1967.

White, Stewart Edward. *The Unobstructed Universe.* New York: Dutton, 1952.

———. *The Betty Book.* New York: E. P. Dutton, 1937.

Wiitala, Geri Colozzi. *Heather's Return.* Virginia Beach: A.R.E. Press, 1996.

Wilde, Stuart. *Affirmations.* Taos: White Dove,1987.

Xavier, F., and W. Vieira. *The World of Spirit.* New York: Philosophical Library, 1966.

Yost, Casper S. *Patience Worth.* New York: Henry Holt, 1916.

Zaleski, Carol. *Otherworld Journeys.* Oxford University Press, 1987.

Zolar. *Zolar's Book of the Spirits.* New York: Prentice Hall, 1987.

INDEX

Practical Candleburning Rituals

Spells and Rituals for Every Purpose

RAYMOND BUCKLAND

Magick is a way in which to apply the full range of your hidden psychic powers to the problems we all face in daily life. We know that normally we use only 5 percent of our total powers. Magick taps powers from deep inside our psyche where we are in contact with the universe's limitless resources.

Magick need not be complex—it can be as simple as using a few candles to focus your mind, a simple ritual to give direction to your desire, and a few words to give expression to your wish.

This book shows you how easy it can be. Here is magick for fun; magick as a craft; magick for success, love, luck, money, marriage, and healing. Practice magick to stop slander, to learn truth, to heal an unhappy marriage, to overcome a bad habit, to break up a love affair, etc.

Magick—with nothing fancier than ordinary candles, and the twenty-eight rituals in this book (given in both Christian and Old Religion versions)—can transform your life.

0-87542-048-6
210 pp., 5¼ x 8, illus. **$13.99**

Advanced Candle Magick

More Spells and Rituals for Every Purpose

RAY BUCKLAND

Seize control of your destiny with the simple but profound practice of *Advanced Candle Magick.* Ray Buckland's first book on candle magick—*Practical Candleburning Rituals*—explained the basic techniques of directing positive forces and "making things happen." In *Advanced Candle Magick,* you'll use advanced spells, preparatory work, visualization, and astrology to improve and enhance your results. Create a framework conducive to potent spellwork through the use of planetary hours, days of the week, herb and stone correspondences, and color symbolism. Create positive changes in your relationships, finances, health, and spirit when you devise your own powerful rituals based upon the sample spells presented in this book. Taking spellworking one step further, Ray Buckland gives you what you've been waiting for: *Advanced Candle Magick.*

1-56718-103-1
288 pp., 5¼ x 8, illus. **$16.99**

Solitary Séance

How You Can Talk with Spirits on Your Own

RAYMOND BUCKLAND

Contacting the spirits of loved ones isn't just for professionals. With the proven techniques in *Solitary Séance*, you can become your own medium and communicate with the spirit world anytime.

Bestselling author Raymond Buckland presents safe and effective methods for conducting a séance. He also discusses the nature of death, the history of spirit communication, and types of mediums. Also explored are new ways to create a psychic shield, connect with spirit guides, and focus with prayer and meditation. With straightforward guidance, Buckland teaches readers to perform nearly twenty techniques for spirit communication, including dreamwork, tea-leaf reading, table tipping, automatic writing, pendulums, crystal scrying, runes, dominoes, numerology, fire gazing, spirit photography, and tarot.

0-7387-2320-7
240 pp., 5 x 7 **$15.99**